EARLY LEARNING IN THE
DIGITAL AGE

Sara Miller McCune founded SAGE Publishing in 1965 to support the dissemination of usable knowledge and educate a global community. SAGE publishes more than 1000 journals and over 800 new books each year, spanning a wide range of subject areas. Our growing selection of library products includes archives, data, case studies and video. SAGE remains majority owned by our founder and after her lifetime will become owned by a charitable trust that secures the company's continued independence.

Los Angeles | London | New Delhi | Singapore | Washington DC | Melbourne

EARLY LEARNING IN THE
DIGITAL AGE

EDITED BY

COLETTE GRAY &
IOANNA PALAIOLOGOU

$SAGE

Los Angeles | London | New Delhi
Singapore | Washington DC | Melbourne

Los Angeles | London | New Delhi
Singapore | Washington DC | Melbourne

SAGE Publications Ltd
1 Oliver's Yard
55 City Road
London EC1Y 1SP

SAGE Publications Inc.
2455 Teller Road
Thousand Oaks, California 91320

SAGE Publications India Pvt Ltd
B 1/I 1 Mohan Cooperative Industrial Area
Mathura Road
New Delhi 110 044

SAGE Publications Asia-Pacific Pte Ltd
3 Church Street
#10-04 Samsung Hub
Singapore 049483

Editor: Jude Bown
Assistant editor: Catriona McMullen
Production editor: Nicola Carrier
Copyeditor: Sharon Cawood
Proofreader: Rosemary McDonald
Indexer: Silvia Benvenuto
Marketing manager: Dilhara Attygalle
Cover design: Wendy Scott
Typeset by: C&M Digitals (P) Ltd, Chennai, India
Printed in the UK

Library of Congress Control Number: 2018953891

British Library Cataloguing in Publication data

A catalogue record for this book is available from the British Library

ISBN 978-1-5264-4682-4
ISBN 978-1-5264-4683-1 (pbk)

At SAGE we take sustainability seriously. Most of our products are printed in the UK using responsibly sourced papers and boards. When we print overseas we ensure sustainable papers are used as measured by the PREPS grading system. We undertake an annual audit to monitor our sustainability.

TABLE OF CONTENTS

NOTES ON THE EDITORS AND CONTRIBUTORS

EDITORS

Colette Gray is a chartered developmental psychologist and principal lecturer at Stranmillis University College. Her research interests include all aspects of underachievement, participatory research that gives voice to the child, ethical considerations and the impact of digital technology on teaching and learning. She has written extensively and has an impressive list of internationally reviewed journal articles, books, chapters, international research conference presentations and key note speeches addressing aspects of child development.

Ioanna Palaiologou is an academic associate of the University College London, Institute of Education, and a psychologist. Her research focuses on ethics in research, child development and implications for pedagogy and the role of technology in early childhood. At the 2017 EECERA annual conference, she was awarded best published paper for 2016 in the journal *European Early Childhood Education Research* for her article 'Children under five and digital technologies: implications for early years pedagogy'.

CONTRIBUTORS

Lorna Arnott is a lecturer in the School of Education, University of Strathclyde. Lorna's main area of interest is in children's early experiences with technology, particularly in relation to social and creative play. She also has a keen interest in research methodologies, with a specialist focus on consulting with children. Lorna is the convener for the Digital Childhoods Special Interest Group as part of the European Early Childhood Educational Research Association and is the editorial assistant for the *International Journal of Early Years Education*.

Gary Beauchamp is Professor of Education and Associate Dean (Research) in the School of Education at Cardiff Metropolitan University. His research interests focus on ICT in education, particularly the use of interactive technologies in learning and teaching. He has published widely in academic journals, as well as writing books, book chapters and research reports. In addition, he has been an Additional Inspector for Estyn, a governor at two primary schools (chair and vice chair) and has served as external examiner for many universities.

Ingvard Bråten is an assistant professor at Western Norway University of Applied Sciences, Bergen. His research focus of the last few years has mainly been concentrated on recycling and how different materials can transform, and how this diversity of materials has an impact on children. When working with digital media in the ECE, he combines this with a concern for small children's need for physical experience and use of their whole body.

Maria Dardanou is a lecturer in the Department of Education and Pedagogics at The Arctic University of Norway. Her research interests centre on digital technology in early childhood education, museums and young children, as well as multicultural education. Maria participates in different national projects in Norway related to research in ECE. She collaborates as researcher with the first Children's Museum in Norway and is co-convener for the Special Interest Group *Digital Childhoods* as part of the European Early Childhood Research Association.

Jill Dunn is a senior lecturer at Stranmillis University College, Belfast. She was a primary school teacher working in Foundation Stage and Key Stage 1 classrooms before moving into teacher education. Jill teaches across BEd, PGCE early years and masters programmes, and her main teaching interests include literacy in the early years and working with parents. Jill completed her EdD focusing on children's views on using popular culture to teach writing. She has also been involved in a number of funded research projects on literacy and the use of iPads in early years education and has published in these areas.

Aderonke Folorunsho is a researcher in the School of Education at the University of Sheffield. Her research interest is in early childhood education with a focus on play and pedagogy and play with digital technology (digital play). She holds a PhD in Education from Canterbury Christ Church University, which explored how children between the ages of 3 and 4 engaged with digital technology in a nursery setting in comparison to traditional classroom activities.

Olga Fotakopoulou is a senior lecturer in Developmental Psychology in the Department of Psychology at Birmingham City University (UK), and programme leader for under-graduate psychology programmes. Olga has worked as a researcher since 2003 in research projects funded by the European Union around human development and education. In addition to her research experience with children and adolescents, she has worked as a counsellor with children, adolescents and students in various educational and clinical settings. She has published widely around cognitive, social and moral development in young and primary school children.

Marie Fridberg is a senior lecturer in Science Education at Kristianstad University in Sweden. She holds a PhD in Medical Science in addition to being an educated preschool teacher and teaches science and technology in early years education. She is part of the research group Learning in Science and Mathematics (LISMA) at Kristianstad University and her research interest is in young children's learning about science, with a special focus on digital technology.

Fay Hadley is a senior lecturer and researcher at the Department of Educational Studies (formerly the Institute of Early Childhood), Macquarie University, Sydney. Fay is the director for Initial Teacher Education and teaches across undergraduate and postgraduate programmes. Her research interests include leadership in early childhood, professional learning and career pathways, partnerships with diverse families, policy and international early childhood education and development.

Debra Harwood is an associate professor within the Faculty of Education at Brock University, Canada. She specialises in teaching and research that focuses on a multitude of aspects related to curriculum and pedagogy in early childhood education. She has led several projects focused on children's playing, thinking and ways of interacting within digitally infused classrooms as well as projects that examine educator pedagogies that support and foster digital literacies.

Maria Hatzigianni is a lecturer in Early Childhood Education at the Melbourne Graduate School of Education, at the University of Melbourne. The use of digital technology within early years education is her main research area. Maria has published widely around the use of technology in early childhood education. Her recent research projects have focused on the use of e-folios; 3D printing and design thinking; and infants/toddlers' use of touchscreen technologies.

Kate Highfield is a lecturer at Swinburne's Department of Education in Australia. Kate's research explores effective technology integration and use, with a focus on potential impacts on learning, pedagogy and play. She spent over a decade working as a classroom teacher and ten years working as a lecturer and researcher at Macquarie University and Charles Sturt University. Kate's current research explores the impact of technology as a tool with young children, parents and educators.

Kelly Johnston is a lecturer with the Department of Educational Studies at Macquarie University, Sydney. Prior to moving to Macquarie, Kelly worked as an early childhood teacher and service director in Australia and New Zealand, in primary school teaching in the UK and also in early childhood licensing and accreditation at both a state and federal level. Her research focuses on the conceptualisations, beliefs and practices of early childhood educators in relation to technology integration within play-based curricula.

Karen Julien is a cognition and learning doctoral student at Brock University, Canada. She is currently focused on innovative and inclusive teaching practices, motivation for writing in early childhood, and the impact of educators' social-emotional skills in STEM classrooms. Karen has enjoyed a career as a teacher and educational researcher with schools and provincial and national associations.

Trine Kofoed is a senior advisor at The Norwegian Agency for International Co-operation and Quality Enhancement in Higher Education; her work focuses on teaching and learning in a digital age. She is also conducting her PhD research at The Arctic University of Norway, focusing on citizenship as an educational ideal in the light of Hannah Arendt's political theory. She has broad experience of kindergarten and has worked both as a kindergarten teacher and as a lecturer in pedagogics in early childhood teacher education at The Arctic University of Norway.

Mari-Ann Letnes is an associate professor in pedagogy and arts and crafts at the Norwegian University of Science and Technology (NTNU). She has conducted several research projects related to children's creative work and aesthetic learning processes in school and kindergarten, as well as children's use of digital technology in creative projects. She has published articles and books, participated as an invited keynote speaker at several conferences in Norway and Sweden, and contributed to paper presentations at international and national conferences.

John Levine is Associate Dean for Learning Enhancement in the Faculty of Science, University of Strathclyde. He is also the Digital Education Champion for the Faculty of Science and Chair of the Departmental Committee on Online and Distance Learning at the Department of Computer and Information Sciences. His research is concerned with general artificial intelligence and machine learning, and the use of computing technology, particularly computer games, in education.

Dane Marco Di Cesare is an assistant professor within the Faculty of Education at Brock University, Canada. His university teaching includes courses related to literacy, technology and effective practices for students with exceptionalities. He has conducted a variety of research activities related to tablet use, multimodality and literacy with students of varying exceptionalities across different grade levels.

Pekka Mertala is a former preschool teacher who currently works as a post-doctoral researcher at the University of Oulu, Finland. His ongoing research focuses on teacher beliefs in technology integration in the context of early childhood education. He is also interested in exploring the possibilities of socio-material theories in understanding young children's dispositions towards digitally enhanced learning activities.

Denise Mitchell was, until recently, a senior lecturer across BA, BEd and PGCE Early Years programmes at Stranmillis University College, Belfast. She began her career as a primary school teacher with a particular passion for, and expertise in, the development of literacy, before moving into teacher education. For more than 20 years, Denise mentored initial teacher educators in the theory and practice of literacy using a range of modalities. She was involved in funded research projects and has published a number of international peer-reviewed journal articles. She is now enjoying her well-earned retirement.

Pamela Moffett is a senior lecturer at Stranmillis University College where she delivers courses in mathematics pedagogy on the BEd (Primary), PGCE (Early Years) and CPD programmes. Her research interests include the development of early number sense and the use of meaningful contexts for children's learning in mathematics. She recently co-authored Number Talk (Centre for Lifelong Learning, 2017), a teaching resource book to promote understanding and use of number language in the early years.

Zoi Nikiforidou is a senior lecturer in Early Childhood at Liverpool Hope University. She teaches undergraduate and postgraduate courses and her research interests relate to methodological and theoretical issues on teaching and learning, with an emphasis on the role of cognition, pedagogy and technology. Zoi is a member of the OMEP UK executive committee and a co-convenor of the Holistic Well-being EECERA SIG.

Jane O'Connor is a reader in Childhood Studies at Birmingham City University where she leads the Rethinking Childhood research cluster. She is the author of *The Cultural Significance of the Child Star* (Routledge, 2008), and co-editor of *Childhood and Celebrity* (Routledge, 2017). Jane has written extensively in the areas of representations of childhood and children and the media, and is currently leading an international project exploring young children's use of touchscreen technology.

Ruby Price has extensive experience in caring for young children, in professional settings and in the home, in the UK and beyond. She gained a first-class degree in Early Childhood studies from Cardiff Metropolitan University and worked as a research assistant on a project (www.itilt2.eu), funded by Erasmus+, investigating how interactive technologies can be used effectively in language teaching.

Michelle Rogers is a senior lecturer within the Centre for Children and Families at the University of Worcester. Her current research interests include children's engagement with technology and the influence and impact this has upon their pedagogy. She is interested in how technology is used by children generally and by students within HE. Michelle is also interested in how children perceive their identity and safety in online environments.

Saara Salomaa is a senior advisor and medial education team leader at KAVI, a Finnish agency with a legal obligation to promote media literacy. She is also in charge of the Finnish Safe Internet Centre project. Her work mainly includes expert consulting, research, lecturing for professionals and producing education resources. She is also conducting her PhD research at the University of Tampere, focusing on early years media education, especially from the viewpoint of practitioners' competencies and awareness.

Gillian Shanks is a PhD candidate at the University of Strathclyde, investigating children's ability to design open-world digital games. The project spans education and computer information science.

Grete Skjeggestad Meyer is associate professor in drama/theatre and Head of the Teacher Education Department at NLA University College in Bergen, Norway. She worked as a teacher in early childhood education and care for 12 years, with specialisms in drama and music. Her main research topics are aesthetic learning, children and media, and teaching and learning methods in early childhood teacher education. She leads the development of the 'INTRO' method, where educators design introductory, immersive, aesthetic experiences that lead to problem-based learning tasks for student teachers.

Klaus Thestrup is an associate professor at the Centre for Teaching Development and Digital Media, Aarhus University in Denmark, where he teaches an online masters programme on digital media and pedagogy. He is also a trained social educator and dramaturg and holds a professional masters in children and youth culture and digital media. He is working on making 'makerspaces' global and teaching playful experimentation.

Nick Young is a lecturer in Primary Education Studies at Cardiff Metropolitan University. He is conducting his PhD research within the area of education technology, focusing on the exploration of collaborative learning supported by technology in the classroom. Nick is a former primary school teacher with international teaching experience.

ACKNOWLEDGEMENTS

The editors and the publisher are grateful for permission to reproduce the following material in this book:

Table 1.1 'Criteria for choosing the applications' from 'Evaluation of digital media for emergent literacy', Hillman, M. and Marshall, J. (2010) *Computers in Schools*, 25 (4): 256–270. Reprinted by permission of the publisher (Taylor & Francis Ltd, www.tandfonline.com).

Figure 5.1 'The components of the TPACK framework' © 2012 by tpack.org. Reproduced by permission of the publisher.

INTRODUCTION

COLETTE GRAY AND IOANNA PALAIOLOGOU

Since the introduction of the terms digital play, digital practices and digital literacies to describe children's interactions with technology, an emerging body of research has begun to examine 'what is actually happening for young children and their play within the digital age' (Stephen and Edwards, 2018: 86) and 'how the digital home experiences of children can be actively engaged to create learning experiences where the "digital child" can obtain literacy skills where they have access to quality educational content' (Palaiologou, 2016: 19). Similarly, terms describing children's repertoire of skills and use of technology form part of their early childhood lexicon and offer a rich topic of exploration for large numbers of researchers around the world.

Empirical research started investigating 'new concepts of play' (Edwards, 2013) to contextualise these interactions, or 'new types of digital play' to conceptualise them (Marsh et al., 2016). Researchers also began to explore children's playful explorations with technology (Yelland, 2016), how they can create a blended space between digital and non-digital playworlds (Fleer, 2017), focusing on the ecological context of children's play (Arnott, 2016) and learning (Gray et al., 2017), moving beyond dichotomising play and learning into 'traditional' meaningful play and learning with no technology and 'new' meaningful play and learning with technology. Allied with these developments, another body of research explores the continuation of children's play between home and their early childhood setting (e.g. Edwards et al., 2017), urging the field to (re)think, (re)conceptualise and (re)examine young children's play and learning in the digital age as 'an urgent need for populations to develop the skills and knowledge required to navigate a complex technological world [. . .] hence it makes sense to focus on the related skills, knowledge and practices of individuals from an early age' (Marsh et al., 2017: 6).

Thus, our intention in this book, taking into consideration the social landscapes and communities of the 21st century, is to reflect the contemporary international research that attempts to understand children's play and learning in a digital age, and how digital literacies are translated into pedagogy that shapes digital in early childhood education. The book draws on international research projects that argue for a different understanding of children's engagement with technology, as social and collective, which allows for diverse sensitivities, methodologies and theoretical underpinnings of early childhood in the digital age. It focuses on exploring pedagogical practices representing a way of digital living, play and learning, respecting children's agency.

To explore the fusion of play and learning in the digital age, this book offers a cross-cultural, international perspective on theoretical and practical views of how digital technologies can be integrated into play-based pedagogy in early childhood education. The book includes chapters from an international perspective on digital practices in early childhood education to seek effective practice that enhances children's play and learning and also smooths the transition from home to early childhood education. The goal of this book is to disseminate practices on how digital technologies are becoming, and have become, part of wider pedagogical practices in early childhood education and to inform the discussion on how digital technologies can be part of an effective pedagogy in ECE. For this reason, as editors we made a deliberate choice not to unify any terminology amongst the chapters (for example, kindergarten, setting, nursery or how each country describes educators, i.e. teachers, pedagogues, practitioners) as it may distort the authenticity of the research reported by the authors of the varying countries included in this international text. The book comprises three parts.

In Part I: Play and learning in a digital age, there are four chapters focusing on playful experiences of children with technology. Chapter 1, based on research conducted in England, examines children's playful encounters with iPads and applications, and shows several different types of engagement when children play with applications. Chapter 2 tackles the very important issue of how open games can be used to amplify creative play in early childhood education in Scotland. Chapter 3, building on Vygotsky's axioms on play, provides an example of a Norwegian research study that showed how children can blend media and non-media play to facilitate the development of their play. This part is concluded with Chapter 4 and an important aspect of early childhood education: the outdoors. Despite the techno myth that technology is limiting children's movement and outdoor experience, the chapter discusses the mobile nature of technology in an English early childhood setting.

Part II: Multimodal spaces, opportunities and agency explores issues around professionalism, training, parental views, children's agency and the importance of bridging the digital divide for children to develop as competent people with digital literacy skills. Chapter 5 takes us back to Norway and seeks to examine what type of digital competencies professionals need to have in order to use technological resources in their practice, as technology itself does not necessarily ensure the amplification of play or enhancement of learning. Chapter 6 brings together cross-national and cross-cultural research from the UK, Sweden, Australia and Greece and discusses parental perspectives and practices of touchscreen technology with infants and toddlers and disputes pervading (birth to age 3) under-researched aged techno myths and moral panic on social media. Chapter 7 presents a practitioner inquiry study based on the Australian Early Years Framework which integrates technology as one of many resources to document and explore the transition to school process, focusing on children's agency. Chapter 8 discusses the issue of digital inequalities in the 21st century and raises issues about the role of early childhood by examining Nigerian pre-primary education and the barriers for the inclusion of technology. Chapter 9 offers an example of how these inequalities can become a barrier for children to embrace their own native language in Irish-medium schools in Northern Ireland. This part concludes with Chapter 10 which, although based in Norway, showcases how technology can support children to communicate with the world and positions them as global citizens in the 21st century.

Part III: Digitally enabled learning in the 21st century explores digital practices for learning through play-based approaches. The first chapter in this section, Chapter 11, explains what digital media education is and, drawing from research in Finnish early childhood education, discusses a pedagogical approach (education-centred approach) for the integration of media education. Chapter 12 takes us to Canada to look at teachers' digital practices, views and efficacy and offers interesting practices for the integration of tablets in everyday life in early childhood education and how they can be blended with non-digital practices. However, like other chapters (e.g. 4, 9, 10) they caution us about the important role that teachers play in developing digital pedagogy. Chapter 13 is similar to Chapter 3 in taking a Vygotksian approach and here the research reports on digital literacy in Norwegian kindergartens to explore how children can utilise technology to transfer their stories into films to make their own meaning and vice versa. Chapter 14, extending the ideas of Chapter 4 that examined play, looks at mobile technology and how it can be used outdoors to enhance learning opportunities and how it may be integrated into the Welsh curriculum. Finally, Chapter 15, building on a research project in Greek preschool education, takes an academic subject approach, mathematics, to showcase how digital manipulatives can engage young children in curriculum subjects.

We hope that this book, which aims to disseminate digital practices from a variety of countries, will help the reader to understand the potentialities of the digital age in constructing a pedagogy for the 'digital child' and place young children at the centre of digital early childhood education. By giving voice to diverse digital practices, we hope that in early childhood education and research we can (re)think the way we do things, move away from techno-tales (Stephen and Edwards, 2018), and conceptualise a pedagogy for the 21st century that understands and embraces the full context of a child's life in the digital age.

REFERENCES

Arnott, L. (2016) An ecological exploration of young children's digital play: framing children's social experiences with technologies in early childhood. *Early Years: An International Journal, 36* (3): 271–287.

Edwards, S. (2013) Digital play in the early years: a contextual response to the problem of integrating digital technologies and play-based learning in the early childhood curriculum. *European Early Childhood Educational Research Journal, 10* (2): 199–212.

Edwards, S., Henderson, M., Gronn, D., Scott, A. and Mirkhil, M. (2017) Digital disconnect or digital difference? A socio-ecological perspective on young children's technology use in the home and the early childhood centre. *Technology, Pedagogy and Education, 26* (1): 1–17.

Fleer, M. (2017) Digital playworlds in an Australian context: supporting double subjectivity. In T. Bruce, P. Hakkarainen and M. Bredikyte (eds) *The Routledge International Handbook of Early Childhood Play*. Oxon: Routledge, pp. 289–304.

Gray, C., Dunn, J., Moffett, P. and Mitchell, D. (2017) *Mobile devices in early learning: developing the use of portable devices to support young children's learning*. Paper presented at Stranmillis University College, 24 May.

Marsh, J., Kumpulainen, K., Nisha, B., Velicu, A., Blum-Ross, A., Hyatt, D., et al. (2017) *Makerspaces in the Early Years: A Literature Review*. University of Sheffield: MakEY Project.

Marsh, J., Plowman, L., Yamada-Rice, D., Bishop, J. and Scott, F. (2016) Digital play: a new classification. *Early Years, 36* (3): 242–253.

Palaiologou, I. (2016) Children under five and digital technologies: implications for early years pedagogy. *The European Early Childhood Research Journal, 24* (1): 1–19.

Stephen, C. and Edwards, S. (2018) *Young Children Playing and Learning in a Digital Age: A Cultural and Critical Perspective*. London: Routledge.

Yelland, N. (2016) iPlay, iLearn, iGrow: tablet technology, curriculum, pedagogies and learning in the twenty-first century. In S. Gurvis and N. Lemon (eds) *Understanding Digital Technology and Young Children: An International Perspective*. London: Routledge, pp. 38–45.

PART I

PLAY AND LEARNING IN A DIGITAL AGE

1

CHILDREN'S PLAYFUL ENCOUNTERS WITH IPADS

ADERONKE FOLORUNSHO AND IOANNA PALAIOLOGOU

CHAPTER OVERVIEW

A plethora of research evidence suggests that digital technology has become a major part of the lives of children and that many homes in developed countries are digitally fluent (e.g. Edwards et al., 2017; Palaiologou, 2016; Plowman, 2015). There has been a dramatic increase, especially in tablet use by children (Dunn et al., 2016), which has overtaken television as children's first choice of digital entertainment (Livingstone et al., 2014). Although we know a great deal about what happens in home life and the inclusion of technology in everyday activities (Plowman, Stephen and McPake, 2010), research on how early childhood education can use these devices is still emerging (Fleer, 2017; Yelland, 2015, 2016). Thus, this chapter, based on a mixed methods study that was conducted in English early childhood education, discusses children's playful encounters with technology and, through observational case studies, explores how children interact with digital devices in their everyday life.

This chapter aims to help you understand:

- what research defines as digital play
- how children interact with digital devices
- how children develop their play with digital devices
- implications for early childhood education.

DIGITAL PLAY

The presence of technologies in children's daily lives has led to the term 'digital play' being introduced to characterise the ways children engage with digital devices (e.g. Bird and Edwards, 2015; Stephen and Plowman, 2014). An emerging body of research, as it will be seen throughout this book, also examines children's digital profiles and the nature of these interactions/encounters to see whether they are playful (Marsh et al., 2016), contribute to children's playful experiences (Arnott, 2016; Danby et al., 2017; Miller et al., 2017) and 'extend play to include them in the repertoire of play experiences' (Yelland and Gilbert, 2017: 33). Some researchers (e.g. Stephen and Edwards, 2018) go further by arguing that traditional views and theories of play are not connected with the use of digital technologies and identify the need for research on 'an alternative theory of digital play' (p. 85). Although there is research that examines traditional play (e.g. Brooker et al., 2014; Wood, 2015) and how it provides a platform for learning for young children, the nature of digital play as a 'new' type of play has not been examined in full. Despite the research, it still seems that early childhood educators are concerned about what digital play entails (Huh, 2017) and whether it has any educational value (Palaiologou, 2016).

The term 'digital play' has been used to describe the range of activities children engage in with digital technology (Kline et al., 2003) and its inclusion in play (Howrey, 2016; Kucirkova, 2017) these digital devices comprise touchscreens (smartphones, tablets) and applications of digital content, video games and internet-connected toys. Regardless of the emerging field of research, some believe and argue that digital play is not real play (Palmer, 2015) and that such technology may cause a decline in spontaneous forms of play (Ferguson, 2015; Kabali et al., 2015; Nathanson, 2015; Radesky et al., 2015). Despite these beliefs, emerging research is beginning to shed light on how children's engagement with digital technology can be viewed as play (Arnott, 2016; Danby et al., 2017; Edwards, 2013; Fleer, 2017; Holloway et al., 2016; Marsh et al., 2016; Slutsky and DeShelter, 2017; Stephen and Plowman, 2014). This body of evidence is significant for early childhood educators because it will help them understand how digital play occurs (Bird and Edwards, 2015; Edwards and Bird, 2017).

Typically, research on children's digital play uses descriptors or types of play associated with non-digital play to frame children's digital engagements. Marsh et al. (2016), for example, examined how apps promote play and creativity by adapting Hughes' (2002) taxonomy of play to their research. The study showed that 'traditional' characteristics of play could be applied in a digital context. They argued that what changed when the children engaged with digital technology was not the type of play, but the context in which the play occurred, meaning that play occurred in a digital context. The characteristics of play did not change because the mode of play changed. Types of play such as symbolic, creative, role, socio-dramatic and collaborative were evident in a digital context (Sullivan and Bers, 2016; Zaman et al., 2016). Yelland (2015, 2016) used the term 'playful explorations' to describe children's engagement with digital technology and proposed that these are about making digital and non-digital activities available for children. She argued that isolating digital activities is not the way forward if we want to understand how digital play occurs. Thus, she urged for the provision of 'contexts so that young children can experience different modes of representations which in turn afford them the opportunity to formulate new understandings about their world' (Yelland, 2015: 235).

To conclude, emerging research argues that the nature of play has not changed but digital activities have changed the context. This identifies the need for more research on what happens when children engage with digital play, as new research shows that children's play is blended between digital and non-digital activities (Bird, 2017; Nuttal et al., 2015; Plowman, 2015; Yelland and Gilbert, 2017). Thus, the research presented by us in this chapter aimed to examine:

- what types of playful encounters occur when children are interacting with digital applications
- what characteristics such encounters entail.

REFLECTIVE TASK

Reflect on the use of digital technology in your life. How do you use technology? Can you identify activities that you can classify as your digital enjoyable time?

THE RESEARCH CONTEXT

This is a small-scale research study conducted in one early childhood setting in southern England within a period of six months (for information on the English context, see Chapter 4). The methodology employed was mixed methods. In this chapter, we report the qualitative findings from:

- semi-structured observations that aimed to collect data about the specific context within which the play encounters with technology were happening
- participant observations.

Over the study period, 168 observations were collected and analysed thematically.

The study focuses on children's interactions with iPads. Prior to the research, the setting was not using mobile technology, such as tablets, and had only a desktop computer that children were using with an adult at certain times during the week for educational activities, such as learning phonics. The iPad was introduced to a class of five boys and nine girls aged 3–4 years as another 'toy' in the class and not something that could be used at certain or fixed times during the day. During play times, the children could pick it up and use it as they would have done with any other toys in the class. After negotiations with the practitioners and for ethical reasons, the iPad was offered offline to children, with the most common applications available being related to literacy and numeracy, although there were also puzzle and painting apps such as Peppa Pig Shopping, Endless 123 and Disney Junior.

To choose the applications, we reviewed a number that were available for young children up to 6 years of age. The choice of applications for this research study was based on six categories of criteria and questions, presented in Table 1.1, that can be used to assess and select digital activities for children. The work of Hillman and Marshall (2010) guided us as to which applications were to be used in agreement with practitioners and parents.

Table 1.1 Criteria for choosing the applications

Domain	Central question	Criteria questions
Interactivity	Is the role of the child integral to the activity?	• Does it allow the child to actively participate? • Does it promote critical and creative thinking? • Does it model decision making and positive problem solving?
Digital literacy	Does it increase the child's familiarity and ability with technology?	• Does it help the child make sense of the world? • Does it teach the child to explore?
Appropriateness	Is it targeted at young children?	• Does it allow the child to experience multiple domains? • Does it contain significant content and outcomes? • Is the digital experience challenging, but not frustrating? • Does the digital world present a positive virtual universe?
Results	Does it provide knowledge of results a child can understand?	• Is there a clear and understood connection between the child's actions, learning responses and the programme (app)'s results? • Is feedback incorporated regularly to guide the child's performance rather than as a display of success/failure or win/lose decision at the end? • Is the feedback easy to interpret?

Domain	Central question	Criteria questions
Participation	Does the programme encourage participation (collaboration) amongst children, parents and teachers?	• Are there programme components that provide parents, caregivers and teachers with information on the programme's goals, ways to participate, the child's experiences and ways to evaluate the child's experiences? • Is the learning experience enhanced when parents, caregivers or teachers participate with the child?

Source: Hillman and Marshall (2010)

Subsequently, the applications in Table 1.2 were selected.

Table 1.2   Digital applications selected in the study

Peppa Pig Shopping	Bird Collection Puzzle	Alphabet Tots
Literacy	Peppa's Paint Box	Puzzle 123
Max and Ruby	Tonia Colour Book	Endless Reader
Hooked Phonics	Lego Game	Pixie Dust Lite
Edu Kids Room	Disney Junior	Endless 123
Tiggly Chef	The Garden	Nursery Rhymes
Art Studio	Not Like the Others	Wild Habitat
Endless Word Play	Stumpy	Play Kids
Animal Puzzle	Leo's Pad	Lumi Kids
Elmo 123	Edu Math 1	Disney Digital Books
Mini School	Mr Potato Head	Bugs and Numbers
Cardtoons	House Hunt	Turtle Math
Addition	Critter Math	Farm 123
Funbrain Jr	Road Trip	Colour Book
Monsters	Fit Brains	Monkey Birthday Party

REFLECTIVE TASK

Reflecting on the criteria presented in Table 1.1, download an application designed for young children and critique it by applying the criteria in the table. How will you rate the interactivity, digital literacy, appropriateness, results and participation? To what extent and in what ways do you think this application can enhance children's play?

TYPES AND CHARACTERISTICS OF DIGITAL PLAYFUL ENCOUNTERS

The result of the observations when children were engaged with applications demonstrated many playful characteristics similar to other studies (e.g. Kucirkova, 2017; Kucirkova et al., 2014). We found that when children engaged with the applications, behavioural, cognitive, emotional, social and physical playful encounters were present. We also found that children disengage with the iPad to move on to other activities. The types and characteristics of children's playful encounters with the apps that emerged from the observations are presented in Table 1.3.

Table 1.3   Types and characteristics of digital playful encounters with the applications

Types of encounters	Characteristics
Behavioural engagement	
	Involvement
	Persistence
	Assertiveness
Cognitive engagement	
	Use of language
	Problem solving
	Symbolic representation
	Creating and constructing
	Categorising
	Selective attention
	Recalling
	Active listening
	Working memory
	Exploration
	Classifying
Emotional engagement	
	Happiness
	Enjoyment
	Frustration
	Empathy
Social engagement	
	Peer engagement
	Give-and-take and interchange activities (reciprocal)
	Cooperation

Types of encounters	Characteristics
	Adult interaction
	Conflict with peers
	Negotiation: Theme and topic of the activity Roles Use of objects (including apps)
Physical engagement	
	Fine motor skills
	Muscular and postural engagement
Disengagement	
	Distraction
	Absence of effort
	Withdrawal

The features of the iPad (i.e. mobility) and the applications (i.e. colour, interactivity, movement) influenced the children's playful encounters. The applications had interactive backgrounds that were bright and colourful and drew children's attention; the children were further attracted by the music playing in the background to each app. These apps had menus that helped the children to navigate to different tasks within the game. This made it easy for them to understand how to navigate the digital activities because they were usually large and colourful. The children also enjoyed getting feedback whenever they completed a task, as is illustrated in the Peppa Pig case study (1.1).

CASE STUDY 1.1:
MAX PLAYS PEPPA PIG

Toby and Max are playing with the Peppa Pig app. The app includes a shopping cart and the children need to navigate it around to do their shopping before moving to the next level. Max holds the iPad and is looking out for the items he needs. He sees on the screen an item in his shopping cart that is not part of the items in his shopping list.

Max: 'I don't need that.'
Toby: 'Then tap on the shopping cart and swipe it out.'
          Max taps on the shopping cart and swipes the item out.

(Continued)

(Continued)

Max:
[talking
to the
screen]

'No, Daddy Pig, don't do that!', he says when the pig on the app puts an item not on Max's list into the shopping cart. After playing a while, he finds all the items he was supposed to collect from the list.

'Good job', says the voice in the game and triumphant music plays.

Both boys give a big smile and say: 'We did it!'

In this instance, Max takes on the role of shopper, tapping on a number of items on the shelves as his avatar Peppa Pig passes them by; this is a playful encounter that can be classified as an 'enactment of real-life scenarios in a digital environment that are based on personal experiences and this can take place through avatars for example going shopping' (Marsh et al., 2016: 6).

Also, there were many instances of creative problem solving during play where the children explored and developed ideas and pictures in a digital context when using Peppa's paint box and Leo's pad, as in case study 1.2.

CASE STUDY 1.2: ADAM'S VIRTUAL LAVA DRAWING ON THE PEPPA PIG APP

Adam taps on George (one of the characters in the app). He moves his finger to the menu and taps on the red paint bucket. He uses his fingers to spread the red paint all over the screen.

'I'm making lava', he says.

He moves his fingers towards the menu icons and taps the blue paint bucket. He uses his fingers to spread the blue paint across the screen. He does the same with black paint. (See Figure 1.1)

'George is afraid of the dark', he says as he paints.

Peppa's paint box was a favourite digital activity when it came to painting. This app was one of the activities that occurred often in the observations. This showed that the children transferred their interest in drawing and painting to the digital activity that provided them with a stimulating environment without them getting paint on their fingers or having to wear an apron. Furthermore, they could delete their picture and start again if they chose to.

Figure 1.1   Adam's virtual painting

There were also situations where imaginative play in a digital context was observed, as in the examples in case study 1.3.

CASE STUDY 1.3: SARAH PLAYS TIGGLY CHEF

Sarah taps on Tiggly Chef. The game starts and she taps on five bananas, one cherry and five eggs. She is using her right index finger now to tap the ingredients into the bowl. Sarah laughs and looks at the researcher. She appears to enjoy playing the game with the iPad. She makes the chewing sound as she taps on the food prepared. The game ends. She starts the game again excitedly.

'Strawberry', she says excitedly as she taps on two strawberries in the bowl.

She makes a munching noise as she taps on the food prepared.

'I ate it all up', she says happily.

(Continued)

(Continued)

In this instance, Sarah was engaging with activity on the app and pretending that she was eating the food she was preparing virtually. We can see the activity encouraging pretend and imaginative play in a digital context whereby the children made use of their imaginations. This shows that imaginative and pretend play can occur with digital activities as well as non-digital activities. iPads and digital activities can be resources, therefore, that children can use to meet their play needs (Arnott, 2016). The application that Sarah interacted with was a numeracy activity which allows children to learn how to count using food ingredients. Sarah was able to tap on the food ingredients whilst the Chef (on the app) counted the numbers out. Then Sarah went further by imagining that the food was real, and pretending to eat it. Therefore, the intended purpose of the digital activity was achieved. Imaginative play can also occur when children use toy people, animals, cars and houses to create imaginary worlds. In these worlds, they act out stories that they are familiar with or make up new stories or situations from their imaginations. They are in control of the storyline and make and break the rules.

The applications chosen encouraged imaginative play and problem solving, whereby the child was engaging with the virtual characteristics such as the animals getting to a picnic by passing through some hurdles. The applications 'acted as digital placeholders and digital pivots to enhance play' (Fleer, 2017: 303). However, in an earlier study, Stephen and Plowman (2014) caution that digital activities such as these may provide initial motivation and engagement for play and learning but only for a short period of time. They go on to suggest that digital technology specifically created for children should be more open-ended and flexible so that it can easily respond to children's changing interests and relate to their authentic experiences.

REFLECTIVE TASK

After exploring an application for children from the list in Table 1.2, consider what are its advantages and disadvantages. In your practice, how can you use it with the children to amplify their play?

CONCLUSIONS

In our study, we found that when engaging with digital activities children exhibit playful encounters that they also exhibit in non-digital play. As Marsh et al. (2016: 250) suggest, 'what changes in digital context is not so much the types of play possible, but the nature of that play'. The examples provided here illustrate the playful encounters children can have with digital devices in early childhood education. The digital activities provided opportunities for the children to communicate with each other, be creative, self-initiate their interests and be cognitively engaged. Digital activities can provide play opportunities for children in the same way that non-digital activities do. Thus, as elsewhere in the literature on digital play, early childhood education should:

> align and integrate technology and media with other core experiences and opportunities. Young children need tools that help them explore, create, problem solve, consider, think, listen and view critically, make decisions, observe, document, research, investigate ideas, demonstrate learning, take turns and learn with and from one another. (NAEYC and Fred Rogers Center, 2012: 6–7)

The digital applications that children had access to in this project became a platform for their play and offered them opportunities to engage in artistic pursuits such as drawing or imaginative play, such as cooking and eating, where 'efforts and process are more important than the product' (Eliason and Jenkins, 2012: 355) as 'they experience being the one who makes or decides something' (Branscombe et al., 2014: 30).

SUMMARY

In this chapter, we presented a small case study of the playful encounters of children with applications using the iPad. We demonstrated that when engaging with digital activities children exhibit characteristics of play similar to the ones that have been described elsewhere in the literature of non-digital play. The applications amplified children's play and became 'digital placeholders and pivots', where children engaged behaviourally, emotionally, socially, cognitively and physically.

KEY POINTS TO REMEMBER

- Although there is still a body of opinion that claims digital devices do not have a place in early childhood education, we argue that they can become part of the resources valuable to children in their daily life.
- Digital devices can offer children another playful platform where their play is taken in a different context.
- Early childhood education cannot ignore the integration of technology as part of children's playful landscapes, which can become a valuable toy amongst other non-digital toys.

POINTS FOR DISCUSSION

- Reflecting on the curriculum framework you are working within in your practice, discuss what digital devices you could integrate in your daily routine, for what purposes and how you could use them.
- Consider what type of training staff in early childhood education might require in order to amplify children's play in the digital age.
- Consider what might be the advantages and disadvantages in your own context of integrating a variety of digital devices.
- Technology is developing rapidly and children are now moving to more tangible technologies such as internet-connected toys. Read the following article: Marsh, J. A. (2017) The internet of toys: a posthuman and multimodal analysis of connected play. *Teachers College Record*, 119: 1–32, and consider what implications this development in technology might have for your early childhood practice.

FURTHER READING

Danby, S., Davidson, C., Theobald, M., Houen, S. and Thorpe, K. (2017) Pretend play and technology: young children making sense of their everyday social worlds. In S. Lynch, D. Pike and C. Beckett (eds) *Multidisciplinary Perspectives on Play from Birth and Beyond*. Singapore: Springer, pp. 231–245.

Harwood, D. (2017) *Crayons and iPads: Learning and Teaching of Young Children in the Digital World*. London: Sage.

As technology is changing rapidly, the following two articles examine the role of internet-connected toys and how children engage with these:

Holloway, D. and Green, L. (2016) The internet of toys. *Communication Research and Practice*, 2 (4): 506–519.

Yelland, N. (2018) A pedagogy of multiliteracies: young children and multimodal learning with tablets. *British Journal of Educational Technology*, 49 (5): 847–858.

USEFUL WEBSITE

http://digilitey.eu – this website is based on an international project examining how children may use technology effectively. It includes reports, current research and lists of relevant publications.

REFERENCES

Arnott, L. (2016) An ecological exploration of young children's digital play: framing children's social experiences with technologies in early childhood. *Early Years: An International Journal*, *36* (3): 271–287.

Bird, J. (2017) Children's responses to working and non-working digital technologies. In L. Arnott (ed.) *Digital Technologies and Learning in the Early Years*. London: Sage, pp. 99–100.

Bird, J. and Edwards, S. (2015) Children learning to use technologies through play: a digital play framework. *British Journal of Educational Technology*, *46* (6): 1149–1160.

Branscombe, N. A., Barcham, J. G., Castle, K. and Subeck, E. (2014) *Early Childhood Curriculum: A Constructive Perspective* (2nd edn). New York: Routledge.

Brooker, L., Blaise, M. and Edwards, S. (2014) *The SAGE Handbook of Play and Learning in Early Childhood*. London: Sage.

Danby, S., Davidson, C., Theobald, M., Houen, S. and Thorpe, K. (2017) Pretend play and technology: young children making sense of their everyday social worlds. In S. Lynch, D. Pike and C. Beckett (eds) *Multidisciplinary Perspectives on Play from Birth and Beyond*. Singapore: Springer, pp. 231–245.

Dunn, J., Gray, C., Moffett, P. and Mitchell, D. (2016) 'It's more funner than doing work': children's perspectives on using tablet computers in the early years of school. *Early Child Development and Care*, *188* (6): 819–831.

Edwards, S. (2013) Digital play in the early years: a contextual response to the problem of integrating digital technologies and play-based learning in the early childhood curriculum. *European Early Childhood Educational Research Journal*, *10* (2): 199–212.

Edwards, S. and Bird, J. (2017) Observing and assessing young children's digital play in the early years: using the digital play framework. *Journal of Early Childhood Research*, *15* (2): 158–173.

Edwards, S., Henderson, M., Gronn, D., Scott, A. and Mirkhil, M. (2017) Digital disconnect or digital difference? A socio-ecological perspective on young children's technology use in the home and the early childhood centre. *Technology, Pedagogy and Education*, *26* (1): 1–17.

Edwards, S., Nuttall, J., Mantilla, A., Wood, E. and Grieshaber, S. (2015) Digital play: what do early childhood teachers see? In S. Buffin, N. F. Johnson and C. Bigum (eds) *Critical Perspectives on Early Childhood Education*. Palgrave Macmillan's Digital Education and Learning Series. New York: Palgrave Macmillan, pp. 48–66.

Eliason, C. F. and Jenkins, L. T. (2012) *A Practical Guide to Early Childhood Curriculum*. Boston: MA Pearson.

Ferguson, C. J. (2015) Clinicians' attitudes toward video games vary as a function of age, gender and negative beliefs about youth: a sociology of media research approach. *Computers in Human Behaviour*, *52*: 379–386.

Fleer, M. (2017) Digital playworlds in an Australian context: supporting double subjectivity. In T. Bruce, P. Hakkarainen and M. Bredikyte (eds) *The Routledge International Handbook of Early Childhood Play*. Oxon: Routledge, pp. 289–304.

Hillman, M. and Marshall, J. (2010) Evaluation of digital media for emergent literacy. *Computers in Schools, 25* (4): 256–270.

Holloway, J., Green, K. and Stevenson, K. (2016) Digitods: toddlers, touch screens and Australian family life. *Journal of Media and Culture, 18* (5): 1–7.

Howrey, S. (2016) Preparing pre-service teachers to use internet technology for early reading skills: insights from an action research project. *The Journal of Literacy and Technology, 17*: 80–111.

Hughes, B. (2002) *A Play Worker's Taxonomy of Play Types*. London: PlayLink.

Huh, Y. J. (2017) Uncovering young children's transformative digital game play through the exploration of three year old children's cases. *Contemporary Issues in Early Childhood, 18*: 179–195.

Kabali, H. K., Irigoyen, M. M., Nunez-Davis, R., Budacki, J. G., Mohanty, S. H., Leister, K. P. and Bonner, R. L. (2015) Exposure and use of mobile media devices by young children. *Pediatrics, 136* (6): 1044–1050.

Kline, S., Dyer-Witherford, N. and de Peuter, G. (2003) *Digital Play: The Interaction of Technology Markets and Culture*. Montreal: McGill University Press.

Kucirkova, N. (2017) *Digital Personalisation in Early Childhood: Impact on Childhood*. London: Bloomsbury.

Kucirkova, N., Messer, D., Sheehy, K. and Panadero, C. F. (2014) Children's engagement with educational iPad apps: insights from a Spanish classroom. *Computers and Education, 71*: 175–184.

Livingstone, S., Marsh, J., Plowman, L., Ottovordemgentschenfelde, S. and Fletcher-Watson, B. (2014) Young children (0–8) and digital technology: a qualitative exploratory study – national report – UK. Luxembourg: Joint Research Centre, European Commission.

Marsh, J., Plowman, L., Yamada-Rice, D., Bishop, J. and Scott, F. (2016) 'Digital play: a new classification', *Early Years, 36* (3): 242–253.

Miller, J. L., Paciga, K. A., Danby, S., Beaudoin-Ryan, L. and Kaldor, T. (2017) Looking beyond swiping and tapping: review of design and methodologies for researching young children's use of digital technologies. *Cyberpsychology: Journal of Psychosocial Research on Cyberspace, 11* (3): article 6.

Nathanson, A. L. (2015) Media and the family: reflections and future directions. *Journal of Children and Media, 9*: 133–139.

National Association for the Education of Young Children (NAEYC) (1996) *Developmentally Appropriate Practice in Early Childhood Programs Serving Children from Birth through Age 8*. Washington, DC: NAEYC.

National Association for the Education of Young Children (NAEYC) and Fred Rogers Center for Early Learning and Children's Media (2012) Technology and interactive media as tools in early childhood programs serving children from birth through age 8 (Joint Position Statement). Available at: www.naeyc.org/files/naeyc/file/positions/PS_technology_WEB2.pdf (accessed 18 January 2018).

Nuttal, J., Edwards, S., Mantilla, A., Grieshaber, S. and Wood, E. (2015) The role of motive objects in early childhood teacher development concerning children's digital play and play-based learning in early childhood curricula. *Professional Development in Education, 41*: 222–235.

Palaiologou, I. (2016) Children under five and digital technologies: implications for early years pedagogy. *European Early Childhood Education Research Journal, 24* (1): 5–24.

Palmer, S. (2015) *Toxic Childhood: How the Modern World is Damaging Our Children and What We Can Do About It* (new edn). London: Orion.

Plowman, L. (2015) Researching young children's everyday uses of technology in the family home. *Interacting with Computers, 27*: 36–46.

Plowman, L., Stephen, C. and McPake, J. (2010) *Growing Up with Technology: Young Children Learning in a Digital World*. London: Routledge.

Radesky, J. S., Kistin, C., Eisenberg, S., Zuckerman, B. and Silverstein, M. (2015) Parent views about mobile device use around and by young children: implications for anticipatory guidance. Abstract presented at the Pediatric Academic Societies, San Diego, CA, April.

Slutsky, R. and DeShelter L. M. (2017) How technology is transforming the ways in which children play. *Early Child Development and Care, 187*: 1138–1146.

Stephen, C. and Edwards, S. (2018) *Young Children Playing and Learning in a Digital Age: A Cultural and Critical Perspective*. London: Routledge.

Stephen, C. and Plowman, L. (2014) Digital play. In L. Brooker, M. Blaise and S. Edwards (eds) *SAGE Handbook of Play and Learning in Early Childhood*. London: Sage, pp. 330–341.

Sullivan, A. and Bers, M. U. (2016) Robotics in the early childhood classroom: learning outcomes from an 8-week robotics curriculum in pre-kindergarten through second grade. *International Journal of Technology and Design Education, 26* (1): 3–20.

Wood, E. (2015) Interpretivist research in play: the illumination of complexity. In S. Farrell, S. Kagan and S. Robson (eds) *The SAGE Handbook of Early Childhood Research*. London: Sage, pp. 291–303.

Yelland, N. (2015) Playful explorations and new technologies. In J. Moyles (ed.) *The Excellence of Play*. Maidenhead: Open University Press, pp. 225–236.

Yelland, N. (2016) iPlay, iLearn, iGrow: tablet technology, curriculum, pedagogies and learning in the twenty-first century. In S. Gurvis and N. Lemon (eds) *Understanding Digital Technology and Young Children: An International Perspective*. London: Routledge, pp. 38–45.

Yelland, N. and Gilbert, G. (2017) Re-imagining play with new technologies. In L. Arnott (ed.) *Digital Technologies and Learning in the Early Years*. London: Sage, pp. 32–44.

Zaman, B., Nouwen, M., Vanattenhoven, J., de Ferrerre, E. and Van Looy, J. (2016) A qualitative inquiry into the contextualized parental mediation practices of young children's digital media use at home. *Journal of Broadcasting and Electronic Media, 60* (1): 1–22.

2

OPEN–WORLD GAMES
AN EXPLORATION OF CREATIVE PLAY

LORNA ARNOTT, JOHN LEVINE AND GILLIAN SHANKS

CHAPTER OVERVIEW

This chapter considers the potential role of digital devices, and in particular open-world games, as part of early childhood creative play. As part of digital childhoods, it is clear that children are engaging with 'connected' and gaming resources at young ages. Drawing on this engagement, and child-centred pedagogy, we suggest that open-world games offer new opportunities for creative play for young children, bringing creativity into the domain of Science, Engineering, Maths and Technology (STEM).

This chapter aims to develop an understanding of:

- the potential for open-world gaming to foster engagement with young children and offer one possible mechanism for supporting young children's creative play
- how the affordances of open-world games offer similar possibilities to internet-enabled resources in terms of creative expression, linking to Anna Craft's (2012) 4Ps of digital childhood
- how spaces can be created for game play within the early years curriculum and pedagogy, provided that practitioners have the confidence to embrace it.

INTRODUCTION

We know that young children's worlds are digital; that they have access to digital technologies on a daily basis (Dunn et al., 2018; Marsh et al., 2015). As new technologies have advanced and become increasingly user-friendly for young children, there has been a dramatic increase in the use of tablet computers (Dunn et al., 2018). For example, children from around 6 months to 1 year old are engaging with new technologies (Aldhafeeri et al., 2016; O'Connor, 2017); and toddlers are engaged with screen-based applications, YouTube (Dunn et al., 2018) and communication media like Skype (Arnott, 2016). As a result, our youngest citizens have transitioned from consumers (Marsh, 2010) to co-creators of digital media. For example, children, supported by their families, have well-established YouTube channels, such as Ryan's Toy Review – a YouTube channel hosted by a 5-year-old child with 7 million subscribers. Thus, it is clear that new technologies and the ease of online sharing have created a conduit for novices to 'express themselves' through digital media (Zagalo and Branco, 2015). As a result, Craft (2012) argues that early years children in contemporary digital societies are empowered.

There is still disparity, however, between the level and nature of children's engagement with new technologies in home and educational settings, as we see digital difference between the two contexts (Edwards et al., 2017). In order to improve the continuity of learning and transition between children's various ecological systems (Bronfenbrenner, 2009), it is important for practitioners to develop an awareness of children's learning with technologies in informal learning contexts. Indeed, Marsh (2010: 26) suggests that '[virtual] worlds are becoming increasingly prevalent in children's out-of-school lives and it is important that educators become familiar with the way in which children are using these environments in order to build upon these experiences further'.

This chapter helps to make these connections by exploring digital devices, in particular open-world gaming, as a mechanism for fostering children's creative play. Dunn et al. (2018: 820) suggest that tablets help develop motivation and problem solving but also enhance children's creative expression. We suggest that open-world games have the potential to extend this creative expression, in a similar way that the internet offered a route for children to be 'agents of change':

> Internet enabled resources, it is argued, open up the world to the child beyond the playroom, classroom or home. The internet offers possibilities for learning beyond boundaries, across age phases, harnessing motivation, enabling high participation and nurturing creative possibility thinking [which] are all possible if we are brave enough to acknowledge the potency of childhood and youth and to co-create the future. (Craft, 2012: 183)

Throughout the remainder of this chapter, we highlight the current ways that open-world games have been used to foster creativity among children, and how these experiences offer opportunities for 'possibility thinking' (Craft, 2013). We conclude by drawing on the Early Level Curriculum for Excellence in Scotland to demonstrate the possible spaces for open-world gaming.

CREATIVE PLAY AND STEM: OPEN-WORLD GAMING IN EARLY CHILDHOOD

Traditional games in early childhood are well established as a useful method for learning (Danby et al., 2017), particularly in relation to fostering creativity (Davies et al., 2013: 86). In particular, games which allow for role playing (Gee, 2003); safe risk-taking as well as safe opportunities for failure (Duffy, 2006); open and free choice explorations whilst encouraging intrinsic motivation to learn (Craft, 2012) and imagination (Joubert, 2001) offer some of the best opportunities to support creativity. Gaming in early years education is only just beginning to offer these types of opportunities, as we explain throughout this section.

KEY DEFINITION: EDUTAINMENT

Edutainment is the use of *extrinsic* motivation in a game – suitable for things such as rote memorisation. This is typically achieved through the reward of a game-like feature (e.g. achievement/spending of tokens/points, mini-games or 'levelling up' to unlock achievements/ earn badges).

Until recently, the main form of digital game for young children predominantly fell into the 'Edutainment' bracket. Such games mirrored the kinds of traditional drill and practice exercises and extrinsic motivation associated with the transmission model of learning. These games are particularly challenging because the use of extrinsic rewards, such as coins and stickers, disrupts the child's play (Habgood and Ainsworth, 2011).

KEY DEFINITION: SERIOUS GAMES

Serious games use intrinsic motivation to encourage self-taught learning. Games achieve this through challenge, control, fantasy and curiosity (Malone, 1981) (as well as competition, co-operation and recognition).

Whilst extrinsic motivation is not all negative and research suggests that children enjoy these elements of the game (Dunn et al., 2018), the approach is less aligned to the fundamental principles of early years education. Nevertheless, the gamification of education has resulted in a wealth of Digital Serious Games (also called Digital Purposeful Games), albeit typically for older children. These games offer the opportunity for co-constructed meaning making and child-initiated or child-led opportunities for play. The use of challenge within these games can help achieve what Csikszentmihalyi (2014) referred to as a state of flow; when the difficulty of the game increasingly matches the newly developed skills of the individual. Open-world games offer these opportunities for flow but with the added benefit of open and free-choice exploration, facilitating opportunities to ask those all-important 'what if' questions, described in the next section.

KEY DEFINITION: OPEN-WORLD GAMES

Open-world games are those where the player can move around freely in a virtual world and where the gameplay is not linear. This contrasts with games which have a linear narrative and where the player is expected to solve a sequence of problems to achieve some end state, typically the end of a level. In some open-world games, there is no concrete end goal and the player is free to develop their own narrative and style of gameplay.

THE AFFORDANCES OF OPEN-WORLD GAMES FOR CREATIVE EXPRESSION

In most instances, explorations of creativity are discipline-specific, and the value, definitions and function of creativity are debated (Claxton, 2006; Craft, 2005). 'Possibility thinking' is one lens through which to explore creativity. It is concerned with the ways in which people engage with 'what if' thinking; being able to envisage multiple possibilities as solutions to a problem or to consider new ways of working and playing. It is moving beyond asking what a resource can do, towards exploring what we could do with the resource. It's a propensity to think outside the box and what Craft describes as Little C Creativity (Craft, 2012). This relates closely to a key cognitive process known as divergent thinking. Divergent thinking has been defined as a means of generating ideas to solve a problem (Runco and Acar, 2012), where it 'provides the foundation for creative production' (Romero et al., 2012: 424). Indeed, divergent thinking is central to both play and creativity (Russ, 2003).

It is from this perspective that open-world games have so much to offer because the player develops their own narrative; the game does not dictate to the child the objective of the game or how they should operate but rather offers a platform to explore. Of course, closed activities for young children are not without merit, and indeed a child completing jigsaws, for example, is still valuable for problem solving but they do not tap into that 'what if' critical reflection we are describing here. In an open-world game, children can assume several roles through the selection or creation of their lead character, as well as creating or utilising various tools and resources to create a 'world' or virtual space. This links closely with Craft's 4Ps of digital childhoods.

KEY CONCEPT: 4PS OF DIGITAL CHILDHOODS

'Plurality of identities (people, places, activities, literacies), possibility awareness (of what might be invented, of access options, of learning by doing and of active engagement), playfulness of engagement (the exploratory drive) and participation (all welcome through democratic, dialogic voice)' (Craft, 2011: 33).

We unpick the playful element of this conceptualisation in the next section when we address the place of open-world games in early years curriculum and pedagogy.

REFLECTIVE TASK

Audit your setting:

1. Map the affordances of each technological resource to Craft's 4Ps of digital childhood.
2. Observe children playing with the resources and identify instances of possibility thinking and Little C Creativity.

This activity helps reflect on the resources currently available in your practice and the opportunities they present for creative play. Often, we use resources in set ways, because that's the way it has always been done. Reflecting on the affordances of the resource may highlight new ways to incorporate them in our practice and support children's creative play. We may begin to see creativity as something that is fluid in many activities, rather than as something that is reserved for the art or creation areas.

SPACE FOR CREATIVE GAMING AND DIGITAL PLAY IN SCOTTISH PEDAGOGY AND CURRICULUM

One of the key elements in Craft's framework is the focus on 'playfulness'. Indeed, much of the discussion surrounding children's creativity has play at its core. Some say that creativity and pretend play are synonymous or at least very similar in structure and characteristics (Russ et al., 1999; Saracho, 1992). For example, Vygostky (2004: 11) suggested that:

> We can identify creative processes in children at the very earliest ages, especially in their play. A child who sits astride a stick and pretends to be riding a horse; a little girl who plays with a doll and imagines she is its mother; a boy who in his games becomes a pirate, a soldier, or a sailor, all these children at play represent examples of the most authentic, truest creativity.

Yet, the link to play creates challenges for technologies in early childhood. Yelland (2010) suggests that fears arise because there is a perception that technology does not align with the longstanding principle, dating back to the work of Froebel, that children should take part in concrete activities involving physical, malleable objects. From this, the concern has arisen that virtual play is different from 'real' play, despite research demonstrating that 'Play in virtual worlds is not virtual play ... [but is] ... "real" to the users' (Marsh 2010: 35). Thus, practitioners, worldwide, still feel unsure about the place of technologies in play practices (Mertala, 2017: 197).

Such anxiety from practitioners is juxtaposed with the clear focus from policy on the integration of digital devices in early years practice. For example, there are documented spaces for technologies in early years education in Scotland; as the Digital Learning and Teaching Strategy for Scotland states: 'We want to ensure that from the earliest stages of their education, children can begin to develop digital literacy, finding stimulation in early years settings and schools which use digital technology to enrich learning across the curriculum' (Scottish Government, 2016: 38).

Mertala (2017) suggests that one of the problems which may influence practitioners' integration of technologies is that technological educational games (which typically fall into the Edutainment bracket; see above) focus predominantly on academic achievement. They argue that this is at odds with the immediate focus in early years which is about socio-emotional development. Technologies, it is perceived, do not support this socio-emotional development but rather offer a route to knowledge transmission. Whilst academic learning may form an element of practitioners' planning, it is secondary to the founding principles of early years education which focus on meeting the needs of the individual child, through play. The academic knowledge is developed through these

Table 2.1 Mapping the curriculum to properties of open-world gaming and digital childhoods

Characteristics of open-world games for creative play	Mapped to Curriculum for Excellence Early Level Experiences and Outcomes (Education Scotland, 2016)	CFE themes
Advances in game-play technologies, such as motion sensors similar to those used in Xbox Kinect, allow opportunities for children to become immersed in virtual worlds in a more physical sense. In Scotland, we are also aware of primary schools which make use of a green screen, for example. In this sense, their virtual worlds combine an embodied experience. The experiences simultaneously offer an opportunity to unpick the mechanics, engineering and computer science involved in allowing such game play to occur, whilst the children are already motivated and engaged.	Computing Science: • I understand that sequences of instructions are used to control computing technology. (TCH 0-14a) • I can experiment with and identify uses of a range of computing technology in the world around me. (TCH 0-14b) • I can explore computational thinking processes involved in a variety of everyday tasks and can identify patterns in objects or information. (TCH 0-13a) • I can develop a sequence of instructions and run them using programmable devices or equivalent. (TCH 0-15a)	Technologies
As part of an effective learning environment, collaboration with others can be an important assistance to scaffolding learning and encouraging flow (Duffy, 2006; Fisher, 2013). As such, multiplayer games, either face to face or online (when safely facilitated), could improve creative thought processes.	Digital Literacy: • I can explore digital technologies and use what I learn to solve problems and share ideas and thoughts. (TCH 0-01a) • I can explore, play and communicate using digital technologies safely and securely. (TCH 0-03a)	
'Transgressive play occurred when children used features of the apps that were not part of the design, thus transgressing the app producers' intentions ... Play in which children contest, resist and/or transgress expected norms, rules and perceived restrictions in both digital and non-digital contexts' (Marsh et al., 2016: 250). Transgressive play is at the heart of open-world games; children construct their own narratives and are less restricted by the expected goals and aims of the game.	Craft, Design, Engineering and Graphics: • I explore everyday materials in the creation of pictures/models/concepts. (TCH 0-10a) • I explore ways to design and construct models. (TCH 0-09a) • I explore and discover different ways of representing ideas in imaginative ways. (TCH 0-11a)	
The Scottish national guidance for 'Building the Ambition' (Scottish Government, 2014: 49) calls for a learning environment that 'has plenty for the young child to talk about, imagining and creating, reasoning and testing out, sharing and negotiating, talking about the past, present and the future ... Gives time to persevere with inquiry learning and time to start a project and continue it over several days', all of which is entirely achievable within an open-world game environment (Bowman et al., 2015).	Technological Developments in Society and Business: • I enjoy playing with and exploring technologies to discover what they can do and how they can help us. (TCH 0-05a)	

Characteristics of open-world games for creative play	Mapped to Curriculum for Excellence Early Level Experiences and Outcomes (Education Scotland, 2016)	CFE themes
With advances in mobile technologies, gaming has become a 'common' resource in homes. Engaging with computer scientists around game design, as well as having increased autonomy in the structure of the game through open-world gaming, provides an opportunity for children to demonstrate creative thinking, whilst maintaining a focus on 'what makes it go'.	**Planet Earth:** • I have experienced, used and described a wide range of toys and common appliances. I can say 'what makes it go' and say what they do when they work. (SCN 0-04a) **Topical Science:** • I can talk about science stories to develop my understanding of science and the world around me. (SCN 0-20a)	Science
The virtual nature of online gaming offers opportunities to explore contexts and materials which may not be physically safe. The example may be a virtual science lab with dangerous chemicals and reactions. Children can virtually begin to engage with these materials through a science lab game design and be creative in their experimentation without fear of physical danger.	**Materials:** • Through creative play, I explore different materials and can share my reasoning for selecting materials for different purposes. (SCN 0-15a)	
A key focus in open-world games is designing the environment or game 'world'. Children engage with symbolic objects and signs to plan the context, characters and game objectives. N.B. Many other areas of numeracy and mathematics will be relevant, depending on the theme of the open-world game selected by the children.	**Information Handling:** • I can collect objects and ask questions to gather information, organising and displaying my findings in different ways. (MNU 0-20a) • I can match objects, and sort using my own and others' criteria, sharing my ideas with others. (MNU 0-20b) • I can use the signs and charts around me for information, helping me plan and make choices and decisions in my daily life. (MNU 0-20c) **Shape, Position and Movement:** • In movement, games, and using technology I can use simple directions and describe positions. (MTH 0-17a)	Numeracy and Maths

co-constructed meaning-making experiences, but pedagogical planning does not start from the curriculum in a top-down manner as various numeracy or literacy 'Edutainment' games would imply. Thus, there is a clear paradox between the learning needs of young children and game design.

We suggest that appropriately designed open-world games for young children may alleviate some of these challenges because they offer that route to co-constructed meaning making, through a child-centred and child-driven play experience. This process then offers a route to creative expression and creative thinking due to the wealth of possibilities they afford. In order to articulate the links between this type of game play and the possibilities for early level learning, we map some characteristics of digital game play to some of the Scottish Curriculum for Excellence's Experiences and Outcomes. We focus on those immediately related to STEM, to articulate that creativity is not reserved for arts-based subjects but has a key role in digital childhoods (see Table 2.1).

To contextualise links to curriculum and pedagogy, we present cases that demonstrate some of the ways open-world games have been used in education, albeit with older children. Yet we know that children engage with game worlds such as *Minecraft* under 5 years of age (Marsh et al., 2018), and, therefore, similar experiences to those presented below could be considered with younger children too.

CASE STUDY 2.1: SCOTTISH CHILDREN'S GAMING IN EDUCATION

The application of technology in education, to foster creativity, to date has been limited in two ways: (a) the number of applications has been small and has focused on specific areas; and (b) the children targeted by these initiatives and studies have typically been in the later years of primary school or in secondary education. However, these limitations are not inherent in the approach used and we discuss this further at the end of this section. Here, we present two specific initiatives where video games and technological toys are used to foster creativity, teamwork, planning and communication.

The first approach involves the open-world game *Minecraft*. *Minecraft* is an open-world sandbox game in which the gameplay has no specific objective, giving players a great deal of freedom about how to play the game. The game runs in a number of modes: one of these is survival mode in which the player has to collect resources and create structures in order to survive in a hostile world. However, another mode, and one which has become more popular with the players, is creative mode, where the player has full access to all resources and can create large and sophisticated structures, such as replicas of famous historic buildings or reconstructions of ancient cities. Using *Minecraft*, Derek Robertson (see 'Useful websites' at the end of the chapter) allowed teams of children aged 9–11 to become virtual architects and reimagine the waterfront in the city of Dundee in Scotland. The results of the project were interesting and encouraging, and showed that real video games can be used in school to foster creativity. They also demonstrated that these skills can be fostered using a 'pupil-led' approach. In a similar vein, the BBC ran a 'Build it Scotland' initiative for 7–14-year-olds, also using *Minecraft*, but this time to recreate famous Scottish monuments (see 'Useful websites').

The other initiative worth mentioning in this context is First Lego League (see 'Useful websites'). This uses the programmable Lego Mindstorms robotics kit to challenge children of ages 9–16 in teams of up to 10 to design, build and programme their own robot to meet a number of interesting robotic challenges laid out on a standard game board. The challenges are specifically designed to be ones which have a wide range of possible solutions; the judges have noted many times that the robotic solutions adopted by the teams are not the ones that they expected to see. The aim of the initiative is to encourage digital skills, creativity, teamwork, communication and planning. In common with the *Minecraft* work mentioned above, it is also pupil-led, with adults acting in the role of mentor rather than instructor. First Lego League is a worldwide initiative run by FIRST, based in the USA. It is run in the UK and Ireland by the Institute of Engineering and Technology, and in Scotland by Lambda Jam. A new competition run by FIRST and aimed at 6–9-year-olds (First Lego League Jr) has now been launched but is not yet available in Scotland. First Lego League Jr is based on the Lego WeDo robotics kit and software.

Here we begin to see how open-world games, and connected communities, offer a route for children's creative application in STEM subjects, but it's important to note that children in these projects were fully supported and guided in their technology use. From a contextualist perspective, we cannot argue that the resources will support creative play autonomously, thus appropriate guided interaction (Plowman and Stephen, 2007) is still required by practitioners. We are not suggesting that open-world games do the pedagogic work for us; rather, that they offer another medium to engage children and support their creative play.

We suggest the use of digital gaming because we know that children enjoy using technologies in the early years (e.g. Dunn et al., 2018). Early childhood education always comes back to putting the child at the centre (HMIe, 2007) and following the child's thread (Nutbrown, 2011). In contemporary Scottish society, the child's thread is digital. Therefore, we must find ways to marry digital play with the principles of high-quality early years pedagogy. We offer open-world games as a potential solution and as a new idea about digital play, as called for by Edwards and Bird:

Contemporary research suggests that the struggle to effectively use technologies in early childhood education could be addressed by developing new ideas about children's digital play that helps educators to recognize children's activity with technologies in a play-based way. (Edwards and Bird, 2017: 159)

REFLECTIVE TASK

Consider the ways in which you currently use digital devices and games in your practice:

1. Identify links to your own curriculum and map out how the use of technologies can support children's creative play in your setting.
2. Reflect on your own pedagogical planning around technologies – in what ways do you or could you plan to use digital devices for creative play?

SUMMARY

Throughout this chapter, we have very briefly introduced the concept of open-world gaming as a potential route towards supporting young children's creative play. This chapter concludes that by exploring the curriculum and our pedagogical planning from the perspective of creativity and technology as complementary, it may offer a new way of seeing and interpreting our practice and the child's creative digital world. We need to marry the founding principle of early years pedagogy with game play, which includes scaffolding children's interactions with technologies through guided interaction (Plowman and Stephen, 2007), where appropriate.

KEY POINTS TO REMEMBER

*   The possibilities offered by open-world gaming as a potential route for facilitating children's creative expression as part of STEM subjects.
*   That open-world gaming allows for the 4Ps of creativity in digital childhoods (Craft, 2013).
*   That open-world gaming aligns more closely with the principles of high-quality early years play by allowing children to engaged in being co-constructed meaning makers and alleviate some of the previous concerns that game play does not represent 'real' play.

POINTS FOR DISCUSSION

Reflect on your perceptions of digital devices and game play in early childhood:

1. In what ways can you see new technologies (in a broad sense) supporting creative play?
2. What games are currently available which offer the types of creative experiences for children that we describe in this chapter?
3. Consider the ways that the nature of children's play is changing due to the accessibility of technologies – how can this support creative thinking?
4. How crucial is a focus on practitioner engagement when utilising open-world games for creative play in early years education?

FURTHER READING

Arnott, L. (ed.) (2017) *Digital Technologies and Learning in the Early Years*. London: Sage.

Craft, A. (2012) Childhood in a digital age: creative challenges for educational futures. *London Review of Education*, 10: 173–190.

Marsh, J., Plowman, L., Yamada-Rice, D., Bishop, J., Lahmar, J. and Scott, F. (2018) Play and creativity in young children's use of apps. *British Journal of Educational Technology*, 49 (5): 870–882.

Stephen, C., Brooker, L., Oberhuemer, P. and Parker-Rees, R. (eds) (2018) *Digital Play and Technologies in the Early Years*. London: Routledge.

USEFUL WEBSITES

BBC (2017) *Make it Digital: Build it Scotland* – www.bbc.co.uk/programmes/articles/5X5dZ7mnvGN3nh5t8PlP18S/build-it-scotland

Institute of Engineering and Technology (IET) (2017) *First Lego League* – http://firstlegoleague.theiet.org

Robertson, D. (2014) *Minecraft: On the Waterfront*. Blog, 17 November – https://hotmilkydrink.typepad.com/my_weblog/2014/11/minecraft-on-the-waterfront.html

Ryan's Toy Review – www.youtube.com/channel/UChGJGhZ9SOOHvBB0Y4DOO_w/featured

REFERENCES

Aldhafeeri, F., Palaiologou, I. and Folorunsho, A. (2016) Integration of digital technologies into play-based pedagogy in Kuwaiti early childhood education: teachers' views, attitudes and aptitudes. *International Journal of Early Years Education*, 24: 342–360.

Arnott, L. (2016) The role of digital technologies. In I. Palaiologou (ed.) *The Early Years Foundation Stage: Theory and Practice*. London: Sage.

Bowman, N. D., Kowert, R. and Ferguson, C. J. (2015) The impact of video game play on human (and orc) creativity. In G. P. Green and J. C. Kaufman (eds) *Video Games and Creativity*. San Diego, CA: Academic Press, pp. 39–60.

Bronfenbrenner, U. (2009) *The Ecology of Human Development*. Princeton, NJ: Harvard University Press.

Claxton, G. (2006) Thinking at the edge: developing soft creativity. *Cambridge Journal of Education, 36*: 351–362.

Craft, A. (2005) *Creativity in Schools*. London: Routledge.

Craft, A. (2011) *Creativity and Education Futures: Learning in a Digital Age*. Stoke on Trent: Trentham Books.

Craft, A. (2012) Childhood in a digital age: creative challenges for educational futures. *London Review of Education, 10*: 173–190.

Craft, A. (2013) Childhood, possibility thinking and wise, humanising educational futures. *International Journal of Educational Research, 61*: 126–134.

Csikszentmihalyi, M. (2014) Play and intrinsic rewards. In *Flow and the Foundations of Positive Psychology*. Dordrecht: Springer, pp. 135–153.

Danby, S., Davidson, C., Theobald, M., et al. (2017) Pretend play and technology: young children making sense of their everyday social worlds. In D. Pike, S. Lynch and C. A. Beckett (eds) *Multidisciplinary Perspectives on Play from Birth and Beyond*. Singapore: Springer, pp. 231–245.

Davies, D., Jindal-Snape, D., Collier, C., et al. (2013) Creative learning environments in education: a systematic literature review. *Thinking Skills and Creativity, 8*: 80–91.

Duffy, B. (2006) *Supporting Creativity and Imagination in the Early Years*. Maidenhead: Open University Press.

Dunn, J., Gray, C., Moffett, P., et al. (2018) 'It's more funner than doing work': children's perspectives on using tablet computers in the early years of school. *Early Child Development and Care, 188* (6): 819–831.

Edwards, S. and Bird, J. (2017) Observing and assessing young children's digital play in the early years: using the Digital Play Framework. *Journal of Early Childhood Research, 15* (2): 158–173.

Edwards, S., Henderson, M., Gronn, D., et al. (2017) Digital disconnect or digital difference? A socio-ecological perspective on young children's technology use in the home and the early childhood centre. *Technology, Pedagogy and Education, 26*: 1–17.

Education Scotland (2016) Curriculum for Excellence. Available at: www.gov.scot/resource/doc/226155/0061245.pdf (accessed 11 October 2018).

Fisher, J. (2013) *Starting from the Child: Teaching and Learning from 4–8*. London: McGraw-Hill Education.

Gee, J. P. (2003) *What Video Games have to Teach us about Learning and Literacy*. New York: Palgrave Macmillan.

Habgood, M. P. J. and Ainsworth, S. E. (2011) Motivating children to learn effectively: exploring the value of intrinsic integration in educational games. *Journal of the Learning Sciences, 20*: 169–206.

HMIe (2007) *The Child at the Centre: Self-Evaluation in the Early Years*. Livingston: HMIe.

Joubert, M. M. (2001) The art of creative teaching: NACCCE and beyond. In A. Craft, B. Jeffrey and M. Leibling (eds) *Creativity in Education*. London: Continuum, pp. 17–34.

Malone, T. W. (1981) Toward a theory of intrinsically motivating instruction. *Cognitive Science, 5* (4): 333–369.

Marsh, J. (2010) Young children's play in online virtual worlds. *Journal of Early Childhood Research, 8*: 23–39.

Marsh, J., Plowman, L., Yamada-Rice, D., et al. (2015) Exploring play and creativity in pre-schoolers' use of apps: final project report. Available at: www.techandplay.org/reports/TAP_Final_Report.pdf (accessed 11 October 2018).

Marsh, J., Plowman, L., Yamada-Rice, D., et al. (2016) Digital play: a new classification. *Early Years, 36*: 242–253.

Marsh, J., Plowman, L., Yamada-Rice, D., et al. (2018) Play and creativity in young children's use of apps. *British Journal of Educational Technology, 49* (5): 870–882.

Mertala, P. (2017) Wag the dog: the nature and foundations of preschool educators' positive ICT pedagogical beliefs. *Computers in Human Behavior, 69*: 197–206.

Nutbrown, C. (2011) *Threads of Thinking: Schemas and Young Children's Learning*. London: Sage.

O'Connor, J. (2017) Under 3s and technology. In L. Arnott (ed.) *Digital Technologies and Learning in the Early Years*. London: Sage, pp. 87–98.

Plowman, L. and Stephen, C. (2007) Guided interaction in pre-school settings. *Journal of Computer Assisted Learning, 23*: 14–26.

Romero, M., Hyvönen, P. and Barberà, E. (2012) Creativity in collaborative learning across the life span. *Creative Education, 3*: 422–429.

Runco, M. A. and Acar, S. (2012) Divergent thinking as an indicator of creative potential. *Creativity Research Journal, 24*: 66–75.

Russ, S. W. (2003) Play and creativity: developmental issues. *Scandinavian Journal of Educational Research, 47*: 297–303.

Russ, S. W., Robins, A. L. and Christiano, B. A. (1999) Pretend play: longitudinal prediction of creativity and affect in fantasy in children. *Creativity Research Journal, 12*: 129–140.

Saracho, O. N. (1992) Preschool children's cognitive style and play and implications for creativity. *Creativity Research Journal, 5*: 35–47.

Scottish Government (2014) *Building the Ambition: National Practice Guidance on Early Learning and Childcare*. Edinburgh: Scottish Government.

Scottish Government (2016) *Enhancing Learning and Teaching through the Use of Digital Technology: A Digital Learning and Teaching Strategy for Scotland*. Edinburgh: Scottish Government.

Vygotsky, L. (2004) Imagination and creativity in childhood. *Journal of Russian and East European Psychology*, 42: 7–97.

Yelland, N. (2010) New technologies, playful experiences, and multimodal learning. In I. Berson and M. Berson (eds) *High-Tech Tots: Childhood in a Digital World*. Charlotte, NC: Information Age Publishing, pp. 5–22.

Zagalo, N. and Branco, P. (2015) *Creativity in the Digital Age*. London: Springer.

3

FROM PLAY TO MEDIA

A PHYSICAL APPROACH TO DIGITAL MEDIA

GRETE SKJEGGESTAD MEYER AND INGVARD BRÅTEN

CHAPTER OVERVIEW

This chapter offers insight into how play-based pedagogy in media-making can give children media experience and new media play-based initiatives. We argue that play and media do not necessarily start with digital technology or media, but in creativity and bodily experience. We build on Vygotsky's idea (2004: 11) that creativity rooted in play is 'an essential condition for existence'.

We describe a research project looking at how children aged 4–5 years old create a story using physical and neutral objects, which is later transformed into an edited film. The study was conducted in Norway, where the term kindergarten is used to refer to early childhood education settings (for more information on the early childhood education system, see Chapter 5).

Our main theoretical framework is on media play in early childhood (Johansen, 2015; Thestrup, 2011; see also Chapter 13 for more information on media play), children's play and imagination (Vygotsky, 1995), bodily experience (Dewey, 2005; Merleau-Ponty, 1994), the devising process (Oddey, 1999) and the risk to education (Biesta, 2014).

This chapter aims to help you understand:

- how technology can help children create stories using dramatic play and then make it into films
- how children's experiences with technology can be used alongside other materials to facilitate story making
- how children's knowledge of media, such as computer games and movies, is highly relevant when faced with the physical materials they are offered.

THE PROJECT

This chapter is based on a research project that used a case study approach. The project was conducted in three different kindergartens, each having three sessions.

In the first session, we created a story. For this purpose, we used the same physical materials in all three kindergartens. These were small wooden blocks (Figure 3.1) and clay. The children were shown one cardboard box and told that next time all the small blocks would be replaced with large boxes. The children used clay to form figures or other elements to illustrate their story. Working with the materials was intended as preparation for the session that followed. The children talked about what they created as they played, and at times we asked them about their constructions. A video camera on a tripod was placed in a corner of the room to record the story and the building process. We also took pictures of the small constructions using an iPad.

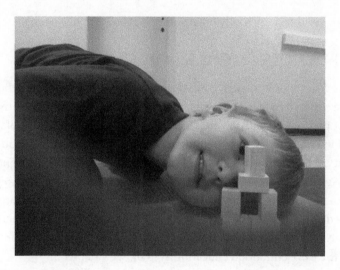

Figure 3.1 The small blocks

In the second session, the room was filled with cardboard boxes. We gathered the children and talked about what we had planned during our last discussion. What had they built using the small bricks and what had they intended to build? Together we agreed on what to build. When a construction with the cardboard boxes was finished, we recorded the scene. Occasionally, the children played and constructed without adult interaction, whilst, at other times, they were gently guided in their play. When we left, the boxes remained in the kindergarten for the children to play with as they wished.

For the third session, we edited the video material, before we presented the film to the children involved. A video camera recorded the children's reaction whilst they watched the film. We asked them to comment if they noted any changes to their story and about their experience of filmmaking. In all three kindergartens, the children watched the films multiple times and invited their peers to watch the finished product.

In the body of this chapter, we focus on findings from the third kindergarten we visited, on the methods used and our theoretical background. This small-scale project involved three girls and two boys (aged between 4 and 5 years) and their class teacher.

MAKING STORIES

We decided to use theatre devising as our method of making a film with the children. In devised theatre, the main focus is on *process* but with the expectation of an end product. We told the children, before starting the work, that our goal was to make a film. Typically, devising and role play/dramatic play are based on collaboration (Kjølner, 2001; Oddey, 1999). In role play, the children are in charge. Conversely, devised theatre usually has some sort of leadership, represented by the theatre group's leader. The devising process strives for equality but may have a leader who decides on the finished product. Kjølner (2001: 79) described devising as 'an attitude towards a production'.

A devising process starts with a stimulus, such as objects or stories. Our project used wooden bricks and cardboard boxes as stimuli; first, we introduced the wooden bricks and in the next session replaced them with cardboard boxes.

Alison Oddey writes that 'the significance of this form of theatre is in the emphasis it places on an eclectic process requiring innovation, invention, imagination, risk, and above all, an overall group commitment to the developing work' (1999: 2). She underlines that 'every group has the right to fail' (1999: 25), an approach that informs our work with children. Devised theatre does not predetermine its outcomes which are unknown at the start of the process. Vygotsky also believed in the importance of process when working with children:

> It must not be forgotten that the basic law of children's creativity is that its value lies not in its results, not in the product of creation, but in the process itself. It is not important what children create, but that they do create, that they exercise and implement their creative imagination. (2004: 72)

Biesta (2014) defines education as a radically open process, which involves the risk of not achieving one's goals. He claims that risk-taking is necessary and that, when pedagogies are open-ended, anything can happen and anything can emerge (Biesta, 2014; Meyer and Eilifsen, 2017). This is the known uncertainty that most arts educators risk. In essence, from the start of this project both the process and the product were at risk and were dependent, amongst other factors, on the group process and the children's initiative and involvement.

In the devising process, it was considered important to secure children's enjoyment in the task, as Vygotsky observed: 'The highest reward that play provides must be the pleasure the child experiences in preparing for the production and from the process of acting itself, and not the success or approval the child receives from adults' (2004: 73).

CASE STUDY 3.1: THE STARTING POINT – DEVISING THE PROCESS WITH FIVE 4- AND 5-YEAR-OLDS

The children are in the room, together with their teacher and two lecturers from the local university college. They sit in a circle on the floor and they each have some small wooden bricks in front of them. We talk about making a film together and that we need stories for the film. The children are building with the bricks and there are many parallel conversations in the room and an atmosphere of deep concentration. Two girls chat and one of them suggests that her bricks resemble a tower. One of them suggests it is the Tower of Rapunzel. An adult repeats the suggestion, and one of the girls wants to take a picture of the tower. There is loud talking, when a boy tries to get attention: 'I have made a doorway, a portal!' His work collapses, he rebuilds his doorway, it collapses again and he rebuilds. At some point, he cries out 'I am making a *Minecraft* portal!' He looks satisfied.

In case study 3.1, which is a re-edited transcription of the video recording, it may be concluded that children use stories from different media: Rapunzel from the animated feature film *Tangled* by Disney (2010) and the portal from the computer game *Minecraft*. The small wooden bricks seemed to remind the boy of the building bricks and portal of *Minecraft*, a game he likes to play. Vygotsky (2004: 16) claims that imagination is dependent on previous experience, but at the same time new in the constructs of fantasy. This theory appeared to be in operation in this scenario. The children used their former media experiences to construct something new, using creative and imaginative processes.

The Swedish media-researcher Rönnberg (1983: 99) calls this phenomenon media play in her report of a project undertaken in Swedish kindergartens aimed at determining how children's play was connected to mass media stories and characters. The Danish media-researcher Thestrup (2011: 66) defined media play as being where 'children play with the media they have access to' (authors' translation). This may include media characters, pictures/stories/communication through film, TV, the internet, concrete digital devices and tools. In case study 3.1, the children's play and film making became media play, as described by Rönnberg and Thestrup, and as illustrated in Figure 3.2.

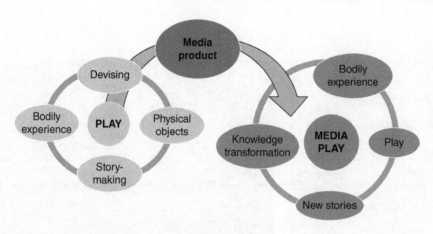

Figure 3.2   Transformation of children's play, through media experience and film production, into media play

---

REFLECTIVE TASK

Reflecting on case study 3.1, discuss your views on how media can be used in your own practice. What advantages and disadvantages might you encounter?

PLAYING THE STORIES AND RECORDING

In session two, the children found cardboard boxes in the room. We told them they could use them to build and develop the play stories devised in the previous session, and that we would video-record the session (see Figures 3.3 and 3.4). Building structures were built and torn down, built and torn down:

The children are playing and building different constructions with cardboard boxes. A doorway is being built. An adult helps the children to make a high portal, and to construct the roof of the portal. The children put a box on the floor of the portal. The boy, who built the portal of the wooden bricks in the first session, is on his way into the portal. He gently steps into the cardboard box on the floor, and exclaims to a teacher, 'One stands a bit like this'. He turns halfway around and then steps out on the other side of the portal: 'Yes, and then we are there.' He explains that the box must be straightened, to be in the middle of the portal. The other children walk through the portal one by one. The other boy walks in and turns around like the first boy, before he carefully steps out on the other side. A girl bends down and goes through as an animal. Only one of the children looks up into the camera.

Figure 3.3 Children play with the materials

Figure 3.4 Cardboard boxes used in the session

In this session, the children continued to use media experiences. The children concentrated on their play and stories. Influenced by the 'Minecraft boy', they joined in the media play. They also built the Rapunzel tower with a girl wanting to be Rapunzel captured in the tower. Some of the children brought the world of Minecraft into new games: 'Look, it is actually a Minecraft car', exclaimed a boy, as he bent a cardboard sheet. A nearby girl pointed at the tower and said 'proper Minecraft'. The children co-operated in making their building higher. As one of the girls moved a stack of boxes, she exclaimed: 'Oh, our beautiful Minecraft house'. The children used their media knowledge to make new stories based on characters and stories from the different media. At this point, the children were in the *devising process* and let the film inform their play.

WATCHING THE EDITED MOVIE

In the third session, we gathered the five children onto mattresses on the floor in front of the wall that functioned as our screen. Having previously edited the film, we presented their collaborative work. We sought to determine their reactions to and comments on the film takes and their story, now transformed into an edited film:

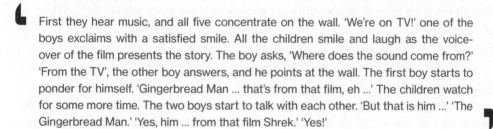

First they hear music, and all five concentrate on the wall. 'We're on TV!' one of the boys exclaims with a satisfied smile. All the children smile and laugh as the voice-over of the film presents the story. The boy asks, 'Where does the sound come from?' 'From the TV', the other boy answers, and he points at the wall. The first boy starts to ponder for himself. 'Gingerbread Man ... that's from that film, eh ...' The children watch for some more time. The two boys start to talk with each other. 'But that is him ...' 'The Gingerbread Man.' 'Yes, him ... from that film Shrek.' 'Yes!'

In the first session, the brown clay seemed to make the children focus on chocolate cookies. To illustrate this focus, the edited film had a still picture of a gingerbread man. The children recognised this as a character from the movie *Shrek*. The film had a voice-over that talked about the magic portal with a soundtrack. One girl commented and pointed at the wall: 'That is such a strange sound.' The soundtrack illustrated their magical transition into a new world, as the children moved through the portal.

A boy got to his feet: 'You have to watch. First like this and then like this!' He shows the others how he stepped into the cardboard box on the floor of the portal and then turned around in what is now the magical portal of the film. When he has finished showing, he sits down again. His action seems to illustrate his reflections on what he himself experienced in real life and what he saw in the edited film.

PLAY AND BODILY EXPERIENCE

As the description above shows, this film project focuses on play and bodily experiences using physical materials. This is a crucial element of the project.

Young children are physical in their approach to the world. Digital tools are sometimes seen as being in contrast to bodily movement. It seems to be generally accepted that children are increasingly sedentary. This possibly finds much of its verification in the expanding use of digital and mass media, in spite of the development of computer and TV games that require body movements. No matter how far technology develops, it will still be an imitation of the physical world. It is our contention that the computer game *Minecraft*, for example, cannot teach a child how to build a house because the physical sense of weight, strength, balance, construction, and so on, is lacking. When a child does a puzzle on the computer, they will not get a sense of losing the pieces, or when colouring in Paint Shop they will not get paint on their fingers. The children of today need to develop digital literacy, but they also need to have physical and bodily experiences in the real world. Things relate to our bodies in different ways.

The philosopher Merleau-Ponty stressed how important our body is in understanding the world. We sense through our body. We understand as a result of our bodily experiences. As such, it is wrong to distinguish between thought and embodied experiences. The philosopher René Descartes launched the thesis: 'I think, therefore I am', as the proof of human existence. Merleau-Ponty believed that rather it should be: 'I can – therefore I am' (1994: 91). Anyone who has seen young children's approach to the world will be able to appreciate Merleau-Ponty's emphasis on bodily experience: children jump, run, taste, listen, crawl, and so on.

As we grow up, our approach to the world changes, but we never grow out of our body. Our sensuous and bodily experiences are an important part of the individual. Many of these bodily experiences happen in close relation to objects. In working with children and digital media, we believe it is important to remember that children should also have physical and bodily experiences. According to Dewey, past experiences are like organs we perceive the world through – like the lungs we breathe with (1980).

In our approach, we emphasised that play and bodily experiences encompass media experiences and are not devoid of the basic nature of childhood. The opposite approach might be where the activities are exclusively based on tools, a computer programme or an application on a tablet. Digital tools give many opportunities well suited for playful use with children, but they can also bind and restrict the natural playfulness of the child.

Digital tools should not replace the experience of physical materials. Rather, the two should complement each other.

REFLECTIVE TASK

- Why do you think young children need experiences that are physically manifested? In your discussion consider:
  - Which physical materials/objects (other than cardboard boxes) could you use as a starting point for story and film making with children? How and why will these

objects function as a stimulus? Try it out in a devising process with children or fellow students.

- Try to make a short film with children or fellow students, using iMovie or something similar. Edit the takes. Your goal is to edit the film as a means of decoding and 'reading' the film together with the children afterwards. Is there a difference between their real-life experience and the shown movie? For example, you can use 'fast forward', 'slow motion' or put in new soundtracks, use stills, etc.

ETHICAL REFLECTIONS

Working with children always requires high ethical awareness. Aubrey (2000: 156) writes that 'ethics means the moral philosophy or set of moral principles underpinning a project'. In our project, it was important to reflect on what it means for children to be filmed in different situations. Today, most children are used to being photographed and filmed, but this is primarily related to home/family situations. Research that captures children on film mastering a situation where they might express joy or sadness requires great sensitivity, with a view to protecting the child's right to demonstrate their feelings in a safe and protected space. The children in our project were aware of the camera but, as they became engrossed in their play, appeared less conscious of its presence. This raises important ethical concerns for researchers, since we need to ensure that the experiences captured on film do not subsequently cause a child to experience regret or discomfort with the content of their depiction. To address these issues, ahead of the premiere to peers and parents, children were able to see and approve/disapprove the film before it was shown.

The stories and examples we present in this chapter are transcriptions of our video material. Working (and doing research) with children requires additional precautions regarding personal protection. Parents, children and teachers must give informed consent ahead of videotaping and for the research process, both in written or oral form depending on ability level. Worthy of note is that this project was also approved ahead of undertaking the study by the Norwegian National Committee for Research Ethics.

Working with children will always be a challenge concerning the balance of power and children's right to participation. This project is based on our own need to learn more about children's relationship with media and digital tools. Nevertheless, it has been important for us that our learning should not happen at the expense of the children. We have emphasised that everything we do in kindergarten should be characterised by a high degree of voluntarism and should be a pleasant experience for the children involved. We had a mutual agreement that if our need for knowledge and progress at any time came into conflict with the children's interests, then we would focus on the rights of the child.

We believe that the project experience should be a pleasurable and beneficial experience for the children, as previously proposed by Vygotsky (2004: 73).

REFLECTIVE TASKS

- According to the UN's Convention on the Rights of the Child, Article 12 (1989) and Norwegian early childhood education legislation (KD 2011, § 1 and 3), a child has an independent right to be heard and to be a decision maker. What consequences does this have for our pedagogical approach to media and to making media products with children?
- When working with children, you will always have to consider the uneven balance of power between a teacher and a child. What ethical considerations should one therefore have when developing a story, play and film project together with children?
- Are there situations where a media project will not benefit the child?
- In having respect for the child presented on film, how can we protect their dignity?

BALANCING THE TEACHER'S LEADERSHIP AND THE CHILDREN'S PARTICIPATION

In the process of making the movie, we wanted the children to experience and play with the physical materials. At the same time, we had a desire to get enough footage to edit into a movie. Here there is a potential conflict between the interests of the children and our research interests. For example, the children showed a greater interest in playing with the materials, whereas our interest was in movie making. Indeed, the session with the children was more about their building opportunities and play than about playful scenes for a film. Consequently, a weakness of our approach lies in the fact that the children had less ownership of the finished movie than we did. Although we took responsibility for editing the video material, we strove to maintain the children's initial ideas. Thus, the final movie showed real-life episodes of children's play, interpreted and narrated by an adult.

REFLECTIVE TASKS

- In what way is it possible to ensure the children's rights to ownership/creativity/ decision making in the film-making process?
- Is it right that teachers/researchers edit the children's film without involving them in the process? Explain your answer, drawing on ethics and theory to justify it.

SUMMARY

In this chapter, we explained how we blended technology and other materials to facilitate children's play. We also showed how media play can become part of children's playful encounters in early childhood education. In our project, when the children saw the film it had similarities with other media products they watch and use, but there were also some important differences. Whilst they see themselves as popular fictional characters in their film, the story is based on their own ideas. Thus, they note that the reinvention of a story can change key elements. In the editing process, we used effects like fast forward and slow motion, voice-overs, and the narrator offering explanations. Using this media experience, the children are heavily involved in the making of the film and are recipients of the process.

We were curious about what would happen after the children saw the movie. Would it nurture new play? The cardboard boxes were still available in their kindergarten. After the participants' peers saw the movie, the teacher told us that those who had been in the film group positioned themselves as experts in how to use the materials and to initiate play. They created new plays, influenced by their film.

Our project indicates that the experience of creating a film and seeing the film product, leads to media play. Through media production and experience of their own film, children's play is transformed.

KEY POINTS TO REMEMBER

- Play, bodily experience and physical materials as a starting point for work on media.
- Devising and the children's right to participation and play.
- Media play as children's play with characters and stories from mass media, films, computer games, the internet, and so on, and their play with digital devices.
- Ethical considerations concerning the vulnerability of children on film.

POINTS FOR DISCUSSION

- Children come with their own media experiences, through television, film, the internet and various digital devices. In early childhood education, we build our work on the children's former experiences and knowledge. The level of digital knowledge connected to media will vary from child to child. Mark Prensky (2001) was the first to use the term 'digital natives'. As Stine Liv Johansen (2015: 22) points out, the main sign of the digital native is that they do not experience so-called new media as new: 'The new media are just media and they have never known a world without them' (Johansen, 2015: 22; our translation). How can this fact have an impact on your work with digital media in ECE?

- Do you have any experience with children's media play? How would you describe it?
- How can you ensure children's play and creativity in your work with digital media in general and film in particular?
- How could one work with children on editing?

FURTHER READING

Biesta, G. J. J. (2014) *The Beautiful Risk of Education*. Boulder, CO: Paradigm Publishers. An exciting book on how education will always have an element of uncertainty and risk in achieving educational goals. The book's main theory is based on John Dewey.

Edwards, S. (2018) *Digital Play*. Encyclopaedia on Early Childhood Development: Play Based Learning. Montreal: Centre of Excellence for Early Childhood Development (CEECD/SKC-ECD).

Merleau-Ponty, M. (2012 [1945]) *Phenomenology of Perception*. New York: Routledge. This classical, philosophical text argues that knowledge of the human being is based on bodily experience and that cognitive processes are interwoven within the body.

Vygotsky, L. S. (2004 [1930]) Imagination and creativity in childhood. *Journal of Russian and East European Psychology*, 42 (1): 7–79. This is a lesser-known article by Vygotsky, describing how creativity is a major part of a child's development and everyday life.

USEFUL WEBSITES

www.bbc.co.uk/guides/zs83tyc;   www.bbc.co.uk/cbeebies/grownups/article-internet-use-and-safety – these sites offer advice on how children can safely use the internet.

www.pbs.org/parents/childrenandmedia/creating-preschool.html – this website offers practical examples of how media can be used with young children.

REFERENCES

Aubrey, C. (2000) *Early Childhood Education Research: Issues in Methodology and Ethics*. London: RoutledgeFalmer.

Biesta, G. J. J. (2014) *The Beautiful Risk of Education*. Bergen: Fagbokforlaget.

Dewey, J. (1980) *Arts as Experience*. New York: Berkley Publishing Group. [Originally published 1934.]

Johansen, S. L. (2015) *Children Live and Learn with Media*. Oslo: Cappelen Damm.

Kjølner, T. (2001) Devised theatre: experimental drama. In B. Rasmussen et al. (eds) *Nordic Voices in Drama, Theatre and Education*. Bergen: IDEA Publications, pp. 73–90.

Merleau-Ponty, M. (1994) *Phenomenology of Perception*. Oslo: Pax. [Originally published 1945.]

Meyer, G. S. and Eilifsen, M. (2017) The challenges of creativity in Norwegian early childhood teacher education. *European Early Childhood Research Journal*, *25* (3): 425–435.

Oddey, A. (1999) *Devising Theatre: A Practical and Theoretical Handbook*. London: Routledge. [Originally published 1994.]

Prensky, M. (2001) Digital natives, digital immigrants. *On the Horizon*, *9* (5). Available at: www.marcprensky.com/writing/Prensky%20-%20Digital%20Natives,%20Digital%20Immigrants%20-%20Part1.pdf (accessed 18 October 2018).

Rönnberg, M. (1983) *Skådelek och medialekar*. [*Harmful play and media games*.] *Early Childhood Research in Denmark IX*. Report of a seminar on children's play in modern industrial society, Committee on Early Childhood Research, Copenhagen, 29–30 August.

Rönnberg, M. (2009) Medieleg – del 2: Re-ludering. [Mediaplay – Part 2: Re-ludering.] *Tidsskrift for Børne & Ungdomskultur*. [*Journal of Child and Youth Culture*], *53*: 119–125.

Thestrup, K. (2011) The experimental community: media play in an educational context. PhD thesis, Institute for Aesthetics and Communication, Aarhus University.

United Nations (UN) (1989) *Convention on the Rights of the Child*. New York: Unicef. Available at: https://downloads.unicef.org.uk/wp-content/uploads/2010/05/UNCRC_united_nations_convention_on_the_rights_of_the_child.pdf (accessed 18 October 2018).

Vygotsky, L. S. (1995) *Imagination and Creativity in Childhood*. Göteborg: Daidalos. [Originally published 1930.]

Vygotsky, L. S. (2004) Imagination and creativity in childhood. *Journal of Russian and East European Psychology*, *42* (1): 7–79. [Originally published 1930.]

4

PLAYING WITH TECHNOLOGY OUTDOORS

MICHELLE ROGERS

CHAPTER OVERVIEW

There is a widespread perception that children are stopped from going outside due to their over-engagement with technology (Edwards et al., 2015). Often in settings in England, children use the outdoor environment for the purpose of 'play without technology'. This chapter explores the possibility of taking technology outdoors and the affordances it provides for children in the early years to fully explore pedagogical possibilities whilst engaging with the outdoor environment. A case study of an early years nursery based in a primary school setting in England was employed to consider the impact and influences that introducing iPads into a forest school presents.

This chapter aims to help you:

- recognise the wide diversity and affordances of mobile technology in the outdoor environment
- gain understanding about children's social presence online
- be able to understand, challenge and apply pedagogic reasoning for taking technology outdoors.

THE ENGLISH CONTEXT

Aubrey and Dahl (2014) considered the impact on early years professionals of aligning the experience and levels of confidence of staff using digital technologies. By extension, the role of children in modelling how best to use iPads to meet their own needs becomes the central issue (Jahnke and Kumar, 2014), rather than staff expectations of how iPads should be used by children. For example, when children share their social presence in the outdoor space with others in the nursery, via remote screen, it allows early years practitioners to 'tune in' to the children's needs to use technology purposefully and in context (Palaiologou, 2014). Similar theories have fuelled the development of training for early years practitioners on the wider and more intuitive ways in which iPads might be used in the outdoor space (Fenty and Anderson, 2014; see also Chapter 14).

It seems that whenever there is detrimental reporting in England on childhood behaviour or health issues, the fault focuses on how children in today's societies engage with the available technology. There is concern that when such demonisation of technology occurs society tends to overlook the fact that technology is purely a tool. Moreover, it is how that tool is used and applied that requires challenge. The affordances of mobile technology exacerbate this demonisation and can be considered detrimental to how young children engage with technology, develop their online presence and become age-aware of the risk factors of using technology. Although there are pockets of technological innovation in England, this knowledge is rarely shared. Implementing good practice necessitates training and questions are being raised concerning the availability of training for staff working in the early childhood education and care (ECE) sector who wish to support and understand how children use technologies effectively and purposefully (Wolfe and Flewitt, 2010).

The evidence presented thus far suggests that ECE in England, as in many countries (Fleer, 2017; Gray et al., 2017; Palaiologou, 2016), requires more digital resources to fully and appropriately engage children with technological experiences and expertise. The focus in this chapter is on multifunctional interactive technologies that encompass interactive media, both digital and analogue, including the use of applications [apps] and a diverse range of software that ensures interaction between child/child and child/adult (NAEYC and Fred Rogers Center, 2012). For example, iPads and tablets are frequently limited by staff who use them to record their daily assessments on the children in their ECE settings. Yet potentially children could use these devices to access interactive storybooks or to take pictures of their constructions of art. Technology in this instance could be used by the children to build a record of their own achievements, thus enhancing all aspects of their developmental growth and well-being. More frequent interaction with technology would also equip children with the knowledge and skills necessary to remain safe in a society dominated by technology.

By the very nature of their size and manoeuvrability, mobile technology has many more affordances than cumbersome personal computers and laptops. At one time, technology appeared to 'go large' with screen sizes becoming impractically large and immobile. However, a change occurred in the development of technology and it was adapted to 'go smaller' to meet consumer requirements. The rapid advancement in mobile technology in the past 18 years ensures that many global societies have access to increasingly sophisticated and advanced devices. However, the level of advancement of mobile technologies is rarely considered, with many people using only a small percentage of the tools and storage contained within them. Seemingly, the drive to update or purchase the latest version of mobile technology is *price*. Consequently, companies design and develop mobile technologies that are consumer-friendly in price and disposability.

REFLECTIVE TASK

Consider your planning over the past month for either a group in your setting or your children. Think about how you have embedded technology into their learning. Engaging with this reflective task will support your understanding of how children learn to use technology purposefully for themselves and to consider their ability with digital devices. The following questions might help you reflect on planning:

- How do you determine a child's digital capabilities?
- What can you do to track their digital development?
- How will this inform the technological affordances you provide?
- How do children use this technology? Is use affected by context?

CASE STUDY 4.1: 'PARENTS AS PARTNERS'

The nursery is attached to a local primary school, which is located in a recognised deprived area of the West Midlands, England. A high percentage of children have English as a second language. Various intervention initiatives are in place to support parents as partners, and to aid language development, community cohesion and outdoor learning, including a forest school initiative. Children attend nursery from 2 years of age, subsidised by government funding; the children who attend the nursery transition into the local primary reception class. The school and nursery work closely to develop joint initiatives, most especially 'parents as partners' who are invited to actively engage with the school and nursery community; there is also a focus on outdoor learning.

This case study focuses on the outdoor initiative and parents as partners, to aid their understanding of their children's digital footprint, the use of mobile technology, tuning parents into digital safety and social presence and the importance of these. Staff used the opportunity to purchase a set of iPads and, after several children showed a reluctance to leave the 'technology' corner, considered how they might use them to support children's digital engagement in the outdoors. Staff observed that four boys (aged between 3:8 and 4:10) consistently monopolised the tablets to play the preloaded apps and games. Azim (3:8), Sam (4:1), Farzul (4:9) and Oli (4:10) were also seen wandering around different areas of the nursery keeping the tablets with them rather than sharing them with others. The boys' key workers identified a need to ascertain whether the boys had access to tablet technology at home and how they might widen the boys' play choices and play spaces. Having consulted with the boys' parents, key workers confirmed that all of the boys had direct or indirect access to tablets and gaming technologies, either their own or those belonging to older siblings or parents. Little was known about the interactions they had online or about how they might use them other than for gaming purposes.

The nursery recognised a need to support the use of technology in outdoor spaces accessible to children in the setting. Recharging points were placed near the forest school and near the climbing frame. A staff member confident in the use of iPads demonstrated to Azim, Sam, Farzul and Oli various ways of capturing and recording information each morning before the forest school began. Within three days, Oli had requested that he take the iPad into the forest school to capture images of frogspawn 'so I can zoom in and see baby frogs'. As the iPads are protected against robust play, Oli was directed about the use of the technology around water, which he accepted, stating that that is why he is not allowed to take his 'mummy's phone into the bathroom because it might fall into the toilet or the bath. It won't work then'. He then went out into the forest school and captured various images of the frogspawn, plus other activities and things which captured his interest. The methodology employed here was informed by the mosaic approach (Clarke and Moss, 2005) and sought to capture Oli's visual thoughts about his environment facilitated by his key worker who sat with him and asked questions about his pictures to inform the development of future planning. Led by Oli, the images and two video recordings were sorted into those which he wanted to delete – at this stage, the criteria which drove his decision to delete were not clear – and those he wanted to save. Images were saved into Oli's file on the hard drive and later used to capture his learning journey. Staff recognised that by placing images and videos into PowerPoint, a software presentation programme, they would have something more dynamic to share with parents when they came into the nursery for parents' evening. Oli was supported in editing the images and in using the crop and enhance app. When this was completed, pictures were uploaded into a digital storybook which was looped onto the setting's web page. No images of children were uploaded onto the site; as Oli suggested, it was about the frogs not the children. If we explore the

(Continued)

(Continued)

concept of consent and assent, it might be argued that Oli's suggestion/decision to only upload these images was *assent*.

Several weeks after the iPads were introduced into the outdoor space, Sam and Farzul tried to locate one of the blue-cased iPads remotely, using a pre-loaded app. Their reason: the available iPads had coloured cases which they neither liked nor wanted to use. Farzul suggested they speak to the children with blue-cased iPads to see if they would change. Farzul and Sam approached their key worker and asked her how they could do this. She demonstrated to Farzul and Sam how to Facetime, then checked to ensure the other iPads were receiving calls. The key worker observed Farzul take steps to contact other iPad users. Another member of staff supported the other children in opening the communication app on the iPad when the call came through. Sam ran to the other group. The children were not in sight but were able to communicate openly and discuss via Facetime their need to exchange iPads. These discussions, using the iPad to capture pictures of what they were seeing and experiencing, informed the other children as to Farzul and Sam's whereabouts in the outdoor space; thus their exchange became about a communication rather than an equipment exchange. Azim, however, did not use the technology affordances of the iPad. Instead, he talked to his mirror image reflected in the iPad cover, exhibiting egocentric speech. He was heard to give commentary on what other children were doing and posed questions, which he continued to answer. A practitioner recognised that he was play acting a previous role-play scenario of where he was a reporter in a 'news office' giving an interview on 'television'. The practitioner set up a desk in the outdoor environment and Azim relocated to the desk within minutes. Staff observed these interactions closely but did not disturb the communication scenes driven by the children.

Oli asked if he could use the sat nav to get to the forest school; his key worker explained that she was not able to do this, as she did not know how. Oli said he would ask his mother to show her. The key worker recognised that this would be an opportunity for parents, if they were able, to share their knowledge with the wider staff and sent a note home to Oli's mum. A week later, Oli's mum attended nursery and showed how this could be done and offered her services to the forest school the next morning. This facilitated a discussion amongst the staff available to support children in documenting their forest school journey over several weeks and in using the sat nav to identify places of local interest. Staff then compiled the stories and videos taken by the children to reinforce the community cohesion that the setting was working towards. A newsletter from the nursery was then sent to parents. Several parents with technology skills offered their time to the nursery to deliver training and to demonstrate digital tools and affordances. Green-screen technologies were then introduced to the children who made their own travel video, supplementing the nursery wall with scenes from the local community to make a realistic panorama. This green-screen technology is now an embedded part of the home corner and changes weekly, dependent on the theme for that week.

REFLECTIVE TASK

- As an early childhood educator, what might your concerns be about Facebook interactions, and what safeguarding measures would you introduce?
- What technological skills might you invite parents to share with the setting to support and enhance their child's learning experiences?

USE OF OUTDOOR PLAY SPACE TO SUPPORT THE USE OF IPADS

Whilst mobile technologies such as iPads are increasingly used in outside spaces, there is a need for ECE practitioners to see the pedagogical value of using it as an additional indoor/outdoor resource. In developing 'A Digital Play Framework', Bird and Edwards (2015) recognised the dilemma faced by many practitioners in ECE, particularly the fact that many staff have yet to realise the pedagogical value and affordances of technology. They also acknowledge that how children learn to use technology through play is not clear and is not fully understood. The staff members in case study 4.1 were concerned with the safety of the equipment. For example, in noting the expense of investing in iPads, staff were keen to protect them from damage, thus limiting their use. Yet, with robust child-friendly covers, there is no reason that portable devices cannot be used in a variety of spaces, including outdoor play areas.

REFLECTIVE TASK

Make time to consider how Bird and Edwards' (2015) framework might be used to support your own and your setting's understanding about how children are learning to use the affordances of mobile technology.

ENGAGING STAFF TO APPRECIATE THE AFFORDANCES OF TECHNOLOGY AND THE IMPLICATIONS FOR TRAINING

A significant area of weakness within England in ECE is the lack of shared communication regarding best practice, especially regarding technology. Formby (2014) recognised that only 43% of ECE staff access apps for children in their setting on iPads, whilst some

84% said they used specific apps and did not deviate or change these apps; and yet this multi-billion-pound industry has launched one billion apps designed specifically for the 2–5 age market (Dredge, 2013). This finding calls into question the level of confidence ECE practitioners have regarding the use and application of such diverse and easily accessible technological resources.

CHALLENGES STAFF FACED IN FACILITATING PEDAGOGICAL OPPORTUNITIES

According to Formby (2014), the majority (74.8%) of practitioners in England believe it is important to use technology with young children; however, 43% lack the technological resources and 38% lack the financial capital necessary to invest in technology. Budgetary cuts and austerity measures continue to reduce funding to ECE. Subsequently, this limits children's exposure to and familiarity with technology and their understanding of social presence and online safety (Lyons and Tredwell, 2015). Ingleby (2014) recognises a critical need for practitioners in ECE to be fully trained to engage with the latest technologies and identifies the current status of continuing professional development for staff in England, regarding technology as the 'house that jack built'.

There is a rising need for the development of professional ECE networks and forums to support and share best practices in technology use. Case study 4.1 highlights the fact that a limited number of staff were confident in using the iPads with children. Yet, by observing the children and the ways in which they identified the affordances of the technology, staff were able to learn from the children who were at ease and innovative in their use of technology.

When the case study was shared with staff, some argued that what was observed and recorded was not necessarily 'play'; for them, 'play' is the process of engaging with the 'play equipment'. These views were based on the fact that these members of staff view iPads only as recording and reporting tools for assessment. Yet the children observed recognised how they could use the technology as a playful tool to enhance their learning experiences.

REFLECTIVE TASK

Reflect on case study 4.1 and discuss the learning which took place for both the children and adults in the setting.

CHALLENGES PARENTS FACE IN TODAY'S DIGITALLY EQUIPPED SOCIETY

There is a presumption that parents should be able to keep their children safe whilst online and that it is parents' responsibility to ensure safe technology use. However, some parents are ill-equipped to understand the intricacies of using technology safely. Although they are, more often than not, a generation of people who have grown up with technology, issues such as digital footprints, digital identities and digital rights have only recently presented as ethical and moral dilemmas.

LEADING THE WAY BY OBSERVING CHILDREN'S PRACTICES AND OWNERSHIP OF TECHNOLOGICAL SPACES

Whilst the Early Years Foundation Stage statutory framework (DfE, 2017a, b) sets out the required framework for preschool learning objectives, it generally rather than specifically mentions technology. If iPads and other forms of mobile technology are to be considered ECE resources, then practitioners should have policy direction and be informed about the advantages they bring to teaching and learning. Yet that does not seem to be the case. In case study 4.1, it was evident that the innovative practice of using iPads to talk remotely to other children in the setting, or using iPads for navigation purposes, came from the children's prior experiences of using the technology or seeing it modelled at home. They were able to apply a wider pedagogical context to technology, rather than hold to a fixed technological perspective. This phenomenon can be likened to a cardboard box, which becomes a bus, a boat or a spacecraft. Children's imagination is not limited to the use of the object; thus tools may be used for different playful purposes. Research by Plowman et al. (2008) found that young children 'acquire a wide range of competencies when interacting with technologies at home, but they were developed in ways which were not necessarily the result of direct teaching' (p. 316). Family practices in using technologies are influential in preparing children to be introduced to new technology in context and also outside that context. Offering these opportunities may support children's engagement, communication and self-expression: these skills can help facilitate a child's transition to school.

It is also a necessity for practitioners to model effective safety practices whilst using technologies; this does not mean when purely online but when taking images, and storing and exploring the images taken. In the case study, there were a number of issues which were not explored in the body of this chapter; for example, what happens when images capture other children who do not want to be included? Clarification on proto-col and ownership of the images should be explored in a safe and appropriate way with children. To ensure that children, staff and parents are clear about their rights and the responsibility associated with posting using social media, which leaves an indelible digital footprint, frank and open discussions are warranted (Gronn et al., 2014).

SUMMARY

Mobile technology is a growing phenomenon, with huge potential for the early years sec-tor. It remains, however, under-resourced and there is a real danger that the progress of technology will outpace the sector's ability to keep abreast of the rapidly changing digital landscape. Settings with iPads and tablet devices, as in the case study included in this chapter, tend to limit their use to staff assessments of children rather than to realise their potential as an additional teaching and learning child-centred and child-led resource. Extending the use of digital technology to embrace outdoor spaces, offers children great opportunities to be engaged more innovatively in child-led play-based activities. In the final analysis, staff who are not digital natives require training and continuing profes-sional development to enhance their practice and to share good practice with others in the sector through shared ECE networks.

KEY POINTS TO REMEMBER

- Images and video – what can be posted safely? What children see as important from the case study should raise questions about their right to online advocacy [safe spaces for children to explore online safety – what is dangerous and what is not to engage in, in online spaces]. Whilst the online rights of children continue to be a subject of concern (Livingstone et al., 2012; NSPCC, 2018), it would be beneficial for the ECE sector to con-sider and align digital policies.
- Evidence-based research may be used to inform good practice, which can then be dis-seminated at a national and an international level to ECE policy makers and educators.
- In the larger study, a lack of professional development opportunities was a concern mentioned several times. This small-scale case study recognised that not all staff were equipped to extend children's learning opportunities; consequently, succession planning is necessary with technology-based teaching and learning. Rather than rely on one or two trained professionals to support innovative technology practices, settings should draw on the wealth of experience parents may bring to the table, thus ensuring the development of parent/practitioner partnerships.

POINTS FOR DISCUSSION

- How can you integrate a range of technology into your setting to bridge the children's home and school experiences with digital technology?
- Discuss the use of technology within play and whether it optimises a different type of play.
- Is technology merely a tool that facilitates ways of playing?
- How can ECE settings keep pace with the continued developments in technology?

FURTHER READING

Bird, J. and Edwards, S. (2015) Children learning to use technologies through play: a Digital Play Framework. *British Journal of Educational Technology*, 46 (6): 1149–1160.

Kutscher, M. L. (2017) *Digital Kids: How to Balance Screen Time, and Why it Matters.* London. Jessica Kingsley.

Rogers, M. and Tyler, L. (2017) Learning in a digital age. In J. Musgrave, M. Savin-Baden and N. Stobbs (eds) *Studying for your Early Years Degree: Skills and Knowledge for Becoming an Effective Practitioner.* London: Critical Publishing.

USEFUL WEBSITES

Livingstone, S., Blum-Ross, A., Pavlick, J. and Ólafsson, K. (2018) In the digital home, how do parents support their children and who supports them? Parenting for a Digital Future: Survey Report 1. LSE, Department of Media and Communication. Available at: www.lse.ac.uk/media-and-communications/assets/documents/research/preparing-for-a-digital-future/P4DF-Survey-Report-1-In-the-digital-home.pdf

NSPCC (2018) Online Safety. Available at: www.nspcc.org.uk/preventing-abuse/keeping-children-safe/online-safety/?utm_source=googleandutm_medium=cpcandutm_campaign=GEN_-_Safety_-_[BMM]andutm_term=protecting_children_onlineandgclid=CjwKCAjwiurXBRAnEiwAk2GFZrVvtW1rROZlZCFnU0GlJe7CPhnSEt axXILopYLG4ywa_6-dI6ll1hoCNrMQAvD_BwEandgclsrc=aw.ds

Paciga, K. A. and Donohue, C. (2017) *Technology and Interactive Media for Young Children: A Whole Child Approach Connecting the Vision of Fred Rogers with Research and Practice.* Latrobe, PA: Fred Rogers Center for Early Learning and Children's Media at Saint Vincent College. Available at: www.fredrogerscenter.org/wp-content/uploads/2017/07/Technology-and-Interactive-Media-for-Young-Children.pdf

REFERENCES

Aubrey, C. and Dahl, S. (2014) The confidence and competence in information and communication technologies of practitioners, parents and young children in the Early Years Foundation Stage. *Journal of Early Years: An International Research Journal, 34* (1): 94–108.

Bird, J. and Edwards, S. (2015) Children learning to use technologies through play: a digital play framework. *British Journal of Educational Technology, 46* (6): 1149–1160.

Clarke, A. and Moss, P. (2005) *Spaces to Play: More Listening to Young Children Using the Mosaic Approach*. London: National Children's Bureau.

Department for Education (DfE) (2017a) *Statutory Framework for the Early Years Foundation Stage: Setting the Standards for Learning, Development and Care for Children from Birth to Five*. London: DfE.

Department for Education (DfE) (2017b) *Early Years Foundation Stage Guidance*. London: DfE.

Dredge, S. (2013) Digital kids: how children are using devices, apps and media in 2013. Available at: http://theguardian.com/technology/2013/Oct/31/digitalkids-devices-apps-media (accessed 1 February 2017).

Edwards, S. H., Skouteris, A., Nolan, A. and Henderson, M. (2015) Young children's internet cognition: understanding digital technologies and young children. In S. Garvis and N. Lemon (eds) *An International Perspective*. New York: Routledge, pp. 38–46.

Fenty, N. and Anderson, E. (2014) Examining educators' knowledge, beliefs and practices about using technology with young children. *Journal of Early Childhood Teacher Education, 35* (2): 114–134.

Fleer, M. (2017) Digital pedagogy: how teachers support digital play in the early years. In L. Arnott (ed.) *Digital Technologies and Learning in the Early Years*. London: Sage.

Formby, S. (2014) *Practitioners' Perspectives: Children's Use of Technology in the Early Years*. London: National Literacy Trust.

Gray, C., Dunn, J., Moffett, P. and Mitchell, D. (2017) Mobile devices in early learning: evaluating the use of portable devices to support young children's learning. Report funded by the Belfast Regeneration Fund and commissioned by the Education Authority for NI. Available at: www.stran.ac.uk/media/media,756133,en.pdf (accessed 18 October 2018).

Gronn, D., Scott, A., Edwards, S. and Henderson, M. (2014) 'Technological me': young children's use of technology across their home and school context. *Technology, Pedagogy and Education, 23* (4): 439–454.

Ingleby, E. (2014) The impact of changing policies about technology on the professional development needs of early years educators in England. *Professional Development in Education, 41* (1): 144–157.

Jahnke, I. and Kumar, S. (2014) Digital didactical designs: teachers' integration of iPads for learning centred processes. *Journal of Digital Learning in Teacher Education, 30* (3): 81–88.

Livingstone, S., Haddon, L. and Görzig, A. (eds) (2012) *Children, Risk and Safety on the Internet: Research and Policy Challenges in Comparative Perspective.* Bristol: Policy Press.

Lyons, C. D. and Tredwell, C. T. (2015) Steps to implementing technology in inclusive early childhood programs. *Computers in Schools: Interdisciplinary Journal of Practice, Theory and Applied Research, 32* (2): 152–166.

NSPCC (2018) Online safety. Available at: www.nspcc.org.uk/preventing-abuse/keeping-children-safe/online-safety/?utm_source=googleandutm_medium=cpcandutm_campaign=GEN_-_Safety_-_[BMM]andutm_term=protecting_children_online andgclid=CjwKCAjwiurXBRAnEiwAk2GFZrVvtW1rROZlZCFnU0GlJe7CPhnSEtaxXIL opYLG4ywa_6-dI6ll1hoCNrMQAvD_BwEandgclsrc=aw.ds (accessed 18 October 2018).

Palaiologou, I. (2016) Children under five and digital technologies: Implications for early years pedagogy. *The European Early Childhood Research Journal, 24* (1): 5–24. (DOI:10.10 80/1350293X.2014.929876, first published online 2014).

Plowman, L., McPake, J. and Stephens, C. (2008) Just picking it up? Young children learning with technology at home. *Cambridge Journal of Education, 38* (3): 303–319.

Wolfe, S. and Flewitt, R. (2010) New technologies, new multimodal literacy practices and young children's metacognitive development. *Cambridge Journal of Education, 40* (4): 387–399.

PART II

MULTIMODEL SPACES, OPPORTUNITIES AND AGENCY

5

IT IS NOT ONLY ABOUT THE TOOLS! PROFESSIONAL DIGITAL COMPETENCE

MARIA DARDANOU AND TRINE KOFOED

CHAPTER OVERVIEW

The aim of this chapter is to stimulate thinking about the importance of developing professional digital competence in early childhood education (ECE). Professional digital competence can be considered a concept that addresses both teachers' individual digital competence and the use of ICT in kindergarten and its potential to support children in all developmental domains whilst they play and learn. This chapter is based on research in Norway that has shown that ECE teachers there require more knowledge of and competence in the pedagogical use of ICT, especially regarding creative and productive activities with children. Additionally, there seems to be a lack of knowledge on the part of teachers around addressing ethical issues with regards to digital technology.

Furthermore, the chapter presents a Technological Pedagogical Content Knowledge (TPACK) framework and model as an example of how professional digital competence may be practised in ECE.

This chapter aims to help you to:

- develop an understanding of the complexity of the term digital competence and the theoretical debate related to educational tasks in a knowledge society
- reflect on what professional digital competence means in ECE regarding the role of the teacher
- offer case studies regarding digital judgement and the TPACK model.

DIGITAL COMPETENCE IN THE KNOWLEDGE SOCIETY

In recent years, digital competence has become a key concept in discussions of the kind of skills and understanding we all need in a knowledge society. It has, however, been interpreted in various ways (e.g. digital literacy, ICT literacy, digital competence, ICT competence, digital citizenship, digital judgement and media literacy) in policy documents, in academic literature, and in teaching, learning and certification practices. Nevertheless, all of these terms highlight the need to handle technology in the digital age (Gallardo-Echenique et al., 2015).

Digital competence has been analysed from several linguistic, cultural and disciplinary backgrounds. Digital competence is a multimodal and complex concept constantly changing with the development of media (Søby, 2016). UNESCO (2009: 9) defined *media education* as that which 'provides the critical knowledge and the analytical tools that empower media audiences to function as autonomous and rational citizens, enabling them to make informed use of the media'.

Digital literacy, another concept that is closely related to digital competence, was introduced by Glister in 1997. Glister (1997) first used and defined the term digital literacy by putting emphasis on critical thinking abilities rather than on technical skills. This concept has a longer tradition than digital competence and is usually understood as a combination of technical-procedural, cognitive and emotional social skills. According to Nawaz and Kundi (2010), there are two paradigms to digital literacy and two broader theories about the nature and the role of ICT in the learning process: instrumental/behaviourist and substantive/constructivist. The instrumental view considers technology as a 'tool' with no inherent value, whilst the substantive view argues that technology is not neutral and has positive or negative impacts (2010). Taking this reflective and critical approach, some authors suggest that digital literacy cannot be limited to a purely utilitarian and reductive view of certain digital skills but is linked to a broader, more critical view of society in an area of technological revolution (Erstad, 2010; Kahn and Kellner, 2005).

POLICY FRAMEWORKS FOR UNDERSTANDING DIGITAL COMPETENCE IN EUROPE

The European Commission (EC) has promoted several initiatives in order to encourage the development of digital literacy in EU Member States. In the *Recommendation on Key Competences for Lifelong Learning*, digital competence is defined as involving 'the confident and critical use of Information Society Technology (IST) for work, leisure and communication' (EC, 2006: 13).

A more recent study that aimed to identify, select and analyse current frameworks concerning digital competence identified the following competences: information management, communication, content creation, safety and problem solving (Ferrari, 2013). Additionally, the following definition is proposed:

> Digital competence can be broadly defined as the confident, critical and creative use of ICT to achieve goals related to work, employability, learning, leisure, inclusion and/or participation in society. Digital competence is a transversal key competence which, as such, enables us to acquire other key competences (e.g. language, mathematics, learning to learn, cultural awareness). It is related to many of the 21st century skills which should be acquired by all citizens, to ensure their active participation in society and the economy. (Ferrari, 2013: 2)

Although the concept of digital literacy seems to be the one most widely used internationally, the term digital competence is often used synonymously, especially in the European context (Ferrari, 2013; Krumsvik, 2008). Digital competence is regarded as a core competence in policy papers but it is not yet a stable concept (Søby, 2016). Whilst some perceive digital competence as the technical use of ICT, others define it more broadly as knowledge application or as 21st-century skills. Even though each author or organisation emphasises different aspects, they all agree that digital literacy or competence is a multidimensional concept entailing a complex integration of technical skills, cognitive (e.g. problem solving, critical thinking skills) and meta-cognitive processes as well as civic and ethical awareness.

A central pedagogical question concerns what it means to grow up in today's media and technology community, and what implications the media has for children's learning and development. Today's children and young people are the first generation to have grown up with digital media and the internet as integral aspects of their everyday lives. Consequently, they are exposed to both the positive and negative impacts of digital technologies – factors that cannot be ignored by ECE settings. Staff are therefore required to consider young children's competence in the use of digital technology, whilst reflecting on the child's media learning needs in kindergarten and at school. Allied with the children's needs, thought must be given to the teacher's ability to use ICT with a good pedagogical-didactic understanding that aligns this aspect of teaching and learning with other subject areas: in other words, consideration must be given to the professional and digital competence of ECE teachers (Krumsvik, 2007). The importance of teachers' professional development in the area of ICT competences was confirmed by the UNESCO project *ICT Competences Standards for Teachers* (UNESCO, 2008). UNESCO's framework emphasised 'that it is not enough for teachers to have ICT competences and be able to teach them to their students. Teachers need to be able to help the students become collaborative, problem solving creative learners through using ICT' (UNESCO, 2011: 3).

ECE IN NORWAY: WELFARE AND EDUCATION IN A LIFELONG LEARNING PERSPECTIVE

In order to create a holistic and coherent aim for education, the government Stoltenberg II moved kindergarten from the Ministry of Children and Family Affairs to the Ministry of Education during the change of government in 2005. With this action, the Norwegian government aimed to fulfill a promise to parents about full day care coverage, high quality and low prices; this is considered to be the most important welfare reform in Norway in modern times.

All children in Norway between the ages of 1 and 5 have the right to a free kindergarten place, with children starting their formal education at 6 years of age. The kindergarten has a Framework Plan for the Content and Tasks of Kindergartens with seven interdisciplinary areas, where documentation and children's participation are central (Norwegian Ministry of Education and Research, 2017). The Norwegian ECE tradition adopts a holistic view of children where care, education, play and learning are integrated. In White Paper 24 (Norwegian Ministry of Education and Research, 2012a: 10), the kindergarten is highlighted as the first part of the Norwegian educational system and as a part of a flexible welfare system. Therefore, it should also be a good arena for children's development and the first stage of lifelong learning.

The Norwegian government adopted a new purpose clause for kindergartens and primary schools in 2008 that came into force in 2010 (Norwegian Ministry of Education and Research, 2010). This provision deals with the kindergarten's social mandate and explains the values underlying the kindergarten's activities and the traditions to which it is to be further developed. Furthermore, it is based on fundamental respect for everyone in a multicultural and diverse society, and on sharing values across different cultures. Thus, it expresses society's change in the view of children and of adults' responsibility to treat children as equal individuals. According to the overall aim of kindergartens, they should both create well-being in childhood and give children a good basis for lifelong learning and active participation in a democratic society (Norwegian Ministry of Education and Research, 2012a).

ICT AND DIGITAL SKILLS IN THE NORWEGIAN CURRICULUM

Since 2006, digital skills have been one of five basic abilities required by the Norwegian primary curriculum, together with the development of children's communication, written, literacy and numeracy skills (Norwegian Directorate for Education and Training, 2006). More recently (Norwegian Directorate for Education and Training, 2012), the development of digital skills has been given greater prominence with a definition provided that includes four sub-categories: 1. Search and process; 2. Produce; 3. Communicate; and 4. Digital judgement. As indicated below, these skills are aligned with other subject areas:

The development of digital technology has changed many of the conditions for reading, writing and oral forms of expression. Consequently, using digital skills is a natural part of learning both in and across subjects, and their use provides possibilities for acquiring and applying new learning strategies while at the same time requiring new and increased powers of judgement. (2012: 12)

Conversely, teachers in kindergartens have much less direction on the early development of children's digital skills. For example, in the Norwegian Framework Plan for the Content and Tasks of Kindergartens the use of ICT is broadly described in one sentence which points out that 'children should have the opportunity to experience how digital tools can be used for play, communication and the gathering of information' (Norwegian Ministry of Education and Research, 2011: 24). Unclear, however, were the reasons *why* it was considered important for children to develop digital skills or *how* these skills might be aligned with other subject areas. Similarly, the document failed to explain the digital outcomes required at this level or how the development of digital skills might be assessed. By 2013, The Norwegian Centre for ICT Education had published a report providing information on a portal that shared images, books, films, audio files and articles on themes related to teaching, with pedagogical tips for kindergarten teachers (2013: 4). Yet, by 2015, Jacobsen, Kofoed and Loi noted a continued deficit in the pedagogical experience, knowledge and competence of ICT available to ECE teachers in Norway.

The Framework Plan for the Content and Tasks of Kindergartens remains under continued review and a new plan was launched in August 2017. The new framework refers to digital judgement as being a part of kindergarten's digital practice (Norwegian Ministry of

Education and Research, 2017: 11) and requires each kindergarten to develop an annual plan outlining the way the learning areas will be adapted to meet educational activities, to include objectives for children's participation, and how these are to be attained and evaluated (Engel et al., 2015). The amended framework also explains *how* teachers *will* provide children with the opportunity to use digital tools for experimenting, playing, learning and thinking/wondering (Norwegian Ministry of Education and Research, 2016).

At pre-service level, The National Curriculum Regulations for Kindergarten Teacher Education stipulates the need for teachers' professional practices to become proficient in the use of digital devices with expertise in embedding them across contexts and subject areas (Norwegian Ministry of Education and Research, 2012b). It also highlights the need for pre-service kindergarten student teachers to gain competence in the pedagogical role of digital devices in children's play and learning, and to be creative and critical in their use (see, for example, Subject: Children's development, playing and learning) (2012b). Nevertheless, the term professional digital competence is not used to describe this area of kindergarten student teachers' pre-service education, nor is the term digital judgement mentioned in the curriculum. This creates a mismatch between pre-service and in-service policy requirements.

PROFESSIONAL DIGITAL COMPETENCE IN ECE: THE ROLE OF THE TEACHER

Krumsvik (2007) provides a definition of digital competence specifically for teachers: 'Digital competence is the teachers' ability to use ICT with a good pedagogical, didactic ICT understanding and to be aware of how this might impact the learning strategies and educational formation of pupils' (p. 68). Thus, Krumsvik (2007) argues that teachers distinguish themselves from other technology users by their focus on education and teaching, rather than everyday use and entertainment. This is in line with Bjønnes' (2015) definition of professional digital competence as a part of a comprehensive educational and pedagogical philosophy, where the digital aspect involves having technical skills, being able to use technology as an integral part of the pedagogy, and a reflective and conscious approach to children's use of technology.

Several studies in the Norwegian context have shown the perspectives of early childhood teachers' views and attitudes towards ICT in the early years (Jacobsen Kofoed and Loi, 2016; Jacobsen, Loftsgarden and Lundh, 2013; Jernes et al., 2010). They showed that teachers generally express positive attitudes and views, but they point to their lack of knowledge regarding the pedagogical use of ICT in ECE. At the same time, international research shows that teachers' lack of professional development, support or pedagogical understanding in the use of ICT in ECE, can affect children's experience with digital technologies (Kalas, 2013; Kerckaert et al., 2015). According to Sandvik et al. (2012), early childhood teachers need to identify strategies for supporting learning with ICT that will enable a balance between child-initiated and adult-led activities. Furthermore, they claim that the communicative role of the teacher and how the digital devices are integrated in daily activities are relevant to the children's learning outcomes. This is in line with Plowman and Stephen (2005, 2007) who argue that developing appropriate practices, which apply in any other types of children's learning experience, can make the use of technology effective. Since digital practices in the ECE area are to a high degree affected by early childhood teachers' attitudes and views, it is, therefore, important to equip teachers with high levels of digital competence in order for them to use ICT to support children's critical thinking and critical awareness (Hardersen and Guðmundsdóttir, 2012). Therefore, professional digital competence is a complex thing addressing knowledge, skills and attitudes for the creative, critical and reflective use of digital technologies.

DIGITAL JUDGEMENT IN ECE

Judgement has been a central theme for both psychology and philosophy. For psychology, judgement is related to cognitive development and the decision-making process. On the other hand, the notion of judgement is connected to a number of philosophical approaches – for example, Aristotle's concept of ethics as involving practical wisdom, skills and judgement or phronêsis, and Kant's critical philosophy of higher-order functions including reflective judgement (Solberg, 2010). Judgement refers to the use of common sense, as well as to how to practise common civility, regardless of whether individual interactions are virtual or in person. Digital judgement can be considered one of the most important elements included in the concept of digital competence, as some of the main aspects of digital judgement involve critical and ethical reflection, interaction, privacy and netiquette (Hardersen, 2016: 151). Therefore, digital judgement refers to a wise and justifiable use of digital media and the internet; and of being critical of virtual sources whilst taking into consideration privacy and copyright issues.

The term digital citizenship refers to: 'the need for adults and children to be responsible digital citizens through an understanding of the use, abuse, and misuse of technology as well as the norms of appropriate, responsible, and ethical behaviors related to online rights, roles, identity, safety, security, and communication' (NAEYC and Fred Rogers Center, 2012: 10). Digital safety is vital for the implementation of technology with young children.

Practices regarding digital judgement in ECE refer both to early childhood teachers' practices as well to children's practices. As Røkenes and Krumsvik (2014) observed, early childhood teachers should adopt critical attitudes and judgement when, for example, they choose a new application on the tablet for the children; the teacher needs to investigate and judge the quality and the pedagogical use of an application or a game, as he/she is responsible for the experience the children are exposed to in the kindergarten. Practising digital judgement in ECE requires first that the teachers themselves understand what digital judgement means, and, therefore, that they are able to exercise it with children in different situations. The way we share pictures and experiences on the internet with others can be an appropriate opportunity to discuss ethical issues and considerations and develop positive attitudes towards use of the internet through reflection (Røkenes and Krumsvik, 2014).

CASE STUDY 5.1: BEING A GOOGLE 'LEADER'

It is November and the kindergarten is working on the theme of 'diversity', with India the focus. The plan is to 'travel' to India with the help of the internet. A group of four children (aged 5) and one teacher, Maja, are engaged in the activity and search Google to find pictures from India and of children's everyday life in India. Alex, one of two boys involved in the activity, claims that he has been 'on Google' many times with his father and has been looking at pictures of his favourite types of cars and trucks.

The teacher takes the opportunity to ask Alex to 'be the leader' and show everyone how we search using Google, where we have to click, and promises to help Alex write the words. Alex seems excited to show the other children how 'to click' and how to use the mouse. Alex asks the teacher to type on the search area 'Indian children'. When the teacher types the words, Alex clicks the enter button and a large number of pictures of children in India appear on the screen. All of the children ask questions such as 'are those the clothes children in India wear?' 'do they go to school with elephants?' and 'what kind of food do children in India eat? Do they eat pizza?' Maja tries to answer the questions about food and clothes when, suddenly, one of the children, Thea, asks: 'But so many pictures ... has anyone asked them to take pictures of them so we can see them? ... those two children [pointing at one of the pictures that shows two children] seem to be sad ... Is it because they did not want their picture taken so we could see them?'

Maja takes this opportunity to discuss whether we should ask others if we can take pictures of them. Additionally, she asks if the children have experienced having their picture taken when they didn't want it taken and had it uploaded to the kindergarten's blog or internet site. She also asks if they prefer to be asked or informed about where the pictures will be uploaded and who should see them.

REFLECTIVE TASKS

- Reflect on case study 5.1 and on the concept of digital judgement in ECE. To what extent is children's consent practised and discussed by staff, parents and children in the kindergarten setting?
- Give other examples of activities or situations where the teacher could introduce ethical and critical consideration being given to children's use of the internet and media.

TECHNOLOGICAL PEDAGOGICAL CONTENT KNOWLEDGE (TPACK): A HOLISTIC APPROACH TO PROFESSIONAL DIGITAL COMPETENCE

Technological pedagogical content knowledge (TPACK) is a framework for the educational, pedagogical and didactical use of technology that is based on Shulman's (1986) model of pedagogical content knowledge (Angeli et al., 2016; Koehler and Mishra, 2009; Mishra and Koehler, 2006). More specifically:

- Technology knowledge (TK) addresses knowledge about various technologies.
- Content knowledge (CK) addresses knowledge about subject areas.
- Pedagogical knowledge (PK) addresses knowledge about the processes and practices of teaching and learning.
- Pedagogical content knowledge (PCK) addresses knowledge which concerns the process of teaching.

Furthermore:

- Technological content knowledge (TCK) refers to knowledge of how technology can create new representations for specific contents.
- Technological pedagogical knowledge (TPK) concerns knowledge of how various technologies can be used in teaching and understanding, and that using technology may change the way teachers teach (Koehler and Mishra, 2009).

Technological pedagogical content knowledge (TPACK; Figure 5.1) addresses knowledge about the complex interplay and interaction amongst the three basic components of knowledge (CK, PK, TK) that a teacher requires to deliver appropriate pedagogical methods and technologies (Chuang and Ho, 2011: 101–102).

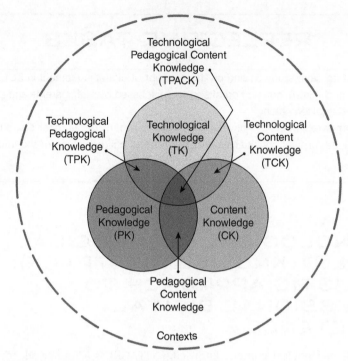

Figure 5.1   Components of the TPACK framework

Source: http://tpack.org

Although the TPACK framework focuses on technological knowledge, both content and pedagogical knowledge are equally important in informing curricular development. Nevertheless, TPACK can improve teacher education and professional development (Hsu et al., 2013; Kildan and Incikabi, 2015; Voogt and McKenney, 2016). For example, the TPACK framework can inform teachers' pedagogical reasoning by encouraging them to reflect on and justify their choice of teaching approaches, teaching content and learning activities, and thus aid their professional development (Koh and Chai, 2016; Voogt and McKenney, 2016). As Mishra and Koehler (2006: 1024) observe, TPACK has given teachers 'a language to talk about the connections that are present (or absent) in conceptualisations of educational technology', and, paraphrasing, to fulfill the relationship between content and technology, providing a wider context in the way pedagogy can use technology.

Using technology, pedagogy and content knowledge together provides a solid foundation for learning that can constantly evolve and develop. The teacher's role is important in the choice of which technology and in what way didactically and pedagogically it can be used in different activities, situations and contexts (Bjønnes, 2015).

CASE STUDY 5.2: TPACK

This example of an activity using the TPACK model involves a group of 10 children aged 5 years old.

TPACK COMPONENTS

The three basic components are:

- **Technological knowledge**: use of interactive whiteboard and GeoGebra (www.geogebra.org)
- **Content knowledge**: the content of the activity focuses on fundamental skills related to forms and, more specifically, circles
- **Pedagogical knowledge**: the instructional strategy for this lesson would be the use of collaborative learning.

Their intersections lie as follows:

- Pedagogical content knowledge (PCK):
    - **Define**: GeoGebra is a technology that supports the content goals of this activity.
    - **Describe**: for this activity, children will find the circles and place them on the right side of the screen.
    - **Support**: GeoGebra allows children to make connections across a number of different mathematical disciplines.
- Technological content knowledge (TCK):
    - **Define**: the interactive whiteboard (T) is a very effective technological tool for facilitating collaborative learning.
    - **Describe**: in this activity, the interactive whiteboard and GeoGebra are used to present various forms and to allow children to explore more closely the concept of circles.
    - **Support**: according to Solvie (2004), the digital/interactive whiteboard can be considered an organisational tool for different activities.
- Technological pedagogical knowledge (TPK):
    - **Define**: interactive whiteboards can promote collaborative based learning.
    - **Describe**: the activity employs different activities with forms, such as categorizing, pairing, etc. A positive outcome of those activities will result in the teacher's role moving to that of facilitator thus encouraging children's engagement.
    - **Support**: the activity provides opportunities for children's collaborative learning.
- Technological pedagogical and content knowledge (TPACK):
    - **Define**: the interactive whiteboard is an effective tool to use with gaming/simulation learning for foundational mathematic development.
    - **Describe**: consider how the interactive whiteboard might be used to facilitate an activity that engages children and teachers in placing different forms into groups.
    - **Support**: the technology and instructional strategy listed has many positive attributes, according to research findings: Incorporating the digital whiteboard in our practice as a tool to teach early literacy skills may help us reach young children in many positive and powerful ways (Schmidt et al., 2009).

REFLECTIVE TASKS

- Discuss how the TPACK framework may support the teacher's awareness of ICT practices with children.
- Plan your own activity using the TPACK framework.

SUMMARY

This chapter focused on different interpretations of digital competence and the theoretical debates related to educational tasks in a knowledge society. Furthermore, we discussed why it is important to develop professional digital competence in ECE professionals, addressing the complexity of knowledge, skills and attitudes for the creative, critical, reflective use of digital technologies with children in kindergarten. We suggested that the TPACK framework offers a model for meeting the pedagogical and didactical needs of kindergarten teachers, and we highlighted in the body of this chapter how digital judgement can be practised in ECE.

KEY POINTS TO REMEMBER

- Digital competence is a concept that can be defined in many different ways – as digital literacy, media literacy, etc. – and refers to the skills, knowledge, views and attitudes in the use of ICT with or without children.
- Digital judgement refers to critical reflection, ethical considerations, consent, empathy and respect with regards to the rights of others in using ICT or to the subject of ICT.
- TPACK is a framework for the implementation of technological pedagogical content knowledge – the knowledge and skills that teachers need to have in order to integrate technology meaningfully in specific content areas.

POINTS OF DISCUSSION

- Discuss how digital judgement can be practised in the documentation of everyday activities in kindergarten. Reflect on the crucial right of the child to privacy and how you can teach children about their rights to give/withhold consent. Is this right always respected in documentation practices in kindergarten?

- Discuss how the different sub-categories regarding digital competence can be integrated with subject content in kindergarten. How with ICT can you help children become collaborative, problem-solving, creative and communicative citizens?

FURTHER READING

Arnott, L. (ed.) (2017) *Digital Technologies and Learning in the Early Years*. London: Sage.

Arnott, L. (2018) Children's negotiation tactics and socio-emotional self-regulation in child-led play experiences: the influence of the preschool pedagogic culture. *Early Child Development and Care*, 188 (7): 951–965.

Danby, S. J., Fleer, M., Davidson, C. and Hatzigianni, M. (eds) (2018) *Digital Childhoods: Technologies and Children's Everyday Lives*. Singapore: Springer.

Marsh, J., Kontovourki, S., Tafa, E. and Salomaa, S. (2017) Developing digital literacy in early years settings: professional development needs for practitioners. A White Paper for COST Action IS1410. Available at: http://digilitey.eu/wp-content/uploads/2017/01/WG2-LR-jan-2017.pdf (accessed 19 October 2018).

USEFUL WEBSITES

Norwegian Centre for ICT in Education – www.udir.no/in-english

Technological pedagogical content knowledge (TPACK) – www.tpack.org

World Economic Forum (8 digital skills) – www.weforum.org/agenda/2016/06/8-digital-skills-we-must-teach-our-children

REFERENCES

Angeli, C., Valanides, N. and Christodoulou, A. (2016) Theoretical considerations of technological pedagogical content knowledge. In M. C. Herring, M. J. Koehler and M. Punya (eds) *Handbook of Technological Pedagogical Content Knowledge (TPACK) for Educators*. New York and London: Routledge, pp. 11–32.

Bjønnes, P. K. (2015) Profesjonsfaglig digital kompetanse i barnehagelærerutdanningen. *Masteroppgave*. [Professional digital competence in early childhood education.] Trondheim: Dronning Mauds Minne Høgskole.

Chuang, H.-H. and Ho, C. J. (2011) An investigation of early childhood teachers' technological pedagogical content knowledge (TPACK) in Taiwan. *Ahi Evran Üniversitesi Eøitim Fakültesi Dergisi, 12* (2): 99–117.

Engel, A., Barnett, W. S., Anders, Y. and Taguma, M. (2015) Early childhood education and care policy review: Norway. OECD 2015. Available at: www.oecd.org/norway/

Early-Childhood-Education-and-Care-Policy-Review-Norway.pdf (accessed 5 May 2018).

Erstad, O. (2010) Educating the digital generation. *Nordic Journal of Digital Literacy*, 1: 56–70.

European Commission (EC) (2006) *Recommendation on Key Competences for Lifelong Learning*. Brussels: EC.

Ferrari, A. (2013) DIGCOMP: A Framework for Developing and Understanding Digital Competence in Europe. Available at: http://ftp.jrc.es/EURdoc/JRC83167.pdf (accessed 15 February 2017).

Gallardo-Echenique, E. E., de Oliveira, J. M., Marques-Molias, L. and Esteve-Mon, F. (2015) Digital competence in the knowledge society. *Journal of Online Learning and Teaching*, *11* (1): 1–16.

Glister, P. (1997) *Digital Literacy*. New York: Wiley.

Hardersen, B. (2016) *App'legøyer og app'estreker? Profesjonsfaglig digital kompetanse i barnehagen.* [*Professional digital competence in kindergarten.*] Latvia: Cappelen Damm Akademisk.

Hardersen, B. and Guðmundsdóttir, G. B. (2012) The digital universe of young children. *Nordic Journal of Digital Literacy*, *7* (3): 221–225.

Hsu, C. Y., Liang, J. C., Chai, C. S. and Tsai, C. C. (2013) Exploring preschool teachers' technological pedagogical content knowledge of educational games. *Journal of Educational Computing Research*, *49* (4): 461–479.

Jacobsen, H., Kofoed, T. and Loi, M. (2016) *Barnehagemonitor 2015. Den digitale tilstanden i barnehagen.* [*Kindergartenmonitor 2015. The digital status of kindergarten.*] Oslo: Senter for IKT i Utdanningen.

Jacobsen, H., Loftsgarden, M. and Lundh, S. (2013) *Barnehagemonitor 2013. Den digitale tilstanden i barnehagen.* [*Kindergartenmonitor 2013. The digital status of kindergarten.*] Oslo: Senter for IKT i Utdanningen.

Jernes, M., Alvestad, M. and Sinnerud, M. (2010) Er det bra, eller? Pedagogiske spenningsfelt i møte med digitale verktøy i norske barnehager. [Is it good, or not? Educational field of excitement in meeting with digital tools in Norwegian kindergartens.] *Nordisk barnehageforskning*, *3* (3): 115–131.

Kahn, R. and Kellner, D. (2005) Oppositional politics and the internet: a critical/reconstructive approach. *Cultural Politics*, *1* (1): 75–100.

Kalas, I. (2013) *Integration of ICT in early childhood education*. X World Conference on Computers in Education, Toruń, Poland, 2–5 July.

Kerckaert, S., Vanderlinde, R. and van Braak. J. (2015) The role of ICT in early childhood education: scale development and research on ICT use and influencing factors. *European Early Childhood Education Research Journal*, *6* (1): 162–172.

Kildan, A. O. and Incikabi, L. (2015) Effects on the technological pedagogical content knowledge of early childhood teacher candidates using digital storytelling to teach mathematics. *Education 3–13*, *43* (3): 238–248.

Koehler, M. J. and Mishra, P. (2009) What is technological pedagogical content knowledge? *Contemporary Issues in Technology and Teacher Education*, *9* (1): 60–70.

Koh, J. H. L. and Chai, C. S. (2016) Seven design frames that teachers use when considering technological pedagogical content knowledge (TPACK). *Computers & Education*, *102*: 244–257.

Krumsvik, R. J. (2007) *Skulen og den digitale læringsevolusjonen.* [*School and the digital learning evolution.*] Oslo: Universitetsforlaget.

Krumsvik, R. J. (2008) Situated learning and teachers' digital competence. *Education and Information Technologies*, *13* (13): 279–290.

Mishra, P. and Koehler, M. J. (2006) Technological pedagogical content knowledge: a framework for teacher knowledge. *Teachers College Record*, *108* (6): 1017–1054.

National Association for the Education of Young Children (NAEYC) and Fred Rogers Center for Early Learning and Children's Media (2012) Technology and interactive media as tools in early childhood programs serving children from birth through age 8 (Joint Position Statement). Available at: www.naeyc.org/files/naeyc/file/positions/PS_technology_WEB2.pdf (accessed 18 January 2018).

Nawaz, A. and Kundi, G. M. (2010) Digital literacy: an analysis of the contemporary paradigms. *Int. J. Sci. Technol. Edu. Res.*, *1* (2): 19–29.

Norwegian Centre for ICT Education (2013) Information and communication technology (ICT) in Norwegian education: ICT contributes to increased quality, enhanced learning and better learning strategies for pupils, apprentices, students and children in kindergarten. Available at: www.iktsenteret.no (accessed 18 May 2018).

Norwegian Directorate for Education and Training (2006) *National Curriculum for Knowledge Promotion in Primary and Secondary Education and Training.* Oslo: Norwegian Ministry of Education and Research. Available at: www.udir.no/globalassets/upload/larerplaner/fastsatte_lareplaner_for_kunnskapsloeftet/prinsipper_lk06_eng.pdf (accessed 15 May 2018).

Norwegian Directorate for Education and Training (2012) *Framework for Basic Skills.* Oslo: Norwegian Ministry of Education and Research. Available at: www.udir.no/contentas sets/fd2d6bfbf2364e1c98b73e030119bd38/framework_for_basic_skills.pdf (accessed 10 January 2017).

Norwegian Ministry of Education and Research (2010) *Endringer i barnehageloven.* [*Changes in children's law.*] Oslo: Norwegian Ministry of Education and Research. Available at: www.regjeringen.no/contentassets/3106a9d16ba943e09d8a42b92dba7918/no/pdfs/prp200920100105000dddpdfs.pdf (accessed 18 May 2018).

Norwegian Ministry of Education and Research (2011) *Framework Plan for the Content and Tasks of Kindergartens.* Oslo: Norwegian Ministry of Education and Research. Available at: www.udir.no/globalassets/filer/barnehage/rammeplan/framework_plan_for_the_content_and_tasks_of_Kindergartens_2011_rammeplan_engelsk.pdf (accessed 11 November 2016).

Norwegian Ministry of Education and Research (2012a) *Meld. St. 24 (2012–2013): Melding til Stortinget Framtidens barnehage.* [*White paper 24 (2012–2013): Message to Parliament about the future kindergarten.*] Oslo: Norwegian Ministry of Education and Research. Available at: www.regjeringen.no/contentassets/2e8ad98938b74226bc7ff395839434be/no/pdfs/stm201220130024000dddpdfs.pdf (accessed 15 June 2017).

Norwegian Ministry of Education and Research (2012b) *National Curriculum Regulations for Kindergarten Teacher Education*. Oslo: Norwegian Ministry of Education and Research. Available at: www.regjeringen.no/globalassets/upload/kd/rundskriv/2012/nasjonale_retningslinjer_barnehagelaererutdanning.pdf (accessed 10 October 2017).

Norwegian Ministry of Education and Research (2016) Høring Rammeplan for barnehagens innhold og oppgaver Høringsutkast pr. 20.10.2016. [Consultation framework for the kindergarten content and assignments hearing draft.] Available at: www.regjeringen.no/contentassets/aba61253bea04517a27dc78838626ae4/horingsnotat-forskrift-om-ramme-plan-for-barnehagens-innhold-og-oppgaver.pdf (accessed 9 June 2016).

Norwegian Ministry of Education and Research (2017) *Framework Plan for the Content and Tasks of Kindergartens*. Oslo: Norwegian Ministry of Education and Research.

Plowman, L. and Stephen, C. (2005) Children, play, and computers in preschool settings. *British Journal of Educational Technology*, *36* (2): 145–157.

Plowman, L. and Stephen, C. (2007) Guided interaction in preschool settings. *Journal of Computer Assisted Learning*, *23* (1): 14–26.

Røkenes, F. M. and Krumsvik, R. J. (2014) Development of student teachers' digital competence in teacher education: a literature review. *Nordic Journal of Digital Literacy*, *9* (4): 250–280.

Sandvik, M., Smørdal, O. and Østerud, S. (2012) Exploring iPads in practitioners' repertoires for language learning and literacy practices in kindergarten. *Nordic Journal of Digital Literacy*, *7* (3): 204–220.

Schmidt, D. A., Baran, E., Thompson, A. D., Mishra P., Koehler, M. J. and Shin, T. S. (2009) Technological pedagogical content knowledge (TPACK): the development and validation of an assessment instrument for preservice teachers. *Journal of Research on Technology in Education*, *42* (2): 123–149.

Shulman, L. S. (1986) Those who understand: knowledge growth in teaching. *Educational Researcher*, *15* (2): 4–14.

Solberg, M. (2010) Om akademisk danning med utgangspunkt i Kants sensus communis og 'Hva er opplysning?' [About academic formation based on Kant's census communis and 'What is enlightenment? ']. *Unipub forlag*: 51–68.

Solvie, P. A. (2004) The digital whiteboard: a tool in early literacy instruction (Teaching Tips department). *The Reading Teacher*, *57* (5): 484–487.

Søby, M. (2016) Digital competence: a password to a new interdisciplinary field. *Nordic Journal of Digital Literacy*, 2006–2016: 4–7.

UNESCO (2008) *ICT Competency Standards for Teachers: Policy Framework*. Paris: UNESCO.

UNESCO (2009) *Mapping Media Education Policies: Visions, Programmes and Challenges*. New York & Huelva: The United Nations Alliance of Civilizations in co-operation with Grupo Comunicar.

UNESCO (2011) Transforming Education: The Power of ICT Policies. Available at: http://unesdoc.unesco.org/images/0021/002118/211842e.pdf (accessed 16 January 2017).

Voogt, J. and McKenney, S. (2016) TPACK in teacher education: are we preparing teachers to use technology for early literacy? *Technology, Pedagogy and Education*, *26* (1): 69–83.

6

PARENTS' PERSPECTIVES ON THE USE OF TOUCHSCREEN TECHNOLOGY BY 0–3–YEAR–OLDS

JANE O'CONNOR, OLGA FOTAKOPOULOU, MARIA HATZIGIANNI AND MARIE FRIDBERG

CHAPTER OVERVIEW

The rise in personal ownership of touchscreen devices such as iPads and smartphones across the Western world in recent years has led to the increasing use of such technology by young children (Kucirkova et al., 2014; O'Connor, 2017; Palaiologou, 2016). However, the extent to which touchscreen technology is incorporated into the lives of infants and toddlers, and indeed whether it should be incorporated at all, is becoming increasingly recognised as an international modern-day parenting dilemma (Cocozza, 2014).

This chapter reports on the findings from an online parental survey completed by over 370 parents of children aged 0–3 years in the UK, Sweden,

Australia and Greece. The findings are discussed within the context of the ongoing debate around the extent to which technology is perceived as a problematic or advantageous aspect of contemporary childhood.

The chapter begins by discussing key data from the surveys and exploring how 0–3-year-olds are using touchscreen devices in families in the four countries included in this study. The aims of the chapter are as follows:

- to identify emerging common practices
- to consider what parents in these different countries perceive as the advantages and drawbacks of their 0–3s using digital technology and the type of information which they would like to be available to them
- to examine implications for supporting parents in guiding their children's use of touch-screen devices and in understanding the ways in which touchscreens are becoming an established part of the daily lives of many of the very youngest children around the world
- to reflect on how 0–3s' use of touchscreens in the home links to early childhood education and how pedagogical practices in the early years need to take account of parental views and domestic usage.

PARENTAL MEDIATION AND THE CONTENTIOUSNESS OF DIGITAL PLAY

Although recent studies have begun to identify that 0–3s can and do make use of touch-screens to play and learn independently of adult mediation (see Cristia and Seidl, 2015; Plowman et al., 2012), it is undeniable that parents are still key gatekeepers in relation to their young children's use of such devices. It follows then that their beliefs and behaviour in relation to parenting, child development and learning are instrumental in the access their 0–3s have to this technology. Previous research has established that parents tend to act according to their definition of being a 'good parent' (Robinson, 2013) with, for example, parents who perceive technology as of benefit to their children's learning allowing them more access to devices than parents who hold the opposite view. Flewitt (2012) has found that parental beliefs have a significant impact on if and how children use digital media in the home environment, with the most positive attitudes reflecting higher rates of usage. Stephen et al.'s (2013) study of preschool children playing and learning with technological resources at home also found that parents' attitudes were the most important factor in young children's access to technology. This is supported by the findings of Verenikina and Kervin (2011) who found that parents have a pivotal role in their child's access to touchscreen devices, with many putting time-limited boundaries in place and preferring their children to play 'educational' games. Such studies indicate that young children's rates of use of touchscreens at home are closely related to their parents' perceptions of the benefits and/or drawbacks of such use.

The wider literature suggests that two dominant discourses inform the debate around parenting and young children's use of technology. The first can be identified as emanating from a perception of children, particularly very young children, as innocent, natural and in need of shielding from the adult world (see Higonnet, 1998). Identifying with this position is associated with protectionist behaviour around children and technology, whereby technology is seen as somehow robbing children of their childhoods (see Palmer, 2007). Adding weight to this perspective in relation to children's health and development are research findings suggesting that the use of screen devices by the very young may impact brain development and cause attention problems (Courage and Setliff, 2009) or lead to 'irregular sleep patterns, behavioural issues, decreased academic performance, negative impact on socialisation and language development' (cited in NAEYC, 2012: 3). Furthermore, in a review of research specifically around mobile and interactive media use by young children, Radesky et al. (2015) note that there is little evidence that 30-month-old children derive any learning benefits from engaging with mobile media and are dependent on 'real-life' interactions for their cognitive and social development.

The alternative and, in many ways, opposing discourse is grounded in the growing recognition of the opportunities technology offers young children in terms of learning, playing and socialising. Also aligned to the concept of the 'good parent' is the belief that encouraging young children to use technology and enabling them to do so leads to better educational outcomes and, in time, a more successful experience in the world of work. This was demonstrated by Vittrup et al. (2016: 43) who explored parental perceptions in the USA of the role of media and technology in young children's lives (2- to 7-year-olds). They found that: 'Overall parents showed positive attitudes toward media, to the extent that they believed media exposure to be vital to children's development and many disagreed with recommendations from expert sources regarding age appropriate screen time.' They reported that 68.5% of the 101 parents surveyed agreed that 'introducing technological tools at a young age prepared children better for tomorrow's work force' and 33% of them believed that 'children may fall behind academically if their use of technological tools is restricted in early childhood' (Vittrup et al., 2016: 49).

The survey findings reported in this chapter gathered parents' views on this issue from the UK, Sweden and Australia, and a small sample from Greece – a group of countries which were selected to reflect the diversity of Western culture in terms of language, religion, education system and social structure (McKay, 2011). In relation to attitudes towards very young children's use of touchscreens, the countries appear to share much common ground as the following 'cultural snapshots' indicate.

In the UK, there has been widespread panic mongering around touchscreen use by 0–3s in the right-wing press (see, for example, Adams, 2014), further establishing the correlation between being a 'good parent' and protecting or limiting your child/ren's access to and use of technology. The rise of outdoor play movements (see Bond, 2013) supports the view that childhood is more suitably aligned with the outdoor, social pursuits of nature rather than the indoor, often solitary, pursuits of technology, and this is also evident in the growing popularity of forest schools and preschools in the UK. However, there is also growing recognition that touchscreen technology can encourage play and creativity (Marsh, 2010; Marsh et al., 2015) and that apps can support learning in early years settings and have a positive educational impact on young children's learning (Kucirkova et al., 2014).

Digital technology in childhood is also a contemporary topic in Swedish society with varying attitudes towards it being expressed in the media. There have been concerns around health issues caused by spending too much time on screen, such as too little physical exercise, with some pediatricians arguing that the use of touchscreen devices leads to early problems with concentration (see Lagercrantz, 2013). However, those responsible for curriculum development defend the benefits of iPads as a tool for young children's learning. Consequently, the vast majority (83%) of 1–5-year-olds in Sweden attend a preschool setting with digital access governed by the national preschool curriculum (Gällhagen and Wahlström, 2011).

In Australia, although the use of technology with young children is a popular topic in the media, the scholarly research with very young children and their engagement with touchscreens is in its embryonic stages (see Rintakorpi et al., 2014). There is a gap in identifying the everydayness of this new technology and parents' voices and concerns. Although the amount of relevant research is still limited, the need for further investigation has been underlined in almost all previous investigations, as a topic of concern to parents, educators and society in general (see Merchant, 2015: 10–11).

Finally, even though the presence of technology in children's lives from a very early age is unquestionable, research with very young children and how they use digital devices is limited in countries which face economic crisis, such as Greece (Nikolopoulou and Gialamas, 2015; Plumb and Kautz, 2015). However, Palaiologou's (2016) study on the use of digital technology by children under 5 in four European countries did include Greece and found that children under 5 are heavy users of a number of digital technologies at home and are 'digitally fluent from a very young age' (2014: 5). Therefore, whilst our survey in Greece is ongoing it was considered important to include the qualitative dimensions of the study in this chapter to further explore parental views in relation to 0–3s and touchscreen use.

The following analysis and discussion adds insight, detail and personal experience to these wider cultural and educational issues by reflecting on the views held by those parents who completed the survey in the four countries.

DATA COLLECTION AND RESEARCH LIMITATIONS

The data for this study was collected via an online questionnaire which was circulated through personal, parenting and professional networks via the researcher in each country.

The only stipulation for respondents to the questionnaire was that the parents or carers completing it should have at least one child under 3 years of age (36 months). The questionnaire was completed by 226 respondents in the UK, 69 in Sweden, 59 in Australia and 18 so far in Greece, with a total number of 370 respondents across the four countries. The total number of children aged 0–3 being reported on was 516 (255 girls and 261 boys).

The adult sample largely consisted of female, middle-class professionals aged between 31 and 40 years of age. A limitation of this study lies in the fact that important perspectives and information from diverse and disadvantaged families are not represented. Therefore, it does not argue that its findings are generalisable, but they offer a starting point in identifying shared parental concerns and experiences in this area.

THEORETICAL FRAMEWORK

Using a theoretical framework which draws on dominant discourses of childhood, the chapter presents and analyses data from the online survey in order to ascertain the similarities and differences in how 0–3s are using touchscreen technology in homes in these different countries, and what parents perceive to be the potential benefits and disadvantages of their usage.

Although there are always points of convergence and shades of grey with any polarised situation, it does appear, as described above, that two dominant discourses are evident in the literature around parenting and children's use of technology. The protectionist ideology, which conceptualises young children as needing to develop 'naturally' with as little technological involvement as possible, contrasts with a more emancipatory perspective, which acknowledges and actively encourages young children's use of technology as being of benefit to their future skills and education. It is useful to locate these discourses around young children and technology in relation to the paradigm of the social construction of childhood (James and Prout, 2003). Within this theoretical framework, childhood is understood as plural and diverse, informed by cultural discourses which influence how children are treated, conceptualised and behaved towards in wider society and how they are parented and educated at home and at school. From this perspective, the data collected for this study has been interpreted as reflecting the opinions, experiences and beliefs of the respondents regarding the specific topic of 0–3s' use of touchscreens, but also in recognition of the diverse ways in which they may understand and construct meanings around early childhood more generally, dependent on their different cultural and social contexts.

Furthermore, as well as the two distinct discourses identified there are multiple variations and interpretations of both positions which parents may draw on at different times depending on their circumstances. For example, a parent may feel uncomfortable allowing their young child(ren) to use touchscreens unsupervised for entertainment but be happy for them to use Facetime or Skype to communicate with grandparents.

The following analysis and discussion reflect the extent to which these positions are held by those who completed the online survey in the four countries and focuses on the views of parents with very young children from 0 to 3 years. Due to the small sample size in Greece, the quantitative data is reported only from the UK, Australia and Sweden, whereas the qualitative data from the survey is reported from all four countries, including Greece.

AN OVERVIEW OF TOUCHSCREEN USAGE IN THE UK, AUSTRALIA AND SWEDEN

Of the parents who responded to the survey in the UK, Australia and Sweden, 67% said their 0–3s used touchscreen devices. Tablets, such as iPads, were the most popular devices used by 0–3s in the UK and Sweden, followed by smartphones. In Australia, smartphones were the most widely used devices, followed by tablets. Surprisingly, Kindles were also identified. This was an unexpected finding for this age group across the three countries, given that Kindles typically require a child to be able to read the words on the screen.

'At home' was by far the most common response to the question of where 0–3s used touchscreens. This finding is consistent with previous research which documented the rise in preschoolers' use of technology at home (see Stephen et al., 2013). For Swedish children, nursery/school was the second most common place, followed by 'in the car'.

The rate of 0–3s using a touchscreen device daily or sometimes was highest in the UK at 66% and then Sweden at 61%. In Australia, the rate of 0–3s using touchscreen devices 'at least once a week' or 'sometimes' was 49% for smartphones and 40.3% for iPads.

According to UK respondents, playing game apps is the most popular use of touchscreens with this age group (92%). For Swedish and Australian children, the most common use involves looking at photos and videos, followed by playing game apps (Sweden) and for communication with family members with applications such as Skype or Facetime (Australia). Using touchscreens for reading books/stories was the least frequent reason for use in Australia (11%), the UK (24%) and Sweden (25%).

PERCEIVED ADVANTAGES OF 0–3S USING TOUCHSCREENS

Parents were asked to indicate the advantages/benefits they perceive for their 0–3s using touchscreens and the responses for each country are shown in Table 6.1.

Table 6.1 Positive reasons for touchscreen use amongst 0–3s

	The UK (N = 226)	Australia (N = 58)	Sweden (N = 69)
They learn new skills	74%	41%	84%
They learn new knowledge	50%	49%	80%
It keeps them occupied	63%	37%	73%
It entertains them	76%	32%	49%
It allows them to be creative	39%	63%	49%
It will help them when they go to school	35%	80%	45%

The use of touchscreens for 'learning new skills' was the highest scoring benefit perceived by parents in the UK and Sweden. This focus on education is also related to 'It will help them when they go to school' which was the highest scoring benefit identified by Australian parents. 'It will help them when they go to school' was the least frequent response for parents from the UK.

Acknowledgement of the ever-increasing role technology will play in the future lives of the children was a common theme in parental responses, as is evident in the typical examples below:

A 'digital native' has advantages we can't understand yet. (Sweden)

They are being introduced to technology that they will be using throughout their life. (UK)

Being a 'good parent' seems to be interpreted here as ensuring that their children are keeping up with technological and social changes. This awareness of the need for future technological skills in such young children is an important indicator of the impact touchscreens may be having on perceptions around very early childhood education and play.

Parents in each country also responded candidly about using touchscreens for more practical reasons such as for distracting or controlling their very young children. For example:

[Their use of touchscreens] gives some free time to parents to do something else. (Greece)

It can be an instant pleaser in places such as the car (my 2-year-old hates car journeys) and occasionally if out eating etc and she is bored of drawing/playing it keeps her still. (UK)

This recognition of very young children's fascination with touchscreens was also evident in parents' reporting of the way in which touchscreens were perceived to enable very young children to express their creativity, pursue knowledge or explore their own identity.

Comments included the following:

> They can follow their interests, choose what they are interested in and pursue it when they want to. (UK)
>
> They do creative activities [such as] puzzles and creations in digital environments. (Greece)

Another interesting category of responses focused on the opportunities touchscreens presented to very young children for communicating and connecting with absent family members, even over very long distances. This was particularly apparent in the data from the UK, Australia and Sweden:

> As a family we skype our parents to catch up on her developments. (Australia)
>
> Allows him to see and 'chat' with grandparents who live far away. (UK)
>
> [Skype] keeps relationships to relatives alive. (Sweden)

In a time of increasingly geographically disparate extended families due to changes in social mobility, employment patterns and globalisation, it is clear that mobile touchscreen devices offer important opportunities for even very young children to develop relationships with distant family (Kelly, 2013). The use of touchscreens for this purpose seemed to be uncontentious for the respondents and no negative comments were made about the facility for babies and toddlers to see and connect with physically absent friends and family.

CASE STUDY 6.1: INDIVIDUAL DIFFERENCES AND TOUCHSCREEN USE AMONGST 0–3S

Ben is 13 months old. He lives with his parents, who are both teachers, and his 6-year-old brother. Ben goes to nursery three days a week where no digital devices are used with children under 2. At home, he sees his brother playing games on the iPad and sees his parents texting and reading on their phones and is very interested in both types of digital device. Ben is not allowed to use the smartphones or iPad as he gets too excited and presses everything at once, closing apps, opening irrelevant pages and dropping the devices. His cousin Sophie is the same age but she is allowed to use specific baby apps on her parents' iPad such as bubble time and drawing sparkles when she is sitting quietly, and also enjoys looking at photos on her mother's phone.

REFLECTIVE TASK

Reflect on case study 6.1 and discuss how you would describe Ben and Sophie's behaviour towards the smartphone and the iPad. Try to observe children under 3 and discuss whether they show similar behaviours towards non-digital material.

PARENTAL CONCERNS AROUND 0–3S USING TOUCHSCREENS

The majority of parents across the UK, Australia and Sweden reported having concerns about their 0–3s using touchscreens (the UK 62%, Australia 76% and Sweden 71%). Responses to this question drew largely on the discourse of childhood innocence, whereby children are perceived as primarily vulnerable and in need of guidance and protection, with the adult knowing best and being the advocate for the child's well-being. There was also evidence of the established and historical polarised debate on children and technology with a substantial number of respondents across the three countries (33%) reporting having no concerns at all about their 0–3s using touchscreens and considering their use as no different from other activities such as reading books, and others being so worried about negative effects that they allow no use at all. For example:

> We have not encouraged our daughter to use a touchscreen. We haven't even let her know it's possible to play games on devices etc. It doesn't seem right to me that she might be potentially able to use a device very competently before she is able to speak properly. (UK)

However, the majority of respondents in the UK, Australia and Sweden allowed their 0–3s to use touchscreens, although 90% of them reported putting limitations on their use (usually between 20 and 30 minutes per day). The range of concerns expressed about the practice often appeared to be compounded by a lack of trusted official guidance and research-based evidence. For example, many parents expressed fears that their child may become over-reliant on or even addicted to their mobile devices. The following comments illustrate the unease many parents expressed about the limits they should be setting around their children's usage of touchscreens:

> I believe screens can be very addictive and can affect the child's ability to self-entertain, to be creative and to take initiative. (Australia)
>
> I worry that he expects to play on it a lot and gets upset if I say no. (UK)
>
> Screens seem to be addictive in a way that books/toys are not. (UK)

Ensuring that their very young children were learning to interact and communicate effectively was extremely important to the questionnaire respondents in the UK, Sweden and Australia. Examples of comments around this issue are provided below and represent significant first-hand observations of how touchscreen use may be interfering with this important area of development:

> In the very young babies if the screen is very close to their face ... it reduces the time they can spend looking at real people's faces and learning social skills. (UK)
>
> My children seem to forget how to be a nice human following a long time on their tablet or iPad. I believe they are better off playing with each other or toys. (Australia)
>
> I don't think it's good for small children. In part because they become asocial and choose the screen over social life and play. (Sweden)

Parental fears also related to ways in which touchscreen use may impact negatively on their child's cognitive, social and physical development (including eyesight). These types of concerns are reflected in the following responses:

> If they use it too much it might prevent them from developing other relevant skills at the right time – but what is too much? (UK)
>
> I think under 2s have enough stimulation from the world around them that they don't need to be overstimulated by videos or apps accessible at all times. (Australia)
>
> Today's children are not allowed to be bored. As soon as anything's boring, the parents hand them a phone or an iPad. (Sweden)
>
> Decreases imagination and creativity, bad for the eyes, not assisting the development of the brain. (Greece)

That very young children learn through play has become accepted in most of the developed world and forms the basis of many curricula and frameworks of early education, as well as informing health and education campaigns aimed at parents (see Patte and Brown, 2012). The strength of this discourse is reflected in the types of concerns many parents in this study have about touchscreens taking these learning opportunities away from their children by replacing traditional forms of play and printed books:

> They very quickly start to want to play only on the iPad rather than anything else. The iPad version of reality is more colourful, easier and more appealing than real life e.g. colouring in an iPad is much easier than on real paper with real pens. For this reason, we limit their use and do not allow access every day. (UK)
>
> I believe excessive use of tablet or similar may seriously damage children's creativity. (Sweden)

One Greek mother explained how practical necessity resulted in her toddler using an iPad but expressed guilt at allowing him to do so, again reflecting the association felt by many parents between being a 'good parent' and limiting access to technology:

> With my oldest child I was almost forced to let him engage with this type of activity due to personal circumstances. My second pregnancy was very hard, I couldn't get up, I had to stay in bed. Unfortunately, due to this situation my child had to spend time playing with technology. This is how it started and continued. After I gave birth, I was alone in the house and had to take care of the new baby. My older son was not very cooperative so again I let him engage with technology to give me time to take care of the baby. I still do that. Yes, he learns things but I am very worried (and I also feel guilty). (Greece)

It seems clear from the types of concerns here and the lack of guidance on the issue that parental worry around 0–3s using touchscreens is an area which needs further research. Indeed, in this survey 95% of UK parents, 58% of Swedish parents and 63% of Australian parents had had no guidance or information relating to their 0–3s using touchscreens from any source. Of the minority of parents who had had some advice, this had generally been sourced by themselves from newspapers, the internet or from professional friends and colleagues. The lack of informed guidance, particularly around 'safe' lengths of time for 0–3s to use touchscreens, was a cause of concern for many survey respondents.

In terms of what parents would like advice on, this was broadly similar across the four countries and can be summarised as follows:

- recommended time limits for usage
- whether 0–3s can become addicted to touchscreen devices
- whether touchscreen use can damage 0–3s' eyesight, concentration, posture or behaviour
- whether touchscreens have any benefit to learning
- if and how touchscreens impact on brain development
- whether touchscreens encourage or curtail young children's creativity and communication skills.

Additionally, Greek and Australian parents also wanted to know about the levels of radiation that emanate from touchscreen devices. As one Greek parent succinctly summed it up, parents want to know, above all else, 'if children win or lose from using touchscreen devices' and they want this information to come from evidence-based research.

REFLECTIVE TASK

Reflect on the above and explore your own attitudes towards 0–3s' use of touchscreen technology with the following questions:

1. 'My child will be disadvantaged if we don't allow her to use touchscreens at home before she starts preschool.' To what extent do you agree with this parent's views?
2. What kind of research evidence would be useful to you in deciding whether or not 0–3s should be encouraged or discouraged to use touchscreens in the home?
3. What is your response to the following statement: 'Guidance about touchscreen use for 0–3s should be consistent across different countries'?

THE ONGOING CHALLENGE OF PARENTING IN AN INCREASINGLY DIGITALISED WORLD

The survey findings discussed in this chapter highlight the extent to which the issue of the use of touchscreen devices by the very youngest children has become a shared dilemma for parents across the developed world. Given the lack of firm empirical evidence and the plethora of opposing discourses around the use of such technology by this age group, it is little wonder that parents are drawing on wider cultural constructs of 'good parenting' and established cultural norms around child development to guide their practice.

In relation to the enduring strength of established early childhood discourses around innocence and naturalness, the findings suggest that these are still very powerful in shaping the perceptions and beliefs of parents of very young children. This is reflected in the concern respondents expressed in relation to touchscreens potentially replacing traditional play and learning and fears around children accessing inappropriate material online. The issue of touchscreens replacing traditional play and learning is related to this, as accepted middle-class constructions of being a 'good parent' have focused on encouraging children to read or be read printed books and express themselves through physically creative and/or outdoor activities. The way touchscreens are used threatens these traditional concepts of play and learning and parents are understandably anxious as to the consequences of this for their children's development and well-being. Concerns were also prevalent around the potentially negative impact of touchscreen use on babies and toddlers' interaction and communication skills. Again, much research has highlighted the importance of talking to babies and encouraging social interaction to ensure healthy emotional and social development (see Whitehead, 2010), and touchscreen use appears to challenge this in ways clearly documented in the parents' responses.

As well as identifying the strength of traditional perspectives on childhood evident in the parental responses, the study also highlighted some novel ways of thinking about early childhood which may have important implications for the way in which very young children are conceptualised, cared for and educated in contemporary society. For example, the references to babies and toddlers needing to build up their technological capital in order to be successful in their future education and careers is a reflection of how touchscreen technology may be impacting on traditional ways of thinking about very early childhood as a time of protection from the 'adult' world of technology (Postman, 1996). There was also much positive feedback on the use of tablets to enable very young children to connect easily with distant family members via Skype or FaceTime, suggesting that it may not be touchscreen technology itself which is seen as a threat to the ideals of very early childhood, but how it is actually used.

In line with earlier studies of children and technology (see Marsh et al., 2005; Palaiologou, 2014; Stephen et al., 2010), some parents have embraced the new medium as a way for their 0–3s to further develop skills and competencies. For others, however, touchscreens represent a threat to cherished ideals around childhood innocence and children's physical, social and emotional well-being (Louv, 2010; Palmer, 2007).

What is particularly interesting from this study is the way in which parents from these different countries are grappling with common problems and worries in relation to their children's use of touchscreens, and appear to be reaching similar, unilateral, decisions about what is appropriate for their 0–3s. Most, for example, put limits of 10–20 minutes on their young children's use of touchscreens. The types of concerns and worries that the parents noted were also of a similar nature. This convergence of parental opinion is worth further exploration and documentation as, given the current paucity of informed guidance in this area, it is becoming a vital source of information in relation to practices amongst the very youngest touchscreen users.

The idea that touchscreen use is not part of what is accepted as 'normal' development (Piaget, 1972; Vygotsky, 1998) is a pervasive one that was evident in the survey responses and reflects a conceptual separation between technological skills and other skills that young children need to develop, as well as a common bias towards more 'natural' occupations for very young children. This was evident in parents' expressions of concern over the way touchscreen use may be replacing the traditional play and learning which characterised their own childhoods in a less technologically saturated time.

Despite the misgivings of many of the parents about the potential drawbacks of their 0–3s using touchscreens, overall the survey findings seem to suggest that Vittrup et al. (2016: 52) are correct when they describe the weakening of what they describe as 'parental scepticism around young children using technology' as rates of usage continue to grow. Even so, there is evidence of reluctance in the responses. For example, one Greek mother laments that 'unfortunately we have to follow the trends of our times'. Comments such as this highlight the universal ongoing tension between personally or culturally held ideals around 'good parenting' and the acknowledged importance of ensuring that children are brought up in a way that equips them to deal with the reality of the world in which we live.

It is now impossible to deny that many 0–3s are part of the technological world and have access to touchscreens within their homes. It is therefore of utmost importance that early care and educational practitioners in the four countries, and beyond, recognise the range of views that parents have around 0–3s' use of touchscreens, and ensure that they have an open and informed dialogue about appropriate practices when planning how to integrate or develop touchscreen usage with the children in their settings.

SUMMARY

This chapter explores the growing trend for infants and very young children to have access to and use of touchscreens for play and learning. It reflects on how parents and caregivers manage and make sense of this practice in their families according to their cultural and social understandings and constructions of early childhood education, care and development. The types of concerns voiced by parents were consistent across the respondents from the different countries, as were many of the benefits that they also perceived for their 0–3s using such technology, suggesting that the use of touchscreen technology by 0–3s is a contemporary parenting dilemma that crosses international boundaries.

What is clear is that more research is needed in this area in order to provide evidence-based guidelines as to best practice with this very youngest of age groups. What is also doubtless is that as these little ones start school, and throughout their education, they will be engaged with technology-supported learning in whatever form that may take in the future. The more practitioners and teachers can understand and communicate with parents in relation to their children's early experiences with touchscreen technology, the easier the transition into formal schooling will be for these children.

KEY POINTS TO REMEMBER

- Rates of 0–3s using touchscreens devices are rising around the world.
- Parents in the countries surveyed share common concerns around 0–3s' use of touch-screens as well as recognising similar benefits.
- More research-based evidence is needed to guide parents in their mediation of touchscreen usage with their 0–3s.
- Early childhood education needs to recognise the range of views and concerns held by parents on this issue.

POINTS FOR DISCUSSION

- In response to this research, discuss what competencies adults/parents should develop to support their young children with the use of touchscreens.
- What do you think the role of early childhood education should be in relation to supporting parents of young children and the use of digital devices?
- In your context, what are the policy guidelines for discussing with parents the use of digital devices with their children?

FURTHER READING

Paciga, K. A. and Donohue, C. (2017) *Technology and Interactive Media for Young Children: A Whole Child Approach Connecting the Vision of Fred Rogers with Research and Practice.* Latrobe, PA: Fred Rogers Center for Early Learning and Children's Media at Saint Vincent College. Available at: www.fredrogerscenter.org/wp-content/uploads/2017/07/Technology-and-Interactive-Media-for-Young-Children.pdf (accessed 18 October 2018).

Stephen, C. and Edwards, S. (2018) *Young Children Playing and Learning in a Digital Age: A Cultural and Critical Perspective.* London: Routledge.

Yelland, N. (2016) iPlay, iLearn, iGrow: tablet technology, curriculum, pedagogies and learning in the twenty-first century. In S. Gurvis and N. Lemon (eds) *Understanding Digital Technology and Young Children: An International Perspective.* London: Routledge, pp. 38–45.

USEFUL WEBSITES

www.childnet.com – guidance and support from a charity for parents and teachers on how to keep children safe when using digital technology.

www.wordsforlife.org.uk – guidance on using technology with the under-5s.

REFERENCES

Adams, G. (2014) The day I realised my toddler was addicted to the iPad. *Daily Mail*, 29 January, p. 14.

Bond, D. (2013) Project Wild Thing. Available at: www.thewildnetwork.com (accessed 3 May 2016).

Cocozza, P. (2014) Are iPads and tablets bad for young children? *The Guardian*, 8 January, p. 12.

Courage, M. L. and Setliff A. E. (2009) Debating the impact of television and video material on very young children: attention, learning, and the developing brain. *Child Development Perspectives, 3* (1): 72–78.

Cristia, A. and Seidl, A. (2015) Parental reports on touch screen use in early childhood. *PLoS ONE, 10* (6): 1–20.

Flewitt, R. S. (2012) Multimodal perspectives on early childhood literacies. In J. Larson and J. Marsh (eds) *The SAGE Handbook of Early Childhood Literacy.* London: Sage, pp. 295–310.

Gällhagen, L. and Wahlström, E. (2011) *Lär och lek med surfplatta i förskolan. [Learn and play with tablet in preschool.]* Stockholm: Natur and kultur.

Higonnet, A. (1998) *Pictures of Innocence: The History and Crisis of Ideal Childhood.* London: Thames and Hudson.

James, A. and Prout, A. (2003) *Constructing and Reconstructing Childhood: Contemporary Issues in the Sociological Study of Childhood.* London: Routledge.

Kelly, C. (2013) 'Let's do some jumping together': intergenerational participation in the use of remote technology to co-construct social relations over distance. *Journal of Early Childhood Research, 13* (1): 29–46.

Kucirkova, N., Messer, D., Sheehy, K. and Panadero, C. F. (2014) Children's engagement with educational iPad apps: insights from a Spanish classroom. *Computers and Education, 71*: 175–184.

Lagercrantz, L. (2013) Mycket tid framför skärm splittrar barns liv. [*A lot of time in front of the screen splits children's lives.*] *Läkartidningen, 110* (1–2): 16–17.

Louv, R. (2010) *Last Child in the Woods: Saving our Children from Nature-Deficit Disorder.* London: Atlantic Books.

McKay, J. (2011) *Understanding Western Society: Vol. 2.* Bedford: St Martin's.

Marsh, J. (2010) Young children's play in online virtual worlds. *Journal of Early Childhood Research, 8* (1): 23–39.

Marsh, J., Hannon, P., Lewis, M. and Ritchie, L. (2017) Young children's initiation into family literacy practices in the digital age. *Journal of Early Childhood Research, 15* (1): 47–60.

Marsh, J., Plowman, L., Yamada-Rice, D. and Bishop, J. (2015) Exploring Play and Creativity in Pre-Schoolers' Use of Apps: Final Project Report. Available at: www.techandplay.org/reports/TAP_Final_Report.pdf (accessed 18 October 2018).

Merchant, G. (2015) Keep taking the tablets: iPads, story apps and early literacy. *Australia Journal of Language and Literacy, 38* (1): 3–11.

National Association for the Education of Young Children (NAEYC) (2012) *Technology and Interactive Media as Tools in Early Childhood Programs Serving Children from Birth through Age 8.* Washington, DC: NAEYC. Available at: www.naeyc.org/files/naeyc/file/positions/PS_technology_WEB2.pdf (accessed 18 October 2018).

Nikolopoulou, K. and Gialamas, V. (2015) Barriers to the integration of computers in early childhood settings: teachers' perceptions. *Education and Information Technologies*, *20* (2): 285–301.

O'Connor, J. (2017) Under 3s and technology. In L. Arnott (ed.) *Digital Technologies and Learning in the Early Years*. London: Sage, pp. 87–98.

Palaiologou, I. (2016) Children under five and digital technologies: Implications for early years pedagogy. *The European Early Childhood Research Journal, 24* (1): 5–24. (DOI:10.10 80/1350293X.2014.929876, first published online 2014).

Palmer, S. (2007) *Toxic Childhood: How the Modern World is Damaging Our Children and What We Can Do About It.* London: Orion.

Patte, M. and Brown, F. (2012) *Rethinking Children's Play*. London: Bloomsbury Academic.

Piaget, J. (1972) *Psychology of the Child*. London: Basic Books.

Plowman, L., Stevenson, O., Stephen, C. and McPake, J. (2012) Preschool children's learning with technology at home. *Computers and Education, 59*: 30–37.

Plumb, M. and Kautz, K. (2015) Innovation determinants and barriers: a tri-perspective analysis of IT appropriation within an early childhood education and care organisation. *Australasian Journal of Information Systems, 19*: 1–22.

Radesky, J. S., Schumacher, J. and Zuckerman, B. (2015) Mobile and interactive media use by young children: the good, the bad, and the unknown. *Pediatrics, 135* (1): 1–3.

Rintakorpi, K., Lipponen, L. and Reunamo, J. (2014) Documenting with parents and toddlers: a Finnish case study. *Early Years, 34* (2): 188–197.

Robinson, K. (2013) *Innocence, Knowledge and the Construction of Childhood*. London: Routledge.

Stephen, C., McPake, J. and Plowman, L. (2010) Digital technologies at home: the experiences of 3- and 4-year-olds in Scotland. In M. Clark and S. Tucker (eds) *Early Childhoods in a Changing World*. Stoke-on-Trent: Trentham Books, pp. 145–154.

Stephen, C., Stevenson, O. and Adey, C. (2013) Young children engaged with technologies at home: the influence of family context. *Journal of Early Childhood Research, 11* (2): 149–164.

Verenikina, I. and Kervin, L. (2011) iPads, digital play and pre-schoolers. *He Kupu, 2* (5): 4–16.

Vittrup, B., Snider, S. and Rose, K. (2016) Parental perceptions of the role of media and technology in their young children's lives. *Journal of Early Childhood Research, 14* (1): 43–54.

Vygotsky, L. S. (1998) Infancy. In R. W. Rieber (ed.) *The Collected Works of L. S. Vygotsky*, Vol. 5. New York: Plenum Press, pp. 207–241.

Whitehead, M. (2010) *Language and Literacy in the Early Years 0–7*. London: Sage.

7

INTEGRATING TECHNOLOGY TO SUPPORT CHILDREN'S AGENCY AND TRANSITION TO SCHOOL

KELLY JOHNSTON, KATE HIGHFIELD AND FAY HADLEY

CHAPTER OVERVIEW

This chapter discusses the value of digital devices such as iPads or tablets in supporting children's agency, understanding and transitions to school. It also focuses on how digital devices can be used in a complementary way with more traditional early learning resources to support learning within play-based pedagogies.

By the end of this chapter, you should:

- have an awareness of the ubiquity of technology and its presence as a cultural tool in many children's lives

- be able to consider how technology can be integrated and used contemporaneously with other tools and resources to support children's play-based learning
- have an understanding of the potential benefits of using digital devices such as iPads, tablets, cameras, videos, voice recording and computers to support children's processes of investigation, exploration and learning as well as their agency and autonomy.

INTRODUCTION

Technology has become an integral part of society and an increasing presence in children's everyday lives (Chaudron, 2015; Palaiologou, 2016). Many children's experiences encompass an ever-growing range of technological resources, including television, computers, gaming consoles, DVD players, mobile phones, hi-tech toys, iPods, touchscreen tablets and household appliances, and other less tangible resources such as the internet (Blackwell et al., 2013; Fleer, 2011; Zevenbergen and Logan, 2008). The increasing pervasiveness of technology creates important considerations for early childhood educators. Development for children (as well as adults) occurs through engaging with resources and practices that are culturally preferred, relevant and predominant (Rogoff, 2003). In this way, technological resources such as digital devices are, or are becoming, cultural tools. Additionally, ongoing use and experience with technology contemporaneously shifts how it features as a cultural tool and how it is experienced in everyday life. This sociocultural stance acknowledges that children have a dynamic relationship with the various contexts in which they interact, including family, early learning settings and the wider community (Rogoff, 1990). As such, it stands to reason that the inclusion of technology in early learning settings should mirror the experiences children have within their family environments, as well as their broader social contexts. This can present a valuable means for consolidating and extending children's experiences with technology as well as fostering an awareness of how things work in the 21st century (Edwards, 2005; Parette et al., 2013).

Advancements in everyday technologies require a reconceptualisation that extends beyond computers to consider more diverse digital devices (Plowman et al., 2012). The way technology is rapidly developing has created new possibilities, experiences and resources that have not existed for previous generations, and as such interpretations and understandings of play as well as child development are changing. The Australian Early Years Learning Framework (EYLF), a document that provides a framework for learning in prior-to-school settings, continues to promote play-based learning and strongly espouses creating links between play and children's social and cultural experience and understanding (DEEWR, 2009; Sumsion et al., 2009). However, beyond being contextually relevant to children, the concept of play is further shifting with diverse interpretations existing between educators of different ages and backgrounds (Yelland, 2011). Technology is often viewed as conflicting with traditional beliefs around what constitutes play-based learning, with some traditional play theorists seeing engagement with technology as outside the realm of 'play'. Increasingly, however, research provides perspectives that challenge such thinking by demonstrating that technology and play-based learning are not dichotomous (Nikolopoulou and Gialamas, 2015; Palaiologou, 2016). If play is defined as being child-led, voluntary, self-motivating and process-based (Barblett, 2010), then technology-based play must be considered as a modality that helps children make sense of their world. Additionally, this chapter suggests that including technology in play-based pedagogies enables children to understand the role of technology in their world.

Play-based explorations of technology lay foundations for children as they experience the continuous advancement of technology, as well as for their increasing interactions with technology. In saying this, it is also important to define and better understand some of the types of technology that children have experience with from an early age as they can have a strong influence on children's emerging understanding of their world. Progressive thinking in terms of increasing the understanding of technology within play-based pedagogies involves identifying the difference between active and passive technology (NAEYC and Fred Rogers Center, 2012). Such an approach draws on technology as being integrated and interactive in the curriculum and includes elements of play. Children's active engagement with technology can be agentic with children afforded opportunities to create, communicate and provide insights into their understanding and ideas. This chapter explores children's agency as observers and documenters and how these processes support the inclusion of their perspectives and the provision of pedagogical approaches and curriculum inclusions that are socially and culturally relevant.

THE AUSTRALIAN CONTEXT: THE EARLY YEARS LEARNING FRAMEWORK (EYLF)

Early learning in Australia, for children in prior-to-school contexts, occurs in a variety of contexts such as long day care, preschool and family day care. These services are available for children between six weeks and 6 years of age. Within these settings, pedagogical practices are underpinned by the EYLF. This framework promotes the belief that children learn best in play-based situations which reflect their home culture and experience (Barblett, 2010; DEEWR, 2009). Advice within the EYLF also encourages educators to engage children in active discussions about their experiences and thinking processes to further extend understanding, knowledge and familiarity (DEEWR, 2009). Technology features in the EYLF as a means to support communication and children's investigation and learning. The importance of recognising technology as a valuable tool in play-based learning, as well as a resource that children will benefit from gaining familiarity with, is also a focus, with guidance in the EYLF stating that 'Children benefit from opportunities to explore their world using technologies and to develop confidence in using digital media' (DEEWR, 2009: 38).

Previously, the inclusion of technology in early learning settings predominantly involved computers as adjunct experiences (Mantei and Kervin, 2007), whereas guidance within the EYLF promotes a holistic approach to curriculum development and experiences for children (DEEWR, 2009). This also aligns with more resent research that identifies the value of integrating technology as a tool along with some more traditional resources within early learning settings (Edwards, 2015; Yelland, 2011). However, the place of technology in early learning curricula remains unclear and its value unrecognised as such debates continue in regards to the appropriateness of technology and screen time within early learning curricula.

CASE STUDY 7.1: AIDING THE TRANSITION TO SCHOOL

This case study draws on the findings of a doctoral research project conducted in three prior-to-school settings in New South Wales, Australia. Central to the study were practitioner inquiry projects where educators investigated the integration of technology within their early learning curricula. One of the studies involved educators at an early learning setting, working with children of between 4 and 5 years of age, exploring ways in which digital technologies could support children to have agency in their transition to school process. The researcher worked with the educators for three months, gaining insight into their beliefs and practices in relation to technology integration, and then worked with the educators for another four months to trial new ideas and approaches to technology integration within their play-based curricula. This case study provides an example of how children's use of touchscreen tablet devices enabled their voices and perspectives to be heard during the transition process to school and also supported their agency and ownership during this process.

WHAT IS PRACTITIONER INQUIRY?

The study involved practitioner inquiry as a professional learning strategy to support educators to increase understanding and ability in integrating technology in socially and culturally relevant ways through play-based learning. Practitioner inquiry involves educators working collaboratively to identify an area of interest and a question they wish to investigate. This question is then integrated and explored through everyday practice.

(Continued)

(Continued)

The practitioner inquiry process provides the opportunity for educators to critically reflect both individually and collectively, to question beliefs and practices and to work towards the systemic change that they identify as useful and beneficial for those involved in their contexts (Groundwater-Smith et al., 2013). This professional learning strategy enables educators to maintain autonomy and agency in their professional learning and also in facilitating change within their early learning services. It is an important approach when introducing new ideas and resources, such as those often associated with digital technologies, as it enables participants to identify the relevance and value of changes before implementing them. These are recognised as key enablers in effective change and development processes (Guskey, 2002).

PRACTITIONER INQUIRY: QUESTION OR ISSUE IDENTIFIED

In this research study, the educators in one early learning setting identified that each year children underwent the process of transition to school but that children experienced this in very different ways. Some schools created strong connections between the children, families, educators and teachers. The early childhood educator was able to speak with the teachers, and families were able to be part of the transitions process. At other schools, families and early years educators were required to leave children at the school gates and only the children took part in the orientation process.

Transitions are recognised as a time of movement, change and potential vulnerability for children, with the support in place to facilitate the process (Dockett et al., 2017). International research indicates that effective transition to school programmes have positive outcomes for children in terms of starting their first year of schooling. This subsequently has a positive effect on longer-term development and dispositions in terms of learning and social engagement (Educational Transitions and Change [ETC] Group, 2011). The EYLF acknowledges children's transitions as one of the practices that underpins learning outcomes and emphasises the importance of connection, communication and agency in the transition processes (DEEWR, 2009). In practice, effective transition to school programmes should help children to develop a sense of familiarity, confidence and belonging between their current and new contexts. This is most successfully achieved when there are connections and collaborations between children, early learning educators, school educators and families (ETC Group, 2011). Often, this does not occur organically and requires mindful co-ordination, planning, engagement and contribution from all stakeholders, with children's voices and agency given pivotal consideration (Dockett et al., 2017).

The early childhood educators on the study identified a need to create connections, understanding and agency for all children during this transition process. Drawing on this basis, a practitioner inquiry focus emerged – 'Using iPads to help children document, understand and become familiar with their individual school transition process and to also share their peers' experiences of transitioning to school'. Digital resources such as photographs, video clips and digital storybooks have been utilised contemporaneously with more traditional resources such as drawing and painting to enable children to explore their ideas, identify concerns or questions and create broad understandings. Interactions and discussions that accompany the development and use of these resources help to create shared understandings between stakeholders and to authentically reflect children's voices.

REFLECTIVE TASK

Reflect on your context as a practitioner and consider:

- What would you want your practitioner inquiry project to investigate in terms of agency and technology with children in your setting?
- Set out your question and the steps you might take to investigate it.

DIGITAL TECHNOLOGY AS AN INTEGRATED TOOL

The overarching aim of the practitioner inquiry process was to help children feel secure, empowered and confident in the transition process. The educators in this service already utilised a number of different forms of technology as integrated resources within the curriculum. Processes within the project included developing digital storybooks on the iPad as documentation that reflected children's engagement in their school transition experience whilst still attending long day care. This was used to reflect children's individual as well as shared experiences and to subsequently create a greater familiarity and understanding to support the transition process (ETC Group, 2011). Sharing experiences would provide the opportunity for children to understand that they may have the same ideas, fears, hopes and expectations in relation to transitioning to school as their peers, just as they may also have different ones. Another aim of the project was to create a resource that children could revisit throughout their ongoing transition process. This would be particularly useful in the six-week period between when they stopped attending their long day-care service and started kindergarten at their new primary school. The digital storybooks were also intended to be a valuable resource for families to draw on and revisit throughout their child's transition to school, particularly one that included the child's voice and perspective.

FOUNDATIONS FOR USING DIGITAL DEVICES

Educators at the service had used touchscreen devices with the children on a daily basis. A tablet was used to document discussions between children and educators at their morning meeting times and was also used to show YouTube clips as provocations and to research additional information to extend children's ideas and thinking during these meetings. Touchscreen tablets were also used to take photographs and videos of children's experiences and investigations. In this way, children developed an understanding of the devices over time and became aware of them as the cultural tools of the early learning service. Additionally, educators reported that some children were familiar with using touchscreen devices such as tablets or smartphones at home and had built a level of knowledge and familiarity with the devices in that context.

EDUCATOR BELIEFS IN RELATION TO THE BENEFITS OF DIGITAL DOCUMENTATION

During the study, the curriculum included digital documentation as a tool to support children to reflect on their own learning as well as the learning of their peers. Educators also noted that families found digital documentation easier to engage with and that sharing children's experiences and learning with families helped to create greater collaboration between families and educators, which in turn made the early learning curriculum more socially and culturally relevant.

IPADS AS A RESOURCE FOR CHILDREN TO DOCUMENT THEIR TRANSITION TO SCHOOL

The educators wanted to utilise digital devices such as cameras, video and iPads to create shared understandings of the school transition process that included each child's perspective. Educators stated that they had previously observed children using digital documentation to revisit their own experiences and to support all children. This encouraged practitioners to place greater emphasis on children's agency by engaging them in the collection and organisation of information on their transition to school. As a group, the children viewed a short video developed by the Australian Government which was designed to help children in early learning services to gain a level of familiarity with school contexts. Elements such as the kindergarten classrooms, children wearing school uniforms, and the school playgrounds were shown. The educator encouraged children to discuss what was similar and what was different to the school that they were visiting as part of the transition to school process. Family members able to attend the school transition visits were asked if a family member or the child might take photographs of areas of interest and bring them back to share with the class. An early learning educator from one school who attended the session took digital photographs and short video segments for later discussion and reflection with the children on the transition process and experience.

PROCESSES INVOLVED IN THE CASE STUDY

Interactions, discussions and the child's perspective were central to all experiences with the iPads. One way that educators facilitated this was to ask questions and encourage conversations about technology use to gain insights into what children already knew. The educators used open-ended questions for the child leading the discussion. These questions specifically targeted the capacities of the application that the educator explained to the group. Additionally, educators supported children's agency and recognised their competence by encouraging them to demonstrate to their peers how to use the iPad applications to create a page in the digital book. The educators enabled children to maintain the lead in terms of explaining and demonstrating. This included scaffolding in the form of helping to draw out children's knowledge and helping to clarify the understanding of others. This process also helped to consolidate the knowledge of the child who was explaining the process. In planning the introduction and implementation of resources and experiences, educators acknowledged the need for explicit instruction, including foundational skills which involved modelling and demonstrating. In this way, educators drew on their understanding of what children already knew, and then explained the new features and concepts of which the children were unaware. They also ensured that experiences using the iPad aligned with elements of play such as being playful, child-led and enjoyable (Barblett, 2010).

The digital storybook experience with the iPad involved a small group of four children at a time. Other children chose to observe the experience and added ideas and comments without trying to touch the device. Children's engagement with and use of the iPad in the digital storybook experience was child-led, moderated and managed. Educators did not need to stay during this activity and were able to move between proximal and distant guidance. This involved working directly with the children as they developed pages for the book, monitoring children's engagement in the digital storybook experience, whilst working with children on different experiences.

DIGITAL TECHNOLOGY ONE OF MANY RESOURCES USED TO DOCUMENT AND EXPLORE THE TRANSITION TO SCHOOL PROCESS

Educator beliefs and practices demonstrated that they were aware of the ways in which technology could be effectively integrated into the curriculum to support the learning goals and aims in place; it was also evident that technology was viewed as a valuable tool to support the process of inquiry and investigation. The iPad was one of many resources available to children in exploring the transition to school process. The teaching intention was for children to engage in ways that best met their interests and preferences. One child brought in a book that had been given to him at his school transition day called *A Special Place* (NSW Department of Education, 2018), which was read with the group. Digital photographs from school visits served as a stimulus for conversation between children and educators during group discussion. Educators reported that some children chose to document their thoughts and experiences with the school transition through painting and drawing. Children talked together throughout this process with the educator transcribing their ideas onto paper. Other children chose to draw using the digital storybook app, again talking with their peers about their ideas and experiences. Children were able to voice-record the narrative to their stories or type text with assistance from the educators.

Educators allowed the children time to familiarise themselves with the iPad and the applications before moving on to the more specific intentional teaching goal of using the iPad to document their transition to school journey. Following intentional teaching, distal guidance (Plowman and Stephen, 2007) was commonly used within this setting. The initial guidance with the resource helped to ensure that children were familiar, confident and capable with the device and the application. Following this, distal guidance enabled children to share their expertise and confidence with aspects of the digital technology and also to learn from the expertise and knowledge of their peers. Enabling children as both 'experts' and 'novices' (Rogoff, 1990) allows extension beyond the teacher/student dyad that is often present in learning interactions. Additionally, this enabled a culture of responsiveness within the service and the children were confident that the educators were consistently available to respond to their questions and to help them navigate through problems.

Digital technologies were included as an integrated tool/resource alongside other resources that children could use to explore and unpack their knowledge on the transition to school process. For example, during the morning sessions children were able to choose to work collectively on their digital storybooks whilst others at the next table were working on drawings and words for their paper-based storybooks. The iPad was accepted as another resource for children to use if it appealed to their interest. Here, educators made comments such as 'They're using skills, having discussions, teaching each other and exploring creativity in different ways' (Teacher 1, Meeting 3) and 'it's more than novelty – they're getting something out of it. They're learning to use it' (Teacher 2, Meeting 2).

RESULTS AND DISCUSSION

Within this context, there were significant changes to how technology was seen and used by staff. In this way, taking photographs and videos of children's play and experiences allowed children to access additional information and perspectives that they had not been aware of when initially participating in the experience. This process was valued by teachers and their shared knowledge became accessible to the learning community. This section outlines findings in terms of agency and belonging; familiarity with the resource; and active engagement.

AGENCY AND BELONGING

When children looked back on the digital documentation of their experiences and interactions in the school transition process, it helped to foster a sense of belonging and reassurance. Revisiting digital documentation also allowed children to observe the roles others played in their experiences and to develop an awareness of the thoughts, actions and perspectives of others as well as how they all worked together as part of a learning community. Blagojevic and Thomes (2008) note that use of digital documentation such as photography is an effective way to provide additional provocations for learning and provides children with a medium through which to voice their perspectives.

Another effective forum for supporting children's agency was the group meetings that the children and educators took part in every morning. These involved the educator using teaching strategies such as modelling and instructing to support children's development of iPad handling skills and to enable independent use of these devices. Educators encouraged children to lead instruction and learning by asking them to demonstrate how to use the digital storybook application. This approach respected children's knowledge, experience and abilities, and promoted children's agency. Within this context, this shift in agency was significant, with the children positioned as *the more knowledgeable other*, using their digital documentation to provoke and support their stance.

FAMILIARITY WITH THE RESOURCE

As outlined, the aim of the practitioner inquiry investigation for the educators was for children to use iPads for a specific purpose, extending their familiarity with touchscreen devices. The educators allowed children time to familiarise themselves with the iPad and applications before moving on to meet the more specific goal of using iPads to document their transition journey. Educators spent several sessions guiding and supporting children as they learnt to use the application. There was a dual acknowledgement that children have a certain level of ability (both individually and collectively) in using iPad applications, and that technology use is not intuitive for children and therefore educator guidance, observation and support are required. A key point here is that children were familiar with seeing touchscreen devices used as a resource and therefore had an understanding of their purpose as an everyday tool, rather than a novelty item. This aligns with the work of Plowman and Stephen (2005) who suggest the value of demystifying and creating knowledge of new technological resources before introducing them as an everyday resource.

Understanding children's familiarity with digital resources as culturally relevant tools is an important first step for educators when considering technology integration in their early learning curricula. There is a misconception that children have an intuitive knowledge of technology due to being born into a world where technology is ubiquitous (Plowman and McPake, 2013). However, effective use of technology within play-based learning requires that children are aware of the relevance of the device to their worlds and also that they are supported to understand how to use the resource. A combination of factors is evident in supporting children's active use of and competencies with digital technologies (Blagojevic and Thomes, 2008); this includes introducing them using explicit instruction and explanation (Edwards, 2015). As children's agency develops, this can be seen as extending Vygotsky's notion of explicit mediation (Edwards, 2015). Another important factor is the educator's perspective. The educator raised concerns that the iPad was costly, noting that 'with the [protective] cover on I feel fine about them having the freedom to explore it, because you don't have to worry about it being damaged [...] they are always really respectful and they've never been rough with it. They're a pretty good group like that now'. In case study 7.1, it appears that when educators have an image of children as capable and competent they are more likely to entrust them with the use of potentially costly digital devices and make provisions to enable access.

ACTIVE ENGAGEMENT

Case study 7.1 demonstrates that active engagement with technology formed the basis of an effective child-led experience. The interactions were pivotal to this experience of using digital technology as an integrated resource to support children's experience of the transition to school process. Interactions were between educators and children, and also between children themselves. Interactions with educators and more capable peers have long been recognised as valuable ways to extend children's thinking (Siraj-Blatchford, 2009; Yelland, 2011).

REFLECTIVE TASK

Considering the importance of effective transitions between early learning services and school, or when a child moves up to the next age group at an early learning service, which apps and technology tools could enable children to document and reflect on their new context? Consider which apps can be used by children, especially those who cannot read and write.

SUMMARY

This chapter offered an example of how technology can be used to facilitate transitions and how technology offers opportunities for children to have agency and autonomy. Children (aged 4–5 years) who were not yet able to read or write were able to record their voices. This allowed for authentic presentation of their perspectives and increased their autonomy and agency.

Given that children's participation in school transition programmes is recognised as a key factor for successful, positive experiences (ETC Group, 2011), this project provides additional benefits and opportunities for social and emotional development. Educators reported that children were discussing the similarities and differences they noticed during their school transition visits. This helped to create shared understandings between children, and also helped to demystify school as a new place of milieu. These transition processes helped to build a sense of confidence, connection and security which supports children to construct understandings between contexts (DEEWR, 2009). Despite the limitations of the case study presented here, as a one-off case, this example of practitioner inquiry provides evidence of how digital tools can be used to extend and promote engagement in transition. Given that transitions to school can be seen as complex times for many young children, the benefits of providing explicit engagement in this process, whilst simultaneously developing children's agency, are significant.

KEY POINTS TO REMEMBER

- It is important for children to develop foundational understandings of the technology they experience in their everyday lives. This will support them to develop as digital citizens as technology continues to advance and change.
- Technology is most effective when integrated alongside more traditional resources within a play-based curriculum.
- Technology integration should build on children's experiences and interests. New resources should be introduced gradually with explicit guidance in a way that reflects and acknowledges children's previous experience and understanding.
- Digital resources can provide children with additional resources to communicate, express their views and share their experience and understanding with others.

POINTS FOR DISCUSSION

- Consider your own transition experiences – what do you recall in relation to these experiences? Reflect on and list these experiences.
- How might digital documentation such as photos or videos be useful in stimulating discussion, reflection and shared engagement in relation to transition experiences?
- As a practitioner, how might you use digital documentation to support the transition process?

FURTHER READING

Dockett, S., Griebel, W. and Perry, B. (2017) Transitions to school: a family affair. In S. Dockett, W. Griebel and B. Perry (eds) *Families and Transition to School*. Cham: Springer, pp. 1–20.

Holloway, J., Green, K. and Stevenson, K. (2016) Digitods: toddlers, touch screens and Australian family life. *Journal of Media and Culture*, 18 (5). Available at: http://journal.media-culture.org.au/index.php/mcjournal/article/view/1024/0 (accessed 20 October 2018).

Kucirkova, N. (2017) *Digital Personalisation in Early Childhood: Impact on Childhood*. London: Bloomsbury.

National Association for the Education of Young Children (NAEYC) and Fred Rogers Center for Early Learning and Children's Media (2012) Technology and interactive media as tools in early childhood programs from birth through age 8. Available at: www.naeyc.org/files/naeyc/PS_technology_WEB.pdf (accessed 20 October 2018).

Palaiologou, I. (2016) Teachers' dispositions towards the role of digital devices in play-based pedagogy in early childhood education. *Early Years*, 36 (3): 305–321.

USEFUL WEBSITE

www.earlychildhoodaustralia.org.au/our-work/digital-business-kit/live-wires – Early Childhood Australia, Live Wires.

REFERENCES

Barblett, L. (2010) Why play-based learning? *Every Child, 16* (3): 4–7. Available at: www.earlychildhoodaustralia.org.au/our-publications/every-child-magazine/every-child-index/every-child-vol-16-3-2010/play-based-learning-free-article (accessed 22 June 2018).

Blackwell, C. K., Lauricella, A. R., and Wartella, E. and Robb, M. (2013) Adoption and use of technology in early education: the interplay of extrinsic barriers and teacher attitudes. *Computers and Education, 69*: 310–319.

Blagojevic, B. and Thomes, K. (2008) Young photographers: can 4 year olds use a digital camera as a tool for learning? An investigation in progress. *Young Children, 63* (5): 66–70.

Chaudron, S. (2015) Young children (0–8) and digital technology: a qualitative exploratory study across seven countries. Joint Research Centre Policy Reports. Available at: http://publications.jrc.ec.europa.eu/repository/bitstream/JRC93239/lbna27052enn. pdf (accessed 22 June 2018).

Department of Education, Employment and Workplace Relations (DEEWR) (2009) Belonging, being and becoming: The early years learning framework for Australia. Available at: https://docs.education.gov.au/system/files/doc/other/belonging_being_and_becoming_ the_early_years_learning_framework_for_australia.pdf (accessed 4 August 2016).

Dockett, S., Griebel, W. and Perry, B. (2017) Transitions to school: a family affair. In S. Dockett, W. Griebel and B. Perry (eds) *Families and Transition to School*. Cham: Springer, pp. 1–20.

Educational Transitions and Change (ETC) Research Group (2011) *Transition to School: Position Statement*. Albury-Wodonga: Research Institute for Professional Practice, Learning and Education, Charles Sturt University.

Edwards, S. (2003) New directions: charting the path for the role of sociocultural theory in early childhood education and curriculum. *Contemporary Issues in Early Childhood, 4* (3): 251–266.

Edwards, S. (2015) New concepts of play and the problem of technology, digital media and popular-culture integration with play-based learning in early childhood education. *Technology, Pedagogy and Education, 25* (4): 1–20.

Fleer, M. (2011) Technologically constructed childhoods: moving beyond a reproductive to a productive and critical view of curriculum development. *Australasian Journal of Early Childhood, 39* (1): 16–24. Available at: http://search.informit.com.au/fullText;dn= 950133451546494;res=IELHSS (accessed 22 June 2018).

Groundwater-Smith, S., Mitchell, J., Mockler, N., Ponte, P. and Rönnerman, K. (2013) *Facilitating Practitioner Research: Developing Transformational Partnerships*. New York: Routledge.

Guskey, T. R. (2002) Does it make a difference? Evaluating professional development. *Educational Leadership, 59*: 45–51. Available at: www.ascd.org/publications/ educational-leadership/mar02/vol59/num06/Does-It-Make-a-Difference%C2%A2- Evaluating-Professional-Development.aspx (accessed 22 June 2018).

Mantei, J. and Kervin, L. (2007) Looking for clarity amongst the challenges faced by teachers as they consider the role of ICT in classroom literacy learning experiences. Paper presented at Future Directions in Literacy: International Conversations Conference, University of Sydney, Australia, September. Available at: http://hdl.handle.net/2123/2335 (accessed 5 November 2018).

National Association for the Education of Young Children (NAEYC) and Fred Rogers Center for Early Learning and Children's Media (2012) Technology and interactive media as tools in early childhood programs from birth through age 8. Available at: www.naeyc.org/sites/default/files/globally-shared/downloads/PDFs/resources/topics/PS_technology_WEB.pdf (accessed 22 June 2018).

Nikolopoulou, K. and Gialamas, V. (2015) Barriers to the integration of computers in early childhood settings: teachers' perceptions. *Education and Information Technologies, 20* (2): 285–301.

NSW Department of Education (2018) A special place. Available at: https://education.nsw.gov.au/public-schools/going-to-a-public-school/media/documents/a-special-place.pdf (accessed 31 October 2018).

Palaiologou, I. (2016) Teachers' dispositions towards the role of digital devices in play-based pedagogy in early childhood education. *Early Years, 36* (3): 305–321.

Parette, H., Quesenberry, A. C. and Blum, C. (2013) Missing the boat with technology usage in early childhood settings: a 21st century view of developmentally appropriate practice. In H. Parette and C. Blum (eds) *Instructional Technology in Early Childhood*. Baltimore, MD: Paul Brooks Publishing.

Plowman, L. and McPake, J. (2013) Seven myths about young children and technology. *Childhood Education, 89* (1): 27–33. Available at: https://pure.strath.ac.uk/portal/files/19053027/Plowman_McPake_2013_seven_myths_about_young_children_and_technology_.pdf (accessed 22 June 2018).

Plowman, L. and Stephen, C. (2005) Children, play and computers in pre-school. *British Journal of Educational Technology, 36* (3): 145–157.

Plowman, L. and Stephen, C. (2007) Guided interactions in pre-school settings. *Journal of Computer Assisted Learning, 23* (1): 14–21.

Plowman, L., Stevenson, O., Stephen, C. and McPake, J. (2012) Preschool children's learning with technology at home. *Computers and Education, 59* (1): 30–37.

Rogoff, B. (1990) *Apprenticeship in Thinking: Cognitive Development in Social Context*. New York: Oxford University Press.

Rogoff, B. (2003) *The Cultural Nature of Human Development*. New York: Oxford University Press.

Siraj-Blatchford, I. (2009) Conceptualising progression in the pedagogy of play and sustained shared thinking in early childhood education: a Vygotskian perspective. *Education and Child Psychology, 26* (2): 77–89.

Sumsion, J., Barnes, S., Cheeseman, S., Harrison, L., Kennedy, A. and Stonehouse, A. (2009) Insider perspectives on developing belonging, being and becoming: the Early Years Learning Framework for Australia. *Australasian Journal of Early Childhood, 34* (4): 4–13.

Yelland, N. (2011) Reconceptualising play and learning in the lives of young children. *Australasian Journal of Early Childhood, 36* (2): 4–12.

Zevenbergen, R. and Logan, H. (2008) Computer use by pre-schooler children: rethinking practice as digital natives come to preschool. *Australian Journal of Early Childhood, 33* (1): 37–44.

8

THE DIGITAL DIVIDE

ACCESS, SKILLS, USE AND IDEOLOGICAL BARRIERS

ADERONKE FOLORUNSHO AND IOANNA PALAIOLOGOU

CHAPTER OVERVIEW

Throughout this book, digital practices in early childhood education (ECE) in developed countries are discussed. However, in many countries around the world there are still issues of access to technology at many levels, such as physical access or lack of digital skills and usage. The term that is used to describe this gap is *the digital divide*, originally coined in the USA by the Department of Commerce's National Telecommunications and Information Administration in 1999. In 2001, the Organisation for Economic Co-operation and Development (OECD) defined the digital divide as the 'gap between individuals, households, businesses and geographic areas at different socio-economic levels with regard both to their opportunities to access ICT and to their use of the internet for a wide variety of activities' (OECD, 2001).

Thus, in this chapter we examine the case of a developing country, Nigeria, and the issues emerging in ECE in relation to factors that impact the digital divide.

This chapter aims to help you to:

- understand the concept of the digital divide and the implications this might have for early childhood education
- explore the different levels of the digital divide: access, use and skills
- explore a fourth dimension of this divide that leads to limited digital participation in early childhood education: the ideological barrier
- understand the practical aspects of factors that contribute to the digital divide, through a case study from Nigeria.

THE DIGITAL DIVIDE

Digital literacy skills are now considered important for:

> social inclusion, quality of life, success in the labour market and economic growth [...] There is an urgent need for every citizen to develop the knowledge, skills and attitudes required to participate in a complex and increasingly digitised society for personal and societal prosperity. (Kumpulainen, 2017: 12)

Although in developed countries children have access to digital devices from the moment of birth (see Chapter 6 for example), there are still children in other parts of the world who do not have access to or use of digital technologies due to economic, military conflict, political, geographical, social, cultural and religious reasons. This uneven access and use of ICT or lack of participation has been examined under the term *digital divide* where the focus is on the:

- individual (Akhter, 2003), which refers to the accessibility of technology amongst people
- organisational (Forman et al., 2005), which refers to the accessibility amongst institutions and companies
- global (Chinn and Fairlie, 2007), which refers to the accessibility amongst countries.

In 2013, the International Telecommunications Union (ITU) described the digital divide as a complex phenomenon with multidimensions and identified three key dimensions of inequalities:

1. Access – difficulties in gaining entry to networks and the available technology.
2. Intensity of use – the time people spend using technology and the internet.
3. Skills – to what extent people are able to use technology and the internet.

In a more recent report by the OECD (2017) which examined the digital divide at international level, they cautioned us:

> ❝ Digital technology has already changed the world – and as more and more children go online around the world, it is increasingly changing childhood [...] But digital access is becoming the new dividing line, as millions of the children who could most benefit from digital technology are missing out. (p. vii) ❞

Although many focus on the digital divide between developing and developed countries, economically and socially disadvantaged groups versus advantaged groups, the digital have-nots and the digital haves, van Dijk (2017) explains the issue as being more complex than that:

> ❝ the term digital divide has caused much confusion. In fact, it is a metaphor that has inspired at least four misunderstandings. First, the metaphor suggests a simple distinction between two divided groups with a yawning gap between them. Second, it suggests that this gap is difficult to bridge. Third, it can imply absolute inequalities between those who are included and those who are excluded, whereas inequalities are of a more relative kind. Finally, the digital divide is not a static and permanent condition. (p. 1) ❞

Despite the accessibility and affordability of ICT in the 21st century, in recent research focusing on education Cruz-Jesus et al. (2016) looked at the international and internal digital divides that exist across 28 European countries. They found that even in developed countries such as Finland there were still gaps in the use of digital technology, and in Mediterranean countries such as Malta, Spain and Portugal these divides were of even more concern. Similarly, Libaque-Saenz (2016) examined the digital divide in Peru, South Korea and Chile under the three levels: access, intensity of use and skills inequalities, and agreed that the phenomenon is complex. They concluded that these barriers can be overcome if strategies are in place for:

1. Provision of high-quality education and broadband technologies.
2. Use of existent infrastructure and resources to increase internet access, while nation-wide backbones are deployed.
3. Identification of those people who need help the most, because we can match the places to serve them.
4. Mechanisms to pull demand, push supply and regulate prices.
5. E-government, e-learning and e-commerce as key services. (2016: 27)

THE ROLE OF EARLY CHILDHOOD EDUCATION: *THE IDEOLOGICAL BARRIER*

Meanwhile, the use of digital devices and their integration in ECE have been the subject of debate for at least the last ten years. Despite research that shows how digital technology can be used with young children, either during their play or to support their learning (e.g. Chapters 2, 3, 4, 14 and 15), there is still resistance to it in early childhood in comparison to other levels of education. This has led to a divided discourse between home – what children are accessing, using and the skills they develop at home – and ECE (Edwards et al., 2017). With the rapid development of ICT, households in developed countries are becoming digitally rich, but ECE is still behind in terms of embracing it (Marsh et al., 2017). Research shows that digital play and learning have not yet been embraced by the ECE sector (Arnott et al., 2019). In examining the reasons for the divide between home and ECE, Palaiologou (2016) addressed three key reasons that in the field of ECE there is still an ideological barrier for its inclusion: (1) teacher's agency, (2) the ambiguity of what is meant with play and (3) concerns around children's safety and well-being. She concluded that these ideological barriers were affecting the integration of digital technologies:

> The factors influencing the integration of digital devices in ECE include external aspects such as resources and training and internal factors such as beliefs and views. This has led to 'a dualism where problems and benefits are pitched against each other' (Fleer 2013a: 57) and play-based pedagogy is separated from children's digital interactions, undermining the integration of digital technologies into ECE [...]. Research cautions us to focus on working 'towards the common goal of increasing children's digital autonomy and critical thinking for a safe and balanced life' (Chaudron 2015: 29) in order to 'bridge the gap between play and technologies' (Edwards 2013: 209). (2016: 308)

Stephen and Edwards (2018) view this barrier as a 'techno-tale' and argue against the ideology that children are exposed to digital divides between home and ECE where playful learning is mainly associated with physical activity and other play resources. Even with the introduction of internet-connected toys (IoToys) that entail physicality, this ideology is still present (Arnott et al., 2018). However, Stephen and Edwards (2018) urge a move beyond any ideological barriers to include technology in ECE because in the digital age:

> even where research shows that children across different socio-economic statuses have access to similar types of technology – the practices to which these technologies are put clearly differ. Children from lower socio-economic groups tend to use technologies in ways that are oriented towards consumption of digital media, whereas children in higher socio-economic groups access technologies for the generation of digital media, searching for information and communication with families and friends. (p. 6)

Even in cases where digital technology is integrated, there are still divisions and although research stresses the importance of integrating technology into early childhood pedagogy and play (e.g. Yelland, 2016), it remains separate from play which 'is considered essential for supporting children's learning, whilst technology is listed as a separate description and skill' (Garvis and Lemon, 2016: 1–2). Thus, ECE continues to debate the role of ICT rather than embrace it:

> Whilst a range of European work has focused on the development of digital literacies for all citizens [...], scant attention has been paid to educational activities that position children as active, creative and critical investigators of and with digital technologies. At present, there is a dearth of knowledge on creating learning opportunities for digital literacies that are inclusive for diverse learners with different capabilities and interests, and that are able to accommodate their different personal situations and objectives and combine, for example, formal and everyday learning practices. (Kumpulainen, 2017: 13)

The role of ECE in children's holistic development has been emphasised in the literature and a body of research shows that high provision is associated with children meeting their full potential in later life. There remains, however, resistance to the inclusion of any form of technology in ECE due to this ideological barrier (Arnott et al., 2019). Daugherty et al. (2014), for example, found that children in low-income families in the USA had less access to ICT than their better-off peers and had fewer opportunities to learn, explore and communicate digitally which, in turn, impacted on their future chances of getting the workforce skills required to succeed in life. They recommended bridging the gap by including technology in ECE to address digital inequalities and to open the door to new learning opportunities for all children.

The importance of digital literacy and acquiring digital skills from an early age is now paramount to functioning effectively in society and to competing in global economies (Van Deursen and Helsper, 2015). Thus, limited or no digital participation, either in the home or educational context, is a serious issue and has inclusion and exclusion implications at all three levels of the digital divide: access, use and skills. We argue, however, that there is a fourth dimension that affects ECE, an *ideological barrier*, which is most evident in more developed countries of the world. In case study 8.1, drawn from research in Nigeria, we explore the practical implications of the other three barriers to the integration of ICT in education: access, use and skills.

CASE STUDY 8.1: THE NIGERIAN CONTEXT – THE ISSUE OF ACCESS, SKILLS AND USE

PRE-PRIMARY EDUCATION IN NIGERIA

ECE in Nigeria is labelled 'pre-primary education' by the National Policy on Education (Ejieh, 2006) and comprises crèche, nursery and kindergarten provision (FRN, 2004). The focus at this stage was to develop children's cognitive and emotional development before their admission to primary school (Ige, 2011). Recognising the need for pre-primary education in the country, it was officially mandated in the National Policy on Education in 1977; revised in 1981, 1998, 2004, 2007 and 2012 (Obiweluozor, 2015). Pre-primary education in the policy is defined as the education given in an educational institution to children aged 3–5 years of age prior to their entering primary school (FRN, 2012). The objectives of the National Policy of Education are as follows:

- effecting a smooth transmission from home to school
- preparing the child for the primary level of education
- providing adequate care and supervision for children whilst their parents are at work
- inculcating in the child a spirit of enquiry and creativity through the exploration of nature and environment, art, music and playing with toys
- developing a sense of co-operation and team spirit
- inculcating social norms
- learning good habits, especially good health habits
- teaching the rudiments of numbers, letters, colours, shapes, forms, and so on, through play. (FRN, 2012)

Pre-primary education in Nigeria is a result of post-colonial development (Ejieh, 2006). Before the British colonised the country in the nineteenth century, there were two major types of education in Nigeria: Islamic education which was strictly religious; and the indigenous system where children were taught practical skills such as those in farming and the domestic domain. It was colonial administrators who had control of the educational system and implemented the British form of education in Nigeria. At that time, only wealthy individuals in Nigeria could afford education. Nigeria gained independence in 1960 and, recognising that the education system was unsatisfactory, established the Universal Primary Educational Policy (Fabunmi, 2005). This initiative afforded free education to children from poor families and provided the opportunity for children to go to school. The need for working mothers to access nursery provision led to the establishment of crèches and nurseries, typically in church premises organised by missionaries in Nigeria (Akinbote, 2006). The Universal Primary Education Policy was, however, abandoned (Ejere, 2011) due to the high demand which led to a shortage of materials (Madugu, 2000). The failing Universal Primary Education was replaced with Universal Basic Education (UBE) in 2004 to provide children's education from pre-primary to secondary school.

Although the National Policy of Education provided the guidelines for operating pre-primary education (FRN, 2012), it did not address curriculum content (Obiweluozor, 2015). Nurseries and day-care centres were left without proper guidelines or standards to follow, leaving them to design their own curriculum (Ejieh, 2006). The curriculum typically being followed in privately owned pre-primary schools and nurseries included numbers, the alphabet, story time, nursery rhymes and the rudiments of reading, writing and arithmetic (2006). This tended to place greater emphasis on the intellectual rather than the holistic development of the child. Teachers remained devoted to teaching children to read, write and memorise facts rather than to recreational and social activities (2006). The playful learning approach recommended in the national policy on pre-primary education was not implemented in most schools because few teachers had been trained in the use of play for instruction and social interaction (2006).

CHALLENGES IN BRIDGING THE DIGITAL DIVIDE IN NIGERIA

ACCESS INEQUALITIES

Allied with weak management, pre-primary education in Nigeria is underfunded (Akinrotimi and Olowe, 2016). Most pre-primary schools in Nigeria have been characterised as having inadequate facilities, materials, learning resources and teachers (Ige, 2011). Insufficient funding undermines the quality of pre-primary education available in Nigeria, particularly affecting staffing (training and child/staff ratios), the provision of learning resources and infrastructure upkeep (Ibhaze, 2016).

A poor infrastructure is one of the main challenges that affect access to digital technology in pre-primary education in Nigeria (Adomi, 2006). Electricity supplies are unstable, with the federal government yet to provide 24-hour electricity to every part of the country. Consequently, citizens must rely on generators. The lack of a consistent electricity supply makes it difficult to access ICT in the classroom. Privately owned pre-primary schools have durable generators and a constant supply of fuel, thus ensuring pupils have access to ICT. Since public schools lack basic resources including books and writing materials, access to ICT is limited by lack of funding and a durable electricity supply. Limited access to the internet is a second infrastructural challenge that the use of ICT poses in pre-primary schools.

Initiatives have been undertaken to integrate ICT into Nigerian education, including: the SchoolNet Nigeria established in 2001 to sustain deployment and access to digital technology in primary and secondary schools; the Computer-in-Schools project

(Continued)

(Continued)

in 2002 to develop computer literacy in secondary schools; the One-Laptop-Per-Child campaign in 2006 which resulted in the provision of a number of laptops for the e-secondary school project. These initiatives, however, never reached pre-primary education.

SKILLS INEQUALITIES

As shown above, access is a major issue for the integration of technology in ECE in Nigeria. However, the lack of qualifications, adequate supervision when in service as well as a lack of in-service training has led to teachers working in ECE lacking knowledge of how to integrate technology in their daily practice. This is a phenomenon that has been addressed in developed countries as well (Nikolopoulou and Gialamas, 2015; Palaiologou, 2016):

> To develop teachers' capabilities to teach design literacy to children [...], their mindset has to be developed. A strong focus on design thinking and complex problem-solving during teachers' professional development can improve their capabilities to manage students' making processes in digital fabrication contexts. They need to build a repertoire of working with miscellaneous materials, advanced technical equipment and software applications and be able to devise new educational practice. (Kjartansdóttir et al., 2017: 40)

USER INEQUALITIES

The OECD (2017) has pointed out that in the twenty-first century digital skills are of high importance for entering the workplace. It stresses that amongst the inequalities worldwide, one that needs to be considered this century is the digital 'gaps in access and skills' (p. 43). It is suggested that these gaps should be 'identified and closed, rather than being an equalizer of opportunity, connectivity may deepen inequity, reinforcing intergenerational cycles of deprivation. In a world where digital access and digital skills increasingly influence children's futures, the contours of global connectivity are troubling' (p. 43).

It is estimated that worldwide there are 346 million young people between the ages of 15 and 24 that do not have access to the internet. One of the continents where these inequalities are obvious is Africa where it is reported that it 'has the highest share of non-users' (OECD, 2017: 43).

Amongst African countries with the lowest ownership of technology and subsequently user inequalities of technology amongst its citizens, is Nigeria. The key factors that impact on the divide are the socio-economic (poor vs rich), gender (men vs women), educational (literate vs illiterate) and geographical divides (urban vs rural).

REFLECTIVE TASK

In case study 8.1, the main reasons for the digital divide are the economy, the lack of infrastructure and the lack of training and professional development. Are there any other factors you can identify that might contribute to the digital divide?

SUMMARY

In this chapter, we have addressed the complex phenomenon of the digital divide. In ECE this divide has two levels: ideological and practical. ECE, especially in developed countries, has not always embraced digital resources as part of the daily routine, often due to concerns around what play is and how children should play, leaving a divide between what children experience at home and what they experience in education. There are many other factors, such as economic, political, military conflicts, geographical, social, and cultural, that impact on each level of the digital divide. In the case study of Nigeria presented here, we saw how the digital divide is based less on ideological differences and more on access, use and skills. What is clear, however, is that ECE can play a crucial role in bridging this divide by embracing ICT in its practice, as has been explored throughout this book.

KEY POINTS TO REMEMBER

- In the twenty-first century, digital literacy is important for young children to develop into competent citizens.
- The gap between people who can access, have skills in and use technology and those who do not, risks creating a 'digital divide'.
- Lack of digital participation can disadvantage a child's development and their ability to achieve their full potential.
- In ECE, this digital divide exists and it is often shaped by ideological barriers as well as the other dimensions (access, use, skills).

POINTS FOR DISCUSSION

- Discuss the key issues that might encourage or prevent the inclusion of digital technology in your context.
- Identify appropriate strategies that can be developed in your context to ensure digital participation and to bridge the digital divide.

- Study Edwards and colleagues' (2017) article in the further reading section below and discuss how ECE can make effective use of technology to bridge the gap between home and school education. Reflect on the curriculum that is used in your context and discuss if and how technology is included in your daily practice.

FURTHER READING

Edwards, S., Henderson, M., Gronn, D., Scott, A. and Mirkhil, M. (2017) Digital disconnect or digital difference? A socio-ecological perspective on young children's technology use in the home and the early childhood centre. *Technology, Pedagogy and Education*, 26 (1): 1–17. This article discusses the divide between home and early childhood education.

Gillen, J. and Kucirkova, N. (2018) Percolating spaces: creative ways of using digital technologies to connect young children's school and home lives. *British Journal of Educational Technology*, 49 (5). This research focuses on how the divide between home and education can be bridged.

Marsh, J., Kumpulainen, K., Nisha, B., Velicu, A., Blum-Ross, A., Hyatt, D., et al. (2017) *Makerspaces in the Early Years: A Literature Review*. University of Sheffield: MakEY Project. This report is based on a literature review and discusses the context of digital practices in ECE; it can be downloaded at http://makeyproject.eu/publications.

USEFUL WEBSITE

http://portal.unesco.org/en/ev.php-URL_ID=15738&URL_DO=DO_TOPIC&URL_SECTION=201.html – this is the official UNESCO site on strategies to bridge the digital divide.

REFERENCES

Adomi, E. E. (2006) Mobile phone usage patterns of library and information science students at Delta State University, Abraka, Nigeria. *Electronic Journal of Academic and Special Librarianship*, 7 (1): 1–11.

Akhter, S. H. (2003) Digital divide and purchase intention: why demographic psychology matters. *Journal of Economic Psychology*, 24 (3): 321–327.

Akinbote, O. (2006) Origin and development of early childhood education. *ECE 112*. Lagos: National Open University of Nigeria (NOUN).

Akinrotimi, A. A. and Olowe, P. K. (2016) Challenges in implementation of early childhood education in Nigeria: the way forward. *Journal of Education and Practice*, 7 (7): 33–38.

Arnott, L., Palaiologou, I. and Gray, C. (2019) An ecological exploration of the internet of toys in early childhood everyday life. In G. Mascheroni and D. Holloway (eds) *The Internet of Toys: Practices, Affordances and the Political Economy of Children's Play*. London: Palgrave Macmillan.

Chaudron, S. (2015) *Young Children (0–8) and Digital Technologies: A Qualitative Study across Seven Countries*. Luxembourg: Publications Office of the European Union.

Chinn, M. D. and Fairlie, R. W. (2007) The determinants of the global digital divide: a cross country analysis of computer and Internet penetration. *Oxford Economic Papers, 59* (1): 16–44.

Cruz-Jesus, F., Oliveira, T. and Bacao, F. (2016) The education-related digital divide: an analysis for the EU-28. *Computers in Human Behavior, 56*: 72–82.

Daugherty, L., Dossani, R., Johnson, E.-E. and Oguz, M. (2014) *Using Early Childhood Education to Bridge the Digital Divide*. Santa Monica, CA: RAND Corporation. Available at: www.rand.org/content/dam/rand/pubs/perspectives/PE100/PE119/RAND_PE119.pdf (accessed 17 October 2018).

Edwards, S. (2013) Digital play in the early years: a contextual response to the problem of integrating digital technologies and play-based learning in the early childhood curriculum. *European Early Childhood Educational Research Journal, 10* (2): 199–212.

Edwards, S., Henderson, M., Gronn, D., Scott, A. and Mirkhil, M. (2017) Digital disconnect or digital difference? A socio-ecological perspective on young children's technology use in the home and the early childhood centre. *Technology, Pedagogy and Education, 26* (1): 1–17.

Ejere, E. I. (2011) An examination of critical problems associated with the implementation of the universal basic education (UBE) programme in Nigeria. *International Education Studies, 4*: 1–10.

Ejieh, M. U. C. (2006) Pre-primary education in Nigeria: policy implementation and problems. *Elementary Education Online, 5* (1): 58–64.

Fabunmi, M. (2005) Historical analysis of educational policy formulation in Nigeria: implications for educational planning and policy. *International Journal of African and African American Studies, 4*: 1–7.

Federal Republic of Nigeria (FRN) (2004) *National Policy on Education* (4th edn) Lagos: NERDC Press.

Federal Republic of Nigeria (FRN) (2012) *National Information and Communication Technology (ICT) Final Draft Policy*. Abuja, Nigeria: Federal Government Press.

Fleer, M. (2013) Digital positioning for inclusive practice in early childhood: the cultural practices surrounding digital tablets in family homes. *Computers in New Zealand Schools: Learning, Teaching, Technology, 25* (1–3): 56–76.

Forman, C., Goldfarb, A. and Greenstein, S. (2005) How do industry features influence the role of location on Internet adoption? *Journal of the Association for Information Systems, 6* (12): 383–408.

Garvis, S. and Lemon, N. (eds) (2016) *Understanding Digital Technologies and Young Children: An International Perspective*. London: Routledge.

Ibhaze, F. O. (2016) Issues and challenges of implementing early childhood education in Nigeria. *International Journal of Scientific and Research Publications, 6* (5): 176–179.

Ige, A. M. (2011) Challenges facing early childhood care, development, and education in an era of Universal Basic Education in Nigeria. *Early Childhood Education Journal, 39* (2): 161–167.

International Telecommunication Union (ITU) (2013) *Measuring the Information Society*. Geneva, Switzerland: ITU.

Kjartansdottir, S. H., Petursdottier, S., Thorsteinsson, G. and Dyrfjoro, K. (2017) Makerspaces in formal education. In J. Marsh, K. Kumpulainen, B. Nisha, A. Velicu, A. Blum-Ross, D. Hyatt, et al. (eds) *Makerspaces in the Early Years: A Literature Review*. University of Sheffield: MakEY Project, pp. 38–46.

Kumpulainen, K. (2017) Makerspaces: why they are important for digital literacy education. In J. Marsh, K. Kumpulainen, B. Nisha, A. Velicu, A. Blum-Ross, D. Hyatt, et al. (eds) *Makerspaces in the Early Years: A Literature Review*. University of Sheffield: MakEY Project, pp. 12–17.

Libaque-Saenz, C. F. (2016) Strategies for bridging the internet digital divide in Peru: A benchmarking of South Korea and Chile. CONF-IRM 2016, Proceedings Paper 17. Available at: http://aisel.aisnet.org/confirm2016/17 (accessed 17 October 2018).

Madugu, J. E. (2000) From universal primary education (UPE) to universal basic education (UBE) in Nigeria: what lessons and what hope? *Journal of Education Studies*, 6: 1–7.

Marsh, J., Kumpulainen, K., Nisha, B., Velicu, A., Blum-Ross, A., Hyatt, D., et al. (2017) *Makerspaces in the Early Years: A Literature Review*. University of Sheffield: MakEY Project.

Nikolopoulou, K. and Gialamas, V. (2015) Barriers to the integration of computers in early childhood settings: teachers' perceptions. *Education and Information Technologies, 20* (2): 285–301.

Obiweluozor, N. (2015) Early childhood education in Nigeria, policy implementation and a way forward. *African Journal of Teacher Education, 4* (1): https://doi.org/10.21083/ajote.v4i1.2930.

Organisation for Economic Co-operation and Development (OECD) (2001) *Understanding the Digital Divide*. Paris: OECD Publications. Available at: www.oecd.org/internet/ieconomy/1888451.pdf (accessed 17 October 2018).

Organisation for Economic Co-operation and Development (OECD) (2017) *The State of the World's Children 2017: Children in a Digital World*. New York: United Nations Children's Fund (UNICEF).

Palaiologou, I. (2016) Teachers' dispositions towards the role of digital devices in play-based pedagogy in early childhood education. *Early Years: An International Research Journal, 36* (3): 305–332.

Stephen, C. and Edwards, S. (2018) *Young Children Playing and Learning in a Digital Age: A Cultural and Critical Perspective*. London: Routledge.

Van Deursen, A. A. and Helsper, E. J. (2015) The third-level digital divide: who benefits most from being online? *Communication and Information Technologies Annual: Digital Distinctions and Inequalities Studies in Media and Communications, 10*: 29–52.

Van Dijk, J. A. G. M. (2017) Digital divide: impact of access. In P. Rössler, C. A. Hoffner and L.van Zoonen (eds) *The International Encyclopedia of Media Effects*. New York: Wiley.

Yelland, N. (2016) iPlay, iLearn, iGrow: tablet technology, curriculum, pedagogies and learning in the twenty-first century. In S. Gurvis and N. Lemon (eds) *Understanding Digital Technology and Young Children: An International Perspective*. London: Routledge, pp. 38–45.

9

DIGITAL INEQUITY, ACCESS AND PROVISION

THE EXPERIENCE OF IRISH-MEDIUM SCHOOLS IN NORTHERN IRELAND

COLETTE GRAY, JILL DUNN, PAMELA MOFFETT AND DENISE MITCHELL

CHAPTER OVERVIEW

The digital revolution has impacted almost every facet of childhood and transformed children's ability to interact, communicate and experience their world (Collins and Halverson, 2018). Indeed, such is its pervasiveness that in 2017 we observed that 'for children growing up in today's world digital technologies are as unremarkable and ubiquitous as electricity, becoming visible only in their absence' (Gray et al., 2017: 14).

The rapid expansion of digital technology in everyday life has yielded a veritable tsunami of scholarly activity undertaken to explore its impact on young children's lives, including their early cognitive development, exploration, play and early educational experiences (Arnott, 2017; Gray et al., 2017; also see Chapters 11, 14 and 15). The popular appeal of these devices owes much to their portability, the lack of ancillary products such as a mouse or keyboard, their light weight, response to simple swiping and tapping actions, accommodation of child-friendly apps and the provision of immediate feedback (Arnott, 2018; Gray et al., 2017, 2019).

Yet, despite the wealth of evidence focused on the impact of digital technology in the field of early childhood education, this chapter reports findings from a lesser examined aspect – specifically the inequity of digital provision, access and resources available to children attending Irish-medium schools in Northern Ireland (NI) that offer an immersion-style educational experience to children of whose parents hold a strong cultural commitment to the acquisition of the Irish language.

The chapter aims to develop understanding on the:

- macro- and micro-level forces that impact the digital learning and teaching experience
- inequity in provision and access to digital technology for many children in early years classrooms
- influence of teachers' dispositions towards the role of digital technology in Irish-medium pedagogy in early years classrooms
- challenges and opportunities of integrating digital technology into early years Irish-medium classrooms.

INTRODUCTION

To set the work in context, this chapter begins with a brief outline of the origins and popularity of the Irish language, and continues by describing the emergence of Irish-medium education in NI before exploring the influence of attitudinal affordances to the inclusion of the role of digital technology as an additional teaching and learning resource to complement the early years curriculum. Case study evidence is included to offer a deep insight into the challenges and benefits of integrating iPads into everyday classroom activities.

ENDANGERED INDIGENOUS LANGUAGES

An old Celtic language, Irish is related to Scottish Gaelic, Manx and Welsh (Laing, 2006) and was once the dominant language of Ireland. Displaced by English in the nineteenth century, its popularity continues to wane and decline, and it is mainly spoken by an ageing population in a few rural areas in the Republic of Ireland (RI) (Nielsen, 2015; O'Beirne Ranelagh, 1994). Irish is, however, only one of the 2,464 endangered indigenous languages listed by UNESCO (Moseley, 2010) including, amongst many others: Mi'kmaq, Malecite, Carrier and Shuswap, Ntlakapamux in Canada (Pereira and Morgan, 2017);

Aboriginal and Torres Straight Island languages in Australia (Queensland Government, 2018); Ainu in Japan and Saami in Russia (Strochlic, 2018).

Whilst it is generally acknowledged that rates of language extinction have risen dramatically in the last century, research suggests that a complex interaction of macro-, exo- and micro-levels forces continue to revitalise endangered languages (Berardi-Wiltshire, 2017; Ricento, 2000). According to Berardi-Wiltshire (2017), micro-level ideologies at local, social, cultural and historical levels have the greatest influence on the resurgence of interest in indigenous languages. An example from Northern Ireland (NI) demonstrates how micro-level forces can radically challenge and inform macro-level policy and practice, thus impacting the educational landscape.

REFLECTIVE TASK

What steps does your setting take to integrate children who do not share the country's dominant language? What digital resources are available to support their transition?

THE EMERGENCE OF IRISH–MEDIUM SCHOOLS IN NI

In contrast with the continued decline of Irish in the RI, in the late 1960s and early 1970s a small group of Irish speakers in NI lobbied the government, demanding parity of esteem between the dominant English and minority Irish languages. The government of the time had little appetite for the promotion of the Irish language or the introduction of Irish-medium schools. Against a backdrop of negativity, in 1971 a small group of dedicated Irish-speaking parents established the first Irish-medium primary school in Belfast, with nine pupils. Within a decade pupil numbers had tripled, with an increasing number of Irish-medium schools opening in response to demand. It was a further 24 years, however, before the sector received funding from the Department of Education (DE) for NI and recognition at policy level.

Despite receiving affirmation in the Good Friday agreement, which sought to bring peace to a politically and religiously troubled NI, demands for the implementation of the clause fuelled the collapse of devolved government and power sharing in 2017 (Moss, 2018).

❝ The Agreement states that: 'All participants recognise the importance of respect, understanding and tolerance in relation to linguistic diversity. Including in Northern Ireland, the Irish language.' (p. 4) ❞

At present, without a functioning local government in NI, decisions regarding educational expenditure are made by unelected civil servants without mandate. Education cutbacks have led to concerns regarding job security (McHugh, 2018) and to claims that the Irish-medium sector is the subject of consistent underfunding (Kelly, 2018). Though mainstream schools are similarly affected, analogous views were raised by case study interviewees.

DIGITAL TECHNOLOGY IN IRISH–MEDIUM SCHOOLS

Evidence suggests that digital technology can benefit early language, literacy and numeracy development (Billington, 2016). In addition, presenting tasks using age-appropriate apps has the potential to increase motivation and enthusiasm for learning and reading preparedness, particularly amongst children living in disadvantaged areas who have difficulty with more traditional approaches to teaching and learning (Gray et al., 2017; MIT, 2016).

According to the Bain report (2016), which examined technology in schools in NI, the benefits of integrating digital technology into classroom learning is particularly important for Irish-medium schools. Bain observed that:

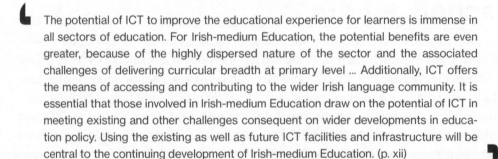

The potential of ICT to improve the educational experience for learners is immense in all sectors of education. For Irish-medium Education, the potential benefits are even greater, because of the highly dispersed nature of the sector and the associated challenges of delivering curricular breadth at primary level ... Additionally, ICT offers the means of accessing and contributing to the wider Irish language community. It is essential that those involved in Irish-medium Education draw on the potential of ICT in meeting existing and other challenges consequent on wider developments in education policy. Using the existing as well as future ICT facilities and infrastructure will be central to the continuing development of Irish-medium Education. (p. xii)

Similar views were expressed by Hallisey et al. (2014), who reported that greater access to wireless communication and internet connection was having a positive impact on the teaching and learning experience of pupils in many Irish-medium schools. Yet, despite its well-documented advantages and the increased availability of digital technology, its integration into educational settings has not been without challenge (Blackwell et al., 2013).

Findings from a study conducted to explore teacher perceptions of a Scottish Gaelic story app for preschool children in Gaelic-speaking schools in Scotland, revealed a tension between teachers' confidence in using iPads and their expectations of meeting curricular demands (McPake and Stephenson, 2016). Given iPads were only introduced to the participating schools at the start of McPake's study, it was not unexpected that teachers felt that they lacked the training and knowledge necessary to fully integrate apps into their teaching and learning. Echoing these findings, Fleer (2013) noted the impact that external factors, at the exo-system level, such as lack of training, poor resourcing and external technological support, had on a teacher's self-efficacy. This, she claims, creates a 'dualism where problems and benefits are pitched against each other' (p. 57), subsequently undermining the integration of digital technology into early years settings.

REFLECTIVE TASK

Self-efficacy is an individual's belief in his/her innate ability to achieve goals. Bandura (1982) described it in terms of an internalised self-belief system – when high, a person is more likely to persist at a challenging task and to perceive their performance positively; when low, an individual is more inclined to abandon the task and to view their efforts as poor.

What strategies would you employ to develop high self-efficacy in a child attempting a challenging task?

In light of similar reports, Edwards et al. (2017) contend that exploring within and between contextual experiences must be understood before assumptions are made about the effective integration of technology into early years education. They conclude that 'understanding settings provides potential for thinking about technology provision in the early years … [and] moves beyond assumptions that technologies should be used in early years settings because they comprise a significant aspect of young children's lives' (p. 14).

THE PRESENT STUDY

In light of the paucity of research on the implementation of digital technology into early years classrooms in Irish-medium schools, here we report findings from a school involved in a project funded by the Belfast Regeneration Office under the auspices of the Education Authority in NI to assess the impact of the use of iPads on children's learning in the Early Years and Foundation Stages of Education (see Gray et al., 2017). Also included is case study evidence from telephone interviews conducted with a further seven schools, bringing the total cohort to eight. Interviews were conducted by telephone, recorded and analysed thematically. Conversations were organised at a time suitable to the interviewee and lasted between 5 and 45 minutes. Worthy of note, the catchment area for seven of the eight schools is marked by endemic social deprivation, generational unemployment and high levels of underachievement. The remaining school is referenced in the chapter.

THEORETICAL FRAMEWORK

Nested within the sociocultural conceptualisations of learning (Vygotsky, 1978), whereby mental processes are viewed as social in origin and mediated through interaction using symbolic representations such as language and cultural artefacts that evolve over time, we sought to determine: equity in the provision of digital resources and the influence of teachers' dispositions towards the role of digital technology in Irish-medium pedagogy in early years classrooms. Given the status of Irish remains at the vagaries of a complex inter-action of contexts, processes, contestations and official policy negotiations, we also draw on the bio-ecological theory (Bronfenbrenner, 2005) that recognises the bi-directional influences that impact the educational system.

CASE STUDY 9.1: THE IPAD PROJECT IN NI

SCHOOL 3

These findings are drawn from interviews with the principal and ICT coordinator involved in the initial research project (Gray et al., 2017).

The principal explained her excitement at being selected for the iPad project. She said:

> given our poor catchment area and the small numbers attending the school (n = 92), we were delighted to be accepted. We have no funding for iPads but believed they would hugely enhance the children's learning experience.

Despite being located in an area of social deprivation, she noted that:

> At home, almost every child in the school has access to a tablet device, Games Console, iPhone or whatever. I suppose you could describe them as media rich. It's essential to capture these skills in the classroom and to make them feel that their home life is valued and important.

Both the principal and the ICT coordinator recalled that the children were delighted with the iPads, and both believe they have increased the children's motivation to learn and their ability to remain on task, and enhanced their communication skills. According to the principal:

> We have really seen an improvement in the work of our underachievers. Some are too timid to write but they make more effort using the iPad. Others move up or down the levels of Maths 3–5 to suit their ability. This increases their independence and they teach each other which is important for their communication and socialisation skills.

According to the ICT coordinator:

> we are extremely enthusiastic about the inclusion of digital technology, our teachers received training prior to its introduction. We spent a considerable amount of time planning how best to use them in class and how to build on a month by month and year by year basis. Obviously that is under review but planning and managing were essential aspects of seamlessly integrating the devices.

She continued:

> Each child is an individual and they work at their own pace using the tablet. Some of our younger ones trace letters on screen, others use work sheets and they all enjoy colouring in and taking their own pictures then adding them into their diary on their iPad. That's another point, they can voice over their name, age and the title of the work. This is an important feature for us, it gives me an opportunity to hear their spoken Irish and to make corrections. Older children record wee stories in Irish.

Asked about innovative practice, she noted that they have been using the iPads both inside and outside the classroom to photograph the changing seasons. With a year 2 class, she is collating the evidence into booklets using Book Creator and noted the children's ability to 'drag and drop' information from one folder to another.

In terms of the difficulties encountered, at first they found the internet signal very weak and they had no online access. A booster was introduced but it took some months before the system worked effectively. Despite these early teething problems, staff felt they received 'great support'. Nevertheless, the key problem remains the lack of available apps for Irish-medium schools in NI. During classroom observations, we noted that all of the apps were in English, limiting the immersion experience of children in Irish-medium schools.

SCHOOL 8

This school principal was enthusiastic about the Irish-medium sector and the role of digital technology in enhancing children's learning. He manages the largest Irish-medium primary school in NI and noted that demand was exceeding supply:

> I'm delighted that we are attracting larger numbers of pupils each year but that is due to the fact that our pupils have a rounded learning experience. We look for every available resource to ensure children have the best opportunity available. I went to an Irish-medium school myself, so I am committed to the sector and I know that the children who leave us are confident, rounded little beings with great potential. We have 20 iPads in the school and can borrow another 10 from a resource

(Continued)

(Continued)

centre if necessary, so we are well equipped. Maths 3–5 is one of the best apps on the market, I only wish there was an Irish version. Unfortunately, the lack of available apps for Irish-medium schools is a problem but we use a range of resources so I honestly don't believe any of our children are disadvantaged.

This interview lasted 45 minutes with the principal inviting us to come and observe classroom practice. He was also keen to learn about other devices which might enhance his children's learning experience.

SCHOOLS 4 AND 5

In contrast to the excited and enthusiastic approach adopted by the previous school principals, two interviewees showed a lack of interest in digital technology; these interviews lasted less than 10 minutes.

The first informed us, 'you're wasting your time. We don't have any devices, just two old computers for years 5 to 7 and, in truth, devices are beyond our means.' Asked, whether she would introduce digital devices into early years classrooms if the money became available, she replied:

No . . . Look, we aren't in a deprived enough area to get grants so we really struggle here. Funding is tight and set to get worse without a working local government, so no I would spend money on getting extra staff to avoid more composite classes. Class sizes are increasing. So, no, I have no real interest in spending money on technology for young children when there are cheaper tried and tested methods. In truth, the Irish-medium sector remains grossly underfunded and children have devices at home to play with.

According to another principal:

[W]e are just too small, badly located and totally under resourced. If you could see the school you would know what I mean. We lack basic classroom resources; we don't have internet connection or Whiteboards. There's no education minister to lobby for funding for the basics, the Irish-medium sector is being badly affected. I advise parents to look on the internet at the CCEA (Council for the Curriculum, Examinations and Assessment) website; they have some Irish speaking apps for children so they can practice using them.

A review of the resources available on the CCEA website revealed that the material is limited, of poor quality and would prove extremely challenging for a young child to manoeuvre.

Included in Table 9.1 is the demographic information gathered for the eight participating schools.

Table 9.1 Demographic information on participating schools

School	Boys	Girls	Total	% Free school meals (FSM)	Digital technology in EYC
1	44	48	92	54	No, interactive whiteboard and 2 C2K computers
2	81	110	191	60	Yes, interactive whiteboard and 2 C2K computers, 10 iPads bought by parents and used with Years 6 and 7 pupils only
3	62	63	125	78	Yes, interactive whiteboard and 2 C2K computers and 6 iPads acquired through grant funding
4	27	33	60	86	No, the school has no WiFi access, 2 C2K computers not linked to net services
5	97	97	194	41	No, the school has no WiFi access, 2 C2K computers not linked to net services
6	74	84	158	60	Yes, interactive whiteboard and 2 C2K computers, Bee-bots and Pre-bots
7	79	86	165	60	Yes, interactive whiteboard and 2 C2K computers
8	177	162	339	64	Yes, well-resourced, interactive whiteboards in all classes, a computer suite, 20 iPads with a further 10 available on loan

Notes: EYC = early years classrooms; 'free school meals' is used as a measure of deprivation by the DE (NI); C2K computers provide teachers and pupils with a range of teaching and learning resources that complement and extend traditional resources.

According to recently published statistics by the DE (NI, 2017–18), the average number of primary school children taking free school meals is 25.9%. Even the most cursory review of Table 9.1 indicates that each of the participating schools has a significantly higher percentage of pupils on free school meals than the national average. Schools 3 and 4 have particularly high levels which are more than triple the national average. Moreover, in discussion the principal of PS3 pointed out that the numbers claiming FSM would be higher but 'for the pride of those who refuse to have their child seen as under privileged'. He estimated that the 78% recorded was more likely to be 84%.

In terms of digital technology, whereas schools 2, 3, 6 and 7 have whiteboards, two computers, and some iPad access, they are available to Year 7 children only in preparation for their transition to secondary school. A number of schools have no WiFi access.

CONCLUSION

Whilst space limits detail, suffice to say that the majority (n = 6) of school principals believe that digital technology plays an important role in early years teaching and learning. As one principal noted:

(Continued)

(Continued)

[M]any of our children come from disaffected families, it is our job to reengage their interest and if that means having different types of resources then that's what we'll get. We fundraise for resources and I apply for dozens of grants, some successful and some not. I believe it's essential to give children the skills they need for a modern society. My only gripe is with the fact that there's a missed marketing opportunity to develop apps for Irish-medium schools. There's a growing market just waiting for someone to fill that gap.

Conversely, several showed less interest in and some antipathy towards the implementation of digital technology in early years classrooms. Chandy (2013: i) claims that a teacher's 'level of competence in using technology and their beliefs and attitudes towards technology play an important role in determining how, how much, and what kinds of technology are incorporated into classroom teaching'.

Developing the point, Palaiologou (2016) surmised that teachers' beliefs and attitudes towards digital technology are a major factor in the successful, or otherwise, integration of these resources into early years teaching and learning. She identifies three conditions that affect teacher attitudes, in summary:

1. Teachers' agency – which involves their experience, attitudes, belief in transformational practice, training and recognition of the benefits for teaching and learning.
2. The ambiguities of play-based pedagogy ideology – reflectively implementing digital resources to complement a play-based pedagogy, offering continuity between home and school.
3. Concerns for the dominance of materiality and for children's safety and well-being – professionals adopting this stance tend to view technological resources as disadvantageous to a child's safety, education, health and well-being. (p. 3)

SUMMARY

Demands for the intergenerational transmission of the Irish language have had a significant impact on NI's political and educational landscape. Rather than a linear, top-down policy-driven approach, cultural beliefs operating at the micro-level provided the impetus for change. In the late 1960s/70s, nine adults successfully challenged the status quo and their actions led to the development of a new sector aimed at reinvigorating Irish, an endangered language. Moreover, such was their success that the sector continues to grow, with many schools oversubscribed and several holding waiting lists. Whilst parity of esteem for the Irish language remains contentious in NI, the debate is frustrated by a complex interaction of social, cultural, political and ideological factors. The collapse of local government has had a significant impact on schools, eroding budgets, staffing levels, increasing class sizes and reducing classroom resources. One principal recalled his anger when asked to:

❝ have a composite class that crossed year groups and stages 2 and 3, I totally refused. It's ridiculous that children's education is taking such a backward step when there is so much potential available to help them succeed in their learning. It's tough enough for a class teacher to teach two year groups but cutting across year groups and learning stages is simply a step too far. ❞

Despite cutbacks and political uncertainty, many Irish-medium schools are keen to implement digital technology into their classroom practice. Self-efficacy, self-belief, confidence, training and support are key factors in determining whether an individual teacher will engage with and identify the potential these devices have to extend and challenge children's early learning experiences. Moreover, the infrastructure to support digital technology, similar to training, must be in place and successfully operating ahead of its introduction in the classroom. Whilst it is not claimed that digital technology is the panacea for underachievement, it may offer teachers another resource to support children's learning, most especially those who struggle with traditional pen-and-paper approaches. As Gray et al. (2017, 2019) report, some children experience a disconnect between pen-and-paper tasks and those presented on screen. Whilst answers to the former provide visible evidence of mistakes, the latter offer children an opportunity to try again with mistakes disappearing from screen and correct answers receiving immediate positive feedback. Moreover, with experience, children can manoeuvre apps, thus gaining independence in their learning by adapting levels to suit their ability.

Worthy of note is the lack of available apps for the Irish-medium sector; this finding highlights a missed marketing opportunity. As pointed out, the sector is growing and, in the main, digitally hungry for apps and devices to aid the teaching and learning of young children through the medium of the Irish language; thus offering them the same curricular opportunities as their peers taught in English-language schools. Whilst many of the children attending Irish-medium schools are *media-rich* at home, there is an inequity in the provision available within and between schools which may ultimately disadvantage children, especially those living in areas of deprivation.

In sum, findings in this chapter may serve to challenge pervading notions of immersion-language schools in media-rich countries. Digital inequity and limited technological access can be easily resolved by governments stating their commitment to parity of esteem, providing equal resources to all schools and, through the development of indigenous language apps and/or language-free apps, complementing and extending the stated aims of the early years curriculum. Whilst children live in *media-rich* homes, many attend *digitally poor* schools that are failing to capture the full potential of their *digitally expert early years* pupils.

REFLECTIVE TASK

Without access to the internet, what digital resources might you introduce into your class-room setting? See Table 9.1 for ideas.

KEY POINTS TO REMEMBER

- The popularity of indigenous languages continues to wane, however, through language intergenerational cultural, social and ideological practices are transmitted.
- Bi-directional influences are complex and multi-faceted. Rather than a linear, top-down policy-driven approach, cultural beliefs operating at the micro-level provided the impetus for change and the introduction of Irish-medium schools in NI.
- Forces operating at the exo- and macro-system levels play a significant role in the allocation of budgets to schools, funding classroom resources, securing staffing levels and maintaining class size. Since NI remains in a state of political flux, there is deep insecurity regarding school budgets and investment, particularly amongst principals of Irish-medium schools.
- Digital technology offers teachers another classroom resource to enhance children's enthusiasm and motivation to learn. Bridging home and school, and reaching educational underachievers are hallmarks of good practice and can be achieved, to some extent, by the implementation of digital technology in early years classrooms.
- Teachers' beliefs about and attitudes towards digital technology are major factors in the successful implementation of these devices in their curricular planning and practice. Whereas some are enthusiastic consumers, others limit their practice and their children's learning experiences to traditional tried-and-tested approaches.

POINTS FOR DISCUSSION

- What signs might identify a young child in danger of falling behind their peer group? If they do not speak the country's dominant language, what strategies might you use to support their learning? If they share the country's dominant language, what strategies might you use to support their learning? *In both instances, consider links with the family and wider community.*

- Consider the range of teaching and learning modalities available to motivate and enthuse young learners. How would you employ mobile devices to maximise all aspects of the early years curriculum?
- What factors might cause some schools to have fewer digital resources than others? How might these challenges be overcome? *Here, you might like to consider links with the family and wider community.*

FURTHER READING

Berardi-Wiltshire, A. (2017) Endangered languages in the home: the role of family language in the revitalisation of indigenous languages. *Revista LinguíStica/Revista do Programa de Pós-Graduação em Linguística da Universidade Federal do Rio de Janeiro [Journal of the Postgraduate Program in Linguistics of the Federal University of Rio de Janeiro]*, *13* (1): 328–348.

Collins, A. and Halverson, R. (2018) *Rethinking Education in the Age of Technology: The Digital Revolution and Schooling in America* (2nd edn). New York: Teachers College Press (Technology, Education – Connections (the TEC series)).

USEFUL WEBSITE

www.trc.ca/websites/trcinstitution/File/2015/Honouring_the_Truth_Reconciling_for_the_Future_July_23_2015.pdf – a report on the Canadian government's approach to displacing indigenous languages.

REFERENCES

Arnott, L. (ed.) (2017) *Digital Technologies and Learning in the Early Years*. London: Sage.

Arnott, L. (2018) Children's negotiation tactics and socio-emotional self-regulation in child-led play experiences: the influence of the preschool pedagogic culture. *Early Child Development and Care, 188* (7): 951–965.

Bain, G. (2016) *The Potential of Irish-Medium Education*. Bangor: Department of Education (DE) Northern Ireland.

Bandura, A. (1982) Self-efficacy mechanism in human agency. *American Psychologist, 37* (2): 122–147.

Berardi-Wiltshire, A. (2017) Endangered languages in the home: the role of family language in the revitalisation of indigenous languages. *Revista LinguíStica/Revista do Programa de Pós-Graduação em Linguística da Universidade Federal do Rio de Janeiro [Journal of the Postgraduate Program in Linguistics of the Federal University of Rio de Janeiro], 13* (1): 328–348.

Billington, C. (2016) *How digital technology can support early language and literacy outcomes in early years settings: A review of the literature.* London: National Literacy Trust.

Blackwell, C. K., Lauricella, A. R., Wartella, E., Robb, M., and Schomburg, R. (2013) Adoption and use of technology in early education: The interplay of extrinsic barriers and teacher attitudes. *Computers & Education, 69,* 310–319. doi: 10.1016/j.compedu.2013.07.024

Bronfenbrenner, U. (2005) *Making Human Beings Human: Bioecological Perspectives on Human Development.* Thousand Oaks, CA: Sage.

Chandy, B. (2013) Examining teachers' technology dispositions and classroom practices within the context of a professional development program: a multiple case study. Dissertation no. AAI3564504, University of Pennsylvania. Available at: https://reposi tory.upenn.edu/dissertations/AAI3564504 (accessed 23 October 2018).

Collins, A. and Halverson, R. (2018) *Rethinking Education in the Age of Technology: The Digital Revolution and Schooling in America* (2nd edn). New York: Teachers College Press (Technology, Education – Connections (the TEC series)).

Edwards, S., Henderson, M., Gronn, D., Scott, A. and Mirkhil, M. (2017) Digital disconnect or digital difference? A socio-ecological perspective on young children's technology use in the home and the early childhood centre. *Technology, Pedagogy and Education, 26* (1): 1–17.

Fleer, M. (2013) Digital positioning for inclusive practice in early childhood: the cultural practices surrounding digital tablets in family homes. *Computers in New Zealand Schools: Learning, Teaching, Technology, 25* (1–3): 56–76.

Gray, C., Dunn, J., Moffett, P. and Mitchell, D. (2017) *Mobile devices in early learning: developing the use of portable devices to support young children's learning.* Presentation and launch of report at Stranmillis University College: A College of The Queen's University of Belfast, 24 May.

Gray, C., Dunn, J., Moffett, P. and Mitchell, D. (2019) Child mentors, virtual tours and adult protégées: young children's experiences with tablet devices. In I. R. Berson, M. J. Berson and C. Gray (eds) *Participatory Methodologies to Elevate Children's Voice and Agency.* Research in Global Child Advocacy Series. Charlotte, NC: Information Age Publishing.

Hallisey, M., Gallagher, A., Ryan, S. and Hurley, J. (2014) *The Use of Tablet Devices in ACCS Schools.* Dublin: Association of Community and Comprehensive Schools.

Kelly, B. (2018) Northern Ireland latest: How did power-sharing at Stormont collapse and what happens if talks break down? *Independent,* 14 February, Available at: www.independent.co.uk/news/uk/politics/northern-ireland-talks-latest-updates-stormont-power-sharing-deal-what-deal-look-sinn-fein-dup-deal-a8207916.html (accessed 14 February 2018).

Laing, L. (2006) *The Archaeology of Celtic Britain and Ireland: c. AD 400–1200.* Cambridge: Cambridge University Press.

McHugh, M. (2018) How budgets are affected by Stormont's collapse. *The Irish News*, April, p. 1.

McPake, J. and Stephenson, C. (2016) New technologies, old dilemmas: theoretical and practical challenges in preschool immersion playrooms. *Language and Education*, *30* (2): 106–125.

MIT (Massachusetts Institute of Technology) (2016) Providing children with tablets loaded with literacy apps yields positive results: project to provide children with tablets loaded with literacy apps reports positive results in Africa, US. *ScienceDaily*, 26 April. Available at: www.sciencedaily.com/releases/2016/04/160426130117.htm (accessed 17 October 2018).

Moseley, C. (ed.) (2010) *Atlas of the World's Languages in Danger* (3rd edn). Paris: UNESCO Publishing. Available at: www.unesco.org/culture/en/endangeredlanguages/atlas (accessed 17 October).

Moss, P. (2018) Northern Ireland: a year without devolved government. BBC Radio 4's *The World Tonight* programme. Broadcast 9 January. London: BBC.

Nielsen, R. (2015) *Why don't the Irish speak Irish?* Whistling in The Wind. Economics, Politics, Religion and Esperanto. Available at: https://whistlinginthewind.org/2015/08/20/why-dont-the-irish-speak-irish/ (accessed 17 October 2018).

O'Beirne Ranelagh, J. (1994) *A Short History of Ireland*. Cambridge: Cambridge University Press.

Palaiologou, I. (2016) Children under five and digital technologies: Implications for early years pedagogy. *The European Early Childhood Research Journal, 24* (1): 5–24. (DOI:10.10 80/1350293X.2014.929876, first published on line 2014).

Pereira, A. and Morgan, J. (2017) What you need to know about indigenous language revitalization. Blog: working effectively with indigenous peoples, 25 April. Available at: www.ictinc.ca/blog/what-you-need-to-know-about-indigenous-language-revitalization (accessed 12 March 2018).

Queensland Government (2018) Preserving Aboriginal languages. Available at: www.qld.gov.au/atsi/cultural-awareness-heritage-arts/preserving-aboriginal-languages (accessed 17 October 2018).

Ricento, T. (2000) Historical and theoretical perspectives in language policy and planning. *Journal of Sociolinguistics, 4* (2): 196–213.

Strochlic, N. (2018) The race to save the world's disappearing languages: every two weeks a language dies – Wikitongues wants to save them. *National Geographic*, 16 April.

Vygotsky, L. S. (1978) *Mind in Society: The Development of Higher Psychological Processes*. Cambridge, MA: Harvard University Press.

10

DIGITAL CITIZENS

HOW PRESCHOOL TEACHERS AND CHILDREN COMMUNICATE IN A DIGITAL AND GLOBAL WORLD

KLAUS THESTRUP

CHAPTER OVERVIEW

This chapter aims to debate the issue of how preschool teachers or social educators, as they are called in Denmark, can work in a globalised, digital world. The chapter aims to provoke discussion and to raise the questions required to move the pedagogical frame of kindergarten and preschool settings beyond the school walls. The chapter is based on four action research projects that took place in Denmark between 2005 and 2017, uses examples from the findings and draws on the principles that informed the new networks of communications developed between these settings and outside agencies.

The chapter aims to help you to:

- develop methods to use digital media in a pedagogical context
- offer practical ideas on how digital media can be used to communicate outside school.

THE RESEARCH CONTEXT

The developmental and research projects that inform this chapter took place mainly in kindergartens and mainly with children between 3 and 6 years of age. Kindergartens are not framed as preschools and operate as part of the school system. Formal education begins at 7 years of age but the vast majority of children start their preschool education when they are 6 years old in class zero. Working parents can send their under-3s to day-care centres staffed by social educators or pedagogues with a degree qualification.

The projects were based on action research and all took place in a context where the practitioners were involved in the planning and development of the projects. The examples mentioned are based on the children in the institution at the time the projects were conducted, drawn from a broad range of social, economic and cultural backgrounds. The research was also based on visual methods (Pink, 2014) and narrative documentation (Henningsen, 2011), with video recordings used as part of the everyday pedagogical methods.

The first project was Digital world citizens (2005–11), where I explored how children and pedagogues use digital media for play and experimentation (Henningsen et al., 2009). Between 2011 and 2012, the focus was on communicating with others in three kindergartens using Facebook (Thestrup, 2012a, 2012b). Simultaneously, my EU project MediaPLAYINGcommunities (2009) developed the idea of digital communication between kindergartens in Europe. In 2015, I was the project leader on one part of a national project about digital tools in kindergartens, Formation in a digital and global world (Thestrup et al., 2015), where 17 kindergartens, 31 pedagogues and consultants, three researchers and 275 children were involved in communicating and producing images and activities through a Google+ group. The final projects (2014–2017) involved a 'cultural exchange' (Lauridsen and Howard, 2017) between two Danish kindergartens and an Italian preschool.

PLAYING WITH MEDIA

In 2007, two pedagogues, 15 kindergarten children (between 4 and 6 years of age) and I invented a game called *camera play*. The idea was simple. We were playing catch-me-if-you-can, with a ball. One threw the ball and the child hit by the ball was out. We replaced the ball with a digital camera. In this variation of catch-me-if-you-can, a child aims the camera at another and if the other is caught on camera they are out. This example typifies an approach which involves play, experimentation, body and space. Later, when kindergartens contacted other kindergartens through the internet, my methods formed the basis for their encounters.

The key component of this game was the use of digital media in the form of a digital camera which was portable, easy to use and offered immediate feedback in the form of pictures. More importantly, catch-me-if-you-can forms part of the children's bodily oriented and playful routine. This example suggests that analogue and digital components are interactive processes that can be easily introduced into a familiar activity.

Underpinning this approach is the notion of 'media play'. It is a term coined in 1983 by Margaretha Rönnberg in response to children transforming elements of narratives from a TV series and movies that, over the years, included digital technologies and narrative elements from, by way of example, computer games (see Chapter 3 for an example of media play). As the term was extended (Rönnberg, 1983) to include new evolving technologies, it was at risk of losing focus. To retain its emphasis, it was more narrowly defined to combine media technologies and media narratives. According to this explanation, children are social actors with the ability to transform their existing play culture by drawing examples from media technologies and/or media narratives. This may involve a momentary change or improvisation, or be maintained over time using the same structures of play or rules of a game (Mouritsen and Qvortrup, 2002). This is also called *interpreting new production*, where children draw on the resources available in their surroundings but interpret them in new ways. What is important here is that they not only repeat an existing form but can also change it (Corsaro, 2005; Kampmann, 2010). This understanding of children's culture is closely connected to a certain understanding of the possibilities of digital media, where individuals can be both a consumer and a producer and use technologies and narratives as inspiration for new games or role play (see Chapter 3 for an example of media play).

So, when 'camera play' was introduced as an idea into the kindergarten context, it became a new form of improvisation. The children suggested alternatives such as using two cameras, a hide-and-seek game involving the whole kindergarten, or taking pictures of shoes, elbows or knees. When asked what they would call these activities, the children suggested *camera play*. Their thinking influenced both this and the following projects mentioned in this chapter. *Camera play* might also be referred to as *tablet play* or *mobile hunt* depending on the technology at hand and the participants involved; it might also embrace *virtual reality play*.

REFLECTIVE TASK

Reflect on the play culture in your context and on how media play might be integrated within it.

THE LIMITS OF THE PEDAGOGICAL SPACE

The EU project MediaPLAYINGcommunities (2007–2009) highlighted the need to identify questions that would inform and speed up the processes necessary to communicate with the world beyond the kindergarten/school. At the time, digital cameras were central to this work. The ideas and examples of media play took some time to implement in the different institutions. This was due to the fact that quite a few settings had to acquire the equipment essential to the process, and began to construct the pedagogical methods based on media play as it was understood and conducted at that time by me, amongst others. The game camera play was amongst those used in the institutions as a demonstration of the way to work and the principles accordingly and provided the basis for other interesting activities (Støvelbæk and MediaPLAYINGcommunities, 2009).

Settings attempted to communicate using Skype, but a few mistakes were made. For example, too many people in each setting attempted to communicate at the same time with no pre-set agenda. Importantly, we did not integrate Skype into our activities. This alerted us to the fact that we were in danger of creating our own problems and of failing to capture the full potential of Skype.

Whilst children's play culture continues to progress, the pedagogical framework around this culture is significant in deciding how it will unfold. Strategies to involve staff from other kindergartens were not in place, raising a number of key questions:

- How could we combine a physical space in one place with a physical space somewhere else?
- When and how should we draw inspiration from the outside?
- What exercises or games should we use?
- How could the kindergarten become a network offering access to any place, at any time, and be prepared to create communication, production and play?

It seemed that both the pedagogical methods and principles for a kindergarten in a globalised and mediatised world were being challenged.

REFLECTIVE TASK

Reflect on the above questions and discuss your ideas about how these can be answered in your context.

CASE STUDY 10.1: COMMUNICATION AND NARRATIVES

Below is an early example of an approach employed in a project conducted in December 2011–12. Three kindergartens worked closely on a number of common Christmas activities.

(Continued)

(Continued)

One of these activities was about two elves, Kallesok and Hanok; Kallesok is the clever and helpful elf and Hanok is the trickster and teaser. For instance, Hanok would hide the children's shoes whilst Kallesok would help find them. The children never saw these characters but found traces of their visits.

Both elves had their own Facebook profile with the three kindergartens sharing access. This meant that the children in each kindergarten could ask the two elves questions and read their answers. The pedagogues opened their Facebook page, read aloud what was written and, based on a discussion with the children, typed in their response. Technically, the pedagogues and the researchers had their own back channel, which was another Facebook space, where they could discuss and decide what would happen next.

In the first instance, one kindergarten devised a story and shared it with the others. Children and pedagogues discussed what Kallesok and Hanok had been doing for the past few years. The pedagogues shared their ideas on the back channel, made suggestions and devised stories. Activities were based on the ideas of the pedagogues and the children. An idea from one child in one kindergarten was to build traps to try to catch Hanok, and soon traps were being drawn on paper and then built.

These traps were filmed and uploaded onto the Facebook page and demonstrated via Skype. So here we effectively used Skype by sharing prepared examples. Each kindergarten demonstrated their traps in action and commented on those of others. The pedagogues on each side made sure that all traps were included. Staff from each kindergarten attended these presentations with pedagogues demonstrating their own activity.

The relationship between synchronous and asynchronous communication was crucial. Skype was not intended to be used alone but was seen as part of the ecology of media. As for Hanok and Kallesok's Facebook page, both pedagogues and children had to accept that they might not get an immediate response, might have to search for Hanok, talk about the elves and/or identify the things he had hidden. Pedagogues could start a search at any time, anywhere in the kindergarten. This ensured that the physical space was important to the activity and could be connected to other physical spaces through a digital channel consisting of both asynchronous and synchronous communication.

Each of the three kindergartens developed their own stories about Kallesok and Hanok. There were no fixed linear narratives containing conflict between the two main characters or a decisive outcome. Instead, the same basic situation might be repeated or changed over time with the story evolving in response to the children's ideas. This facilitated playful improvisation, creativity and problem solving by the children.

Asynchronous communication offered a best fit for the three kindergartens. The understanding of the narrative, the way to use Facebook and the physical activities were centred on what the pedagogues and the children decided in terms of when and how to communicate with the different kindergartens and the Facebook characters in the narrative.

COMMUNICATION ON A LARGER SCALE

The 2015 project involved 17 kindergartens, 31 pedagogues and consultants and 275 children. The project sought to identify how children could become digital world citizens in a global world. We used a simple Google+ group to organise the online part of the project. That was for several reasons; a Facebook group is better suited to ongoing discussions and the sharing of ideas, as described in the first project. The back channel and the common Facebook group were managed by three kindergartens, with two interacting characters, two pedagogues and one researcher. We could stay in the same discussion or easily follow whatever was going on in the group on a daily basis. You could say that our use of Facebook fitted into an ongoing development of activities between small groups in participating institutions who closely followed the development of a shared narrative.

   This aspect of the study was different from the first as it involved more participants. But the Google+ group did solve this new challenge. In the software there is a menu, where you choose who to follow and tasks to work together. When you do this, the posts concerning this cooperation can be seen on the screen. It is also possible to look at the other posts if you want to see what others are doing, but you can control when and how to do this. During the project, we organised use of the platform around the same idea as the earlier project. We cooperated more closely with some of the other partners, but it was possible to get inspiration from others as well.

IN THE PLAYGROUND

We also organised the project in what we named *next practice labs* (Thestrup et al., 2015). This ensured that all of the participants could contribute to the process. Pedagogues, children, consultants and researchers were in the same situation. We worked together to establish the use of digital media in every single kindergarten and we were doing it in a laboratory that could unfold in the midst of everyday pedagogy and practice, in spaces temporarily framed for the purpose.

   We organised the activities in the project in three laboratories. Each one lasted a total of two weeks with a start date for all the pedagogues, consultants and researchers. The launch took place in one of the kindergartens and involved discussions and workshops with the children. During a period of two weeks, pedagogues had to solve tasks and at the end of each laboratory they reflected on their experiences and looked ahead. The first session was about establishing a laboratory in every single kindergarten, the second focused on communicating with other kindergartens in the project and the third looked outwards to the world beyond the project.

In the first laboratory, we played with green-screen technology, which requires a green cloth and an application that makes it possible to combine two different pictures – for instance, a picture of a child placed in a picture of the sky or a video recording so it looked like she was flying. We tried to wrap objects or children in the green cloth, so it looked like they were disappearing or appearing from nowhere or somewhere else. In the second laboratory, we used an application that plays a filmed sequence backwards. So when one kindergarten filmed a short sequence where a stack of plastic boxes were turned over, it looked like they flew up from the ground and stacked them into a tower. Once this was done, other kindergartens followed suit and inspired new versions of this sequence. In the third laboratory, some of the kindergartens travelled virtually into the wider world. Vietnam was the chosen destination. The journey consisted of several elements. Pedagogues went on Google images to find and share images from Vietnam. They used green screen to dance in front of a music video made in Vietnam. They looked at maps to find the country. They made small narratives with an app that made it possible to move small pictures of characters back and forth on a photo background, record it and show it. In this final project, synchronous communication in the form of Skype was also used. It was, for instance, used to sing along simultaneously to the same song even though it often occurred via tablet. Again, this was organised by the pedagogues.

These activities happened outdoors in the playground as well as indoors in the activity rooms. They included body and space and, as there was no script to these activities, everyone engaged in experimentation. As it evolved, the process became increasingly complex as the interactions included others from outside the kindergarten. Importantly, participants did not need to know each other in advance as long as what they saw could be transformed into activities in their own kindergarten – and then posted online.

EXPERIMENTING COMMUNITIES AND OPEN LABORATORIES

The term Next Practice Labs relies on the discussion of other terms: *The Experimenting Community* (Caprani and Thestrup, 2010) and *The Open Laboratory* (Thestrup, 2013/2011). The experimenting community is the name for a community who work together. At the centre of this community is not only the repetition of an existing cultural practice but also the ability to change this very practice partially or completely if needed and wanted. But it also means that everybody involved might change something or be changed. It is not only the child in an educational setting who needs to understand, use and re-mix any given technology or narrative in their media play. It is also the pedagogue, the consultant and the researcher who might add something, learn something or experiment with something. None of the projects I participated in were predicated on a predetermined outcome. Rather, the focus was on *a community of practice* interested in adopting digital media as one of several tools to collectively and creatively construct (Wenger et al., 2009) and engage with others (Gauntlett and Thomsen, 2013).

The open laboratory is open in many forms (Robinson and Thestrup, 2016). It can combine materials, media and narratives. Digital and analogue are seen as entangled in advance (Pink et al., 2016) and can be consciously entangled in a pedagogical process. Existing uses of media, technologies and narratives are deliberately brought together to see what might result. After gathering research and practice in the open laboratory, a new practice is possibly established that can be changed later into a newer version of the laboratory (Thestrup and Robinson, 2016).

The laboratory is used as an open, virtual shared space where people around the world can engage, express views and constructively debate issues of concern. The laboratory is understood by the users as offering a mid-point with access to the near and far. New connections can be established with other labs or construct labs that exist digitally and online, occupying spaces that can include a single platform or a combination of platforms (Sandvik, 2015). They can be thought of as a dynamic media ecology (McLuhan, 1994/1964), created in the laboratory in response to the needs inspired by the social learning environment (Dron and Anderson, 2014).

THE SCREEN

Behind the use of Skype, it appears that pedagogues and children are not used to this software. When the daily encounters in a kindergarten are based on being present in the same time and space involved in physical activities, the risk is that these strategies might be interpreted as an attempt to devise methods for others to copy, though this may not be possible. The screen or any other technology for that matter is neither invisible nor non-existent. Skype or any other screen-based communication system offers a communication platform inside the kindergarten, enabling individuals to see each other through a virtual hole in a wall. Yet we are not sharing the same play or floor space, as we would if we were visiting each other in person. Whilst the idea that a whole group of children might meet with another group of children is perfectly feasible, it is only one way to meet. In the virtual space, children can meet other groups of children and share activities. Singing together is one example of sharing space and time.

The screen is a window offering communication with others. It can be seen as providing access to online worlds such as *Minecraft*. It can be seen as a tool like I-movie and it can be seen as an object in itself, or a screen can be carried around in the same way as a mobile phone. Drawing on the screen using finger movements, partially covering the screen or placing pieces of semi-transparent plastic on it, can change the communication possibilities. The screen itself becomes a way of playing or experimenting and an important way of communicating.

CASE STUDY 10.2:
THE GLOBAL ENCOUNTER

One final example shows some recent developments and what might be the next steps for a kindergarten in a global world. In the period between 2014 and 2017, two Danish and an Italian kindergarten tried to communicate mainly using the application Bookcreator. These kindergartens were also involved in the project mentioned above. This application makes it possible to place sounds, images, drawings and texts on an infinite number of blank pages and, importantly, to share these pages with others. One can, in principle, tell all kinds of narratives as the pages are blank and the different objects can be placed anywhere on the pages. When a narrative is uploaded to a shared space online, it can be downloaded by another access user to their computer/tablet. The narrative can be changed or added to by either user. This new narrative can then be uploaded and the process of change repeated. This method of exchange works best if it involves two kindergartens using the same book. One kindergarten uploads a book and waits for the other kindergarten to connect. Then both can follow the changes and relate to them at the same time.

The reader might recognise the same strategy as in the previous projects, asynchronous communication being important as it fits into everyday life. The content of the asynchronous communication is something that can be developed and used to inspire shared conversations and actions. The physical and local spaces are used as the centre for local activities. An example of the complexity of the issues is the memory game. One kindergarten posts six pictures on a page and the other kindergarten has to guess how they are related. In a traditional memory game, similar pictures are matched, for instance two flowers of the same sort, colour, etc. But this is not quite the way it is done here. Here the children are given the task to find six pictures and to identify possible relations between them. This could be a flower and a bee, but it could also be two objects that have the same colour but in other aspects appear different. The children are involved in the processes around the memory game. They talk about the possible relations between the pictures and why they were chosen, and respond by taking new pictures and making new connections. Prior to this task, the children had already used digital cameras and tablets to take pictures of different objects. They also talked with the pedagogues about how elements might be related and in what way.

This game encouraged children to interpret the aims of another's task and to use it as inspiration for the development of their own activity. It took place in a form that is open to interpretation, change and ongoing construction. The Facebook narratives about the elves and the constant exchange of new ways to film backwards, and so on, on a common site seem to support a pedagogy where the global encounter between many different cultures is, in principle, a real possibility. There is no fixed start or end. There is no need to copy somebody, but the possibility is to inspire and be interpreted. At each stage, children are free to use/not use or copy/not copy another's task. The essence of media play seems to be in improvising new forms of technologies and narratives, with the process defining new formulas that are open to improvisation. The future of a pedagogy in a global world based on media play seems to be the capacity for pedagogues and children to transform whatever they see and hear into ongoing processes of new or partly changed games, or new narratives that work locally or globally.

The pedagogical space exists inside the physical space but it is also framed by digital encounters with the outside world, thus facilitating communication with other individuals, networks and groups. The starting point for most kindergartens might be to recreate, remodel and transform the activities they encounter whilst playing with media. The construction of narratives appears to be a reasonable starting point.

REFLECTIVE TASK

Reflect on case study 10.1 and think of ways that you can use technology to encourage communication in your early childhood education context.

SUMMARY

This chapter offered some examples of how to embark on a voyage to use digital media in its many forms and to do it in the form of Next Practice Labs. The starting point may be what the children play, when they use elements from narratives and what technologies they use and for what purpose. The key to driving the process would be to transform and to include body, space and experiment. Digital and analogue are not opposites of each other but are entangled.

KEY POINTS TO REMEMBER

- The kindergarten is not an isolated pedagogical space but is part of a never-ending world that social educators and children can explore.
- On the way, the children will meet new technologies, new narratives and new cultures; they do not know everything in advance but have to relate to and find uses for it, if possible.
- The pedagogical kindergarten framework is not merely a pedagogy of answers but also a pedagogy of questioning and possibilities.

POINTS FOR DISCUSSION

- Discuss the ways in which technology can be used to communicate with other early childhood education settings in your country and around the globe.
- What benefits can you see in engaging technology in such an activity?
- Reflecting on your own context, what narratives can be created when engaging in such a project?

FURTHER READING

Arnott, L. (2016) An ecological exploration of young children's digital play: framing children's social experiences with technologies in early childhood, *Early Years: An International Journal*, 36 (3): 271–287.

Fleer, M. (2017) Digital playworlds in an Australian context: supporting double subjectivity. In T. Bruce, P. Hakkarainen and M. Bredikyte (eds) *The Routledge International Handbook of Early Childhood Play*. Oxon: Routledge, pp. 289–304.

Slutsky, R. and DeShelter L. M. (2017) How technology is transforming the ways in which children play. *Early Child Development and Care*, 187: 1138–1146.

Thestrup, K. and Robinson, S. (2016) Towards an entrepreneurial mindset: empowering learners in an open laboratory. In P. M. Papadopoulos, R. Burger and A. Faria (eds) *Innovation and Entrepreneurship in Education*. Bingley: Emerald Group, pp. 147–166.

USEFUL WEBSITE

http://creativitylabs.com – The Creativity Labs @ Indiana University is based on an interdisciplinary approach bringing together educators, designers, artists and learning theorists to show how technology can be used with young children.

REFERENCES

Caprani, O. and Thestrup, K. (2010) Det eksperimenterende fællesskab: Børn og voksnes leg med medier og teknologi. [*The experimental community: Children and adults play with media and technology*.] *Læring and Medier* (LOM), 3: 1–39.

Corsaro, W. A. (2005) *The Sociology of Childhood*. London: Sage.

Dron, J. and Anderson, T. (2014) *Teaching Crowds: Learning and Social Media*. Edmonton: AU Press.

Gauntlett, D. and Thomsen, S. B. (eds) (2013) Cultures of creativity: LEGO Foundation report. Available at: http://davidgauntlett.com/creativity/lego-cultures-of-creativity-report (accessed 7 January 2016).

Henningsen, L. (2011) Fortællende visuelle medier – introduktion og perspektiv. [Narrative visual media – introduction and communication.] In I. M. Sørensen (ed.) *Dansk, kultur og kommunikation – et perspektiv.* Copenhagen: Akademisk forlag.

Henningsen, L., Jerg, K. and Thestrup, K. (2009) Billedbevægelser – medieleg i en daginstitution. [When images are changing – mediaplaying in a kindergarten.] *Tidsskrift for Børne- og Ungdomskultur,* 53.

Kampmann, J. (2010) Børnekultur i et institutionsperspektiv – spændingsfeltet mellem leg og læring. [Children's culture in the perspective of institutionalisation – between play and learning.] *Tidskrift for Børne- og Ungdomskultur, 54*: 9–20.

Lauridsen, P. and Howard, P. (2017) *Cultural Exchange.* Unpublished report. Copenhagen: BUPL.

McLuhan, M. (1994/1964) *Understanding Media.* Cambridge, MA: MIT Press.

MediaPLAYINGcommunities (2009) *Mediahandbook.* Bochum, Germany: IBAF.

Mouritsen, F. and Qvortrup, J. (eds) (2002) *Childhood and Children's Culture.* Odense: University of Southern Denmark Press.

Pink, S. (2014) *Doing Visual Ethnography*, 3rd edition. London: Sage.

Pink, S., Ardévol, E. and Lanzeni, D. (eds) (2016) *Digital Materialities.* London: Bloomsbury.

Robinson, S. and Thestrup, K. (2016) Inside the rainbow. Available at: https://youtu.be/YdBekYIC6Hk?list=PLAVS-GEyIPCiFaRypx-1drdEuSxuuvAe2 (accessed 2 April 2017).

Rönnberg, M. (1983) Skådelek och medialekar. [Spectator – and mediaplay.] In C. Bøgh (ed.) *Småbørnsforskning i Danmark IX – Rapport fra seminaret: Børns leg i det moderne industrisamfund. [Research on small children in Denmark IX – report from the seminar: Children's play in the modern industrial society.]* Udvalget vedrørende småbørnsforskning.

Sandvik, K. (2015) *Plot til lyst. [Plotting for fun.]* Aalborg: Aalborg Undervisitetsforlag.

Støvelbæk, F. and MediaPLAYINGcommunities (2009) mPc is what you see. YouTube video. Available at: www.youtube.com/watch?v=GtGHo5oXuUY (accessed 18 October 2018).

Thestrup, K. (2012a) En børnehave møder verden. [A kindergarten meets the world.] *Pædagogisk Extrakt, 1*: 1–15.

Thestrup, K. (2012b) Kallesok er på Facebook. [Kallesock is on Facebook.] *Pædagogisk Extrakt,* 1.

Thestrup, K. (2013/2011) Det eksperimenterende fællesskab. [The Experimenting Community.] VIA Systime.

Thestrup, K. and Robinson, S. (2016) Towards an entrepreneurial mindset: empowering learners in an open laboratory. In P. M. Papadopoulos, R. Burger and A. Faria (eds) *Innovation and Entrepreneurship in Education.* Bingley: Emerald Group, pp. 147–166.

Thestrup, K., Andersen, M. A., Jessen, C., Knudsen, J. and Sandvik, K. (2015) *Delaftale 3: Dannelse I en digital og global verden – digitale redskaber skal understøtte barnets lærings- og dannelsesproces. [Part 3: Formation in a digital and global world – digital tools must support the learning – and formation processes of the child.]* Available at: www.kl.dk/PageFiles/1321042/Delrapport%203%20-%20Dannelse%20i%20en%20digital%20og%20global%20verden.pdf (accessed 7 January 2016).

Wenger, E., White, N. and Smith, J. D. (2009) *Digital Habitats: Stewarding Technology for Communities.* Portland, OR: CPsquare.

PART III

DIGITALLY ENABLED LEARNING IN THE 21ST CENTURY

11

AN EDUCATION–CENTRED APPROACH TO DIGITAL MEDIA EDUCATION

SAARA SALOMAA AND PEKKA MERTALA

CHAPTER OVERVIEW

This chapter presents a pedagogical approach referred to as an *education-centred approach* for digital media education. The chapter is structured around three fundamental questions that all educators need to ask themselves regarding the pedagogical value of digital media:

- What is media education for?
- Who is media education for?
- How should media education be carried out?

With these questions in mind, it is possible to challenge readers to reflect on what it means to be a media educator in early childhood education. The underlying idea of this approach is to stimulate 'media educational consciousness', that is, professional awareness for media education.

The chapter aims to help you to:

- make links between media education and digital practices
- deepen your understanding about media possibilities and challenges in the digital age
- identify the essential parts of pedagogical planning for media education in early child-hood education.

MEDIA EDUCATION IN FINLAND

This chapter is based on our research in five Finnish early childhood education settings and discusses a pedagogical approach referred to as an education-centred approach for media education. Whilst different media are part of children's everyday life in developed countries (Chaudron, 2015), their integration into early childhood education is still limited. For example, in Finland where the basic education curriculum has included media education themes since the early 1970s, the National Core Curriculum of Early Childhood Education 2016 (hereafter referred to as the core curriculum), effective from 2017, is the first curricular early childhood education document that obliges educators to carry out media education, and to examine digital media with children. Thus, it was unsurprising to note the experiences of one teacher at the beginning of the project who commented:

I've never thought of myself as any kind of media educator – I just haven't thought that it belongs here [early childhood education] or is in any way present here in the day-care centre. (Teacher A2)

It is understandable that hasty mediatisation, technologisation and digitalisation of culture and society can lead to uncertainty about professional educators' roles (i.e. Nikolopoulou and Gialamas, 2015; Palaiologou, 2016). Research has also shown that in the field of early childhood education, the term *media education* has strong technical connotations (Kupiainen et al., 2006), which can inform different dispositions towards media education. Another common finding is that practitioners believe that children's lives are filled with media, and their response is to construct a 'media-free' education space (e.g. Lehtikangas and Mulari, 2016; Mertala, 2017b). Others argue that early childhood education practices need to be digitalised; otherwise children whose home environments are filled with media practices might not be motivated to engage in learning activities (Dong and Newman, 2016). In addition, some practitioners seem to have adopted the pro-technology ideology that suggests that '*e is best*' for learning (Ingleby, 2015: 151). Studies also suggest that educators use the (presumed) affordances of digital media as the starting point for pedagogical planning instead of building on their general pedagogical thinking (Mertala, 2017a).

The common factor for all of these findings is that media (in terms of both devices and content), instead of educational thinking, directs educators' views on media education. Furthermore, understanding media only as (digital) devices and content is narrow and ignores the fact that media also includes mediatised communication environments (Meyrowitz, 1999). All aspects of media form the media culture which is the everyday world of today's citizens, including young children (see Chaudron, 2015). The above quote from a teacher offers an illustrative example of how a device-orientated understanding of media can make educators blind to the other ways that media is present in early childhood education. Many types of media culture arise in children's conversations, in the themes of their role play, drawing, writing and crafts, as well as in the print on their clothing.

As previously indicated, the education-centred approach employed in our research is the focus of this chapter and addresses three questions:

- What is media education for?
- Who is media education for?
- How should media education be carried out?

The first question relates to conscious and target-orientated educational choices. The second question challenges readers to reflect on childhoods in media culture. The third question invites readers to benefit from the wide pedagogical possibilities that exploring (digital) media cultures provide. These key questions, alongside the quotations from the empirical data, concretise the conceptual categories that it is suggested are included in media-educational consciousness in early childhood education. These categories include conceptions of the following:

- educational goals and values in relation to media literacy
- human growth and development
- media
- the individual as a media educator and the importance of early childhood education for human growth in media culture.

These conscious or unconscious conceptions have an impact on actualised pedagogical choices. The more aware educators are of their underlying conceptions, the more potential there is for professional development and coherent pedagogical planning (Salomaa, 2016a, 2016b). Before addressing these topics, it is important to explain what is meant by media education in the context of early childhood education and how it relates to digital practices.

REFLECTIVE TASK

What barriers might exist in your early childhood education context for the integration of media? How can they be overcome?

WHAT IS MEDIA EDUCATION?

According to Kupiainen and Sintonen (2009), media education can be defined as 'goal-oriented interaction ... involving the educator, the learner and media culture'; the goal of this interactive process is media literacy (p. 31). Media literacy applies to both traditional and new media and is a broad concept, which may be defined as comprising the ability to access, analyse, evaluate and produce media (Aufderheide, 1993); it also includes participation, social abilities, self-expression and ethics in a media context (Buckingham, 2007; Kupiainen and Sintonen, 2009). Each of these dimensions is included in the Finnish core curriculum's chapters on media education. According to the core curriculum, the task of media education is to provide children with the opportunity to become active and to express themselves in their communities. Children are familiarised with different types of media, such as children's literacy, pictures, audiovisual texts and ICT hardware and software, and teachers are charged with offering them opportunities to experiment with and produce media in a playful manner in a safe environment. Media content, related to children's lives and its veracity, are reflected by and with children. Play, drawing and drama are examples of child-centred methods for exploring media-related themes (FNBoE, 2016).

The Finnish core curriculum's elements – play, arts and drama – illustrate the importance afforded to the social and cultural characteristics of the context where media education is conducted. Contextualisation allows media literacy to be promoted in practice by clarifying its meaning and purposes (see Palsa and Ruokamo, 2015). Consequently, when developing early childhood media education, it is important to ensure from the beginning that a strong connection is created between the common educational objectives of media education and early childhood education. Hence, building on Kupiainen and Sintonen's (2009: 31) classification, we propose the following definition of media education for the early childhood education context:

> media education in institutional early childhood education is goal-orientated interaction involving educators, learners and media culture. The aim is to promote early childhood education's general educational goals by enhancing media literacy.

In Finland, the Early Childhood Education Act 2015 sets out key goals to promote the development and well-being of each child, to support the child's learning environment, to promote lifelong learning and educational equality, and to enable positive learning experiences.

WHAT IS MEDIA EDUCATION FOR? MEDIA LITERACY TO PROMOTE THE GENERAL GOALS OF EARLY CHILDHOOD EDUCATION

When educational goal orientation is expected, it is essential to engage practitioners in a professional dialogue about these objectives. The normative framework is set by legislation and other obligatory guidelines, but the real pedagogical actions are based at local level, even in an individual teacher's planning. What kind of traits, values, skills and abilities should children achieve, learn and develop in early childhood education? The concrete suggestion is to verbalise the targets and objectives of education with 'why' questions. These questions could address the basic nature of early childhood education in relation to media (why is early childhood education/media education important?), or examine early childhood education media activities from a critical perspective, reflecting on the desired goals (why implement pedagogical actions in this way?). With this kind of reflective process, it is possible to pinpoint the objectives to be set as targets for media-education pedagogies. After this, a suitable didactical approach and content can be selected.

The importance of 'why' questions cannot be overemphasised, since goal orientation is one of the key characteristics of professional education. As mentioned earlier, if practices related to digital media are implemented without critical reflection on goals and outcomes, it can lead to routines that may weaken the quality of education. For example, in a study by Mertala (2017a), two teachers were reported to have stopped taking children to visit the theatre because they were now able to show multimedia presentations using a projector. Mertala argued that this approach was shortsighted since it divorced content from the experiential learning children gain from attending a theatrical performance steeped in culture, the arts and the social context. Similarly, Ingleby (2015) noted that whilst teachers were keen to use computers with their children, they had difficulty explaining why they should be used. Whilst 'why' questions appear difficult to answer, they are the ones that give educational value to pedagogical planning. This phenomenon was also acknowledged by one participant in our research who noted that the essential development task was that:

> we would stop and think why we're doing this – what is it that we're after and what are pedagogics really? It's been like, or what I've noticed at least, in the beginning that we are eager to jump into all those activities and methods and ways, but why do we do it? We always have to keep reminding ourselves. (Director A)

Therefore, from an education-centred perspective, it is vital that educators are able to understand how media-educational elements can contribute to the wider objectives of early childhood education, and how to integrate the actions properly both as part of everyday work and in long-term educational planning. One of the teachers set a goal at the very beginning of the development project:

> [t]o sort of bring it into the everyday, that it wouldn't be something separate like we now have this media education thing on Wednesdays. (Teacher C)

Along with the integrative and contextualised approach, the following were also recognised as educational actions promoting emergent media literacy:

> [s]imple everyday things, things we learn in the day-care centre and pre-school anyway, but the good knowledge of what can be a good base for building media competence. (Teacher A2)

According to Teacher A2, supporting the development of good self-esteem and its significance in development are critical in a media relationship. This illustrates Teacher A2's professional understanding of child development in the context of media culture. Both quotations above highlight the importance of methods of integrative pedagogics in early childhood education. One educational action can contribute to many educational objectives, and media literacy can be enhanced alongside several other abilities, namely socio-emotional skills, arts and alphabetical literacy.

WHO IS MEDIA EDUCATION FOR? CHILDHOODS IN A MEDIA CULTURE

The next important question concerns: *who are the children we are educating*? The observations and interpretations of professional educators about children's media relationships are not created through neutral lenses. They are connected to the educator's personal values and perceptions of human beings and their growth and development, as well as those represented by educational institutions. In the interviews, a teacher described media as visible in early childhood education:

> Before, children played at house, or being a car driver, they played the world they lived in. Today, we see them playing the things they see on TV 80 per cent of the time. They play NinjaGo, they play the Dudesons, and then, their play is pretty violent because the cartoons, the animations are pretty violent too. (Teacher A2)

In this excerpt, two childhoods are present: the adult's own childhood, remembered as an adult, and today's childhood, interpreted from the adult's point of view. The first of these is presented in an idealised way compared to the present childhood, to which media has, over time, added the undesired theme of violence. Battle themes are not, however, the invention of modern children's programmes. War and fighting themes reflecting the battle of good and evil are present in traditional stories. Furthermore, the assumption that children's role play would reflect precisely children's media experiences is questionable: children can possess high levels of media-cultural knowledge and role play accordingly, even if they do not have first-hand experience of the particular media (Lehtikangas and Mulari, 2016).

It is also possible that professionals' interpretations *of* children and media are affected by discussions *in* the media. These discussions are often connected to scientific disciplines other than educational sciences, particularly to developmental psychology (Livingstone, 2009). In the public debate, media (mostly digital media) is often seen as unequivocally good or bad in relation to childhood and the effect of media is assumed to be deterministic. In these views, the child's personality, growth environment and the role and possibilities of interaction, upbringing and education are disregarded. An illustrative example of this discourse is the headline of an article on the website of YLE (the Finnish Broadcasting Company): 'Will the kids of the digital world become top experts or grasshoppers?' (Portaankorva, 2015). The 'grasshopper' analogy refers to children's inability to concentrate; children are also portrayed as needing protection against becoming media victims. The 'top expert' discourse then paints a picture of children with innate media skills, of so-called 'digital natives', who, unlike adults, somehow naturally manage media and easily take on the role of expert and educator in all media interactions (Selwyn, 2003). Both these discourses exist in the field of early childhood education (e.g. Mertala, 2017b). For example, the following extract from a teacher illustrates how children are described as born-competent tech-users:

> It's amazing how they [the children] know all these functions. Even though they've never seen this or that mobile phone model, they know how to use them and they don't read the manuals. (Teacher A1)

From an educational perspective, the starting points that emphasise both extremes are insufficient and problematic. The stereotypical conceptions leave hardly any room for children's individuality, or educational effect. The protectionist discourse invalidates the child's subjectivity, describing the child as a passive object instead of an active agent. Conversely, the digital natives' discourse dissipates the educational responsibility of the adults and questions their ability to learn and understand. Children's innate technical skills are seen as the only possible explanation for their skilled activities. This view bypasses children's typical habit of exploring the world through broadminded experimentation, as well as the simple explanation that – thanks to modern technology – using many of today's technical gadgets *is so easy that a child can do it*.

To avoid stereotypical assumptions, cultural change requires educators to use critical reflection to separate their lived childhoods from produced childhoods. It is also essential to build a media-educational policy for the working community, providing a solid educational base and coherence between pedagogies. But how can educators gain access beyond archetypal conceptions and move closer to the childhood children are living now? One of the teachers provided a simple but functional solution:

 We could ask. I think it's important that the child can tell us what it's all about. (Teacher B)

In other words, a good starting point for pedagogical planning is primarily to observe, discuss and utilise the children's own cultural experiences, and to leave out phenomena that have no point of reference in the children's lives. This selective process requires the expertise of early childhood educators: knowledge of the cultural educational context, knowing the children and knowing how to listen to the children, and a pedagogic and educational outlook, self-esteem and judgement.

HOW SHOULD MEDIA EDUCATION BE CARRIED OUT? THE BEST GAME IN THE WORLD

The third big question concentrates on methods of media education: *how should media education be carried out?* As discussed in previous chapters, the chosen resources and methods should contribute to educational goals that are meaningful in the lifeworld of the children and be complementary to overall early childhood education goals. Because of the diverse nature of media, there are countless possibilities to conduct high-quality media education. As stated in the previous chapter, a good starting point is a media phenomenon that is important in children's lives. However, this does not mean that media education should simply reproduce children's existing media experiences. Instead, education should broaden children's understanding about the world and promote skills-active participation.

This section clarifies the process with an example of media education related to digital games. Digital games have become important in the lives of many young children in Western societies (Chaudron, 2015). Children have also reported that playing digital games is what they would like to do with digital media in preschool (Mertala, 2016). Research suggests that playing digital games appears to be the most common way to use digital media in early childhood education (e.g. Blackwell et al., 2016). Superficially, it appears that all is well: children want to play games and educators are responding to this desire with age-appropriate gaming.

However, for educators, playing digital games in early childhood education means using educational games to teach children different curricular subjects, predominantly literacy and maths (Blackwell et al., 2016; Mertala, 2017a). In contrast, children have commented explicitly that what they would like to play in preschool are their favourite (commercial, leisure) games (Mertala, 2016). It appears that there is dissonance between the meaning that educators and children give to playing digital games, and that using digital games cannot be automatically considered as child-initiated pedagogy. Hence, it is questionable whether just 'digitalising' early childhood education would help motivate children to learn, if the digital content does not pay attention to children's cultural interests (see also Wohlwend, 2017). In addition, from a media-educational viewpoint, the pedagogical examination of digital games – this rich and versatile form of culture – should not be reduced simply to game playing, educational or not. This argument builds on Buckingham and Burn's (2007) notion that teaching children about games as a (media) cultural form is a prerequisite for using games to teach other curriculum areas. Thus, from an educational perspective, examining games, playing (as a form of activity) and scrutinising game culture together with the children are all important. Whilst these objectives may sound abstract, if not declamatory, pedagogical practices are not necessarily complex. Case study 11.1 draws from a 2016 early years game project.

REFLECTIVE TASK

- What are the most important educational values and goals for an educator in your context?
- How do these goals and values become apparent when carrying out digital media education?

CASE STUDY 11.1: CHILDREN AS GAME DESIGNERS

The project was based on teachers' observations that digital games are important for children and a significant source for role play and discussion. Hence, teachers wanted to enhance children's understanding of games and know more about children's relationship with games themselves. The teachers opted to have children design games by drawing, which is also one of the suggested methods in the core curriculum. The value

(Continued)

(Continued)

of a design task is that it provides children with an opportunity to critically review existing games, allows them to create something new and provides a first-hand experience of acting from the position of media maker. This allows children to construct understanding about digital games (and other media) as cultural products that result from their makers' choices.

From the perspective of critically evaluating existing games, the design task was a good choice as most children developed new games or modified existing games. For example, one girl designed a game influenced by Super Mario, and explicitly mentioned that 'this is a bit like one game we have at home, but I modified it a bit'. With the modification, she referred to the game character, who, instead of being a moustachioed plumber, was a purple-haired girl. Other children redesigned their favourite games, though many were unfamiliar with or had never played these games. In fact, a child with detailed knowledge of *Minecraft* did not have that game at home. Instead, he gained his knowledge from watching *Minecraft* videos on YouTube and Vimeo.

Based on their drawing themes, the children were divided into small groups and began to design and build their own games from recycled materials. The construction session started by discussing the goals and rules of the game: what is needed to pass or win the game, and how can these factors be concretely implemented in the game?

The following example is from a group whose end result involved an adventure game called *Lego Vampire Battle*. The rules and structure of the game were as follows: players take turns throwing dice and moving Lego figures along a yellow trail across the game board. Whilst circulating, players collect a variety of equipment needed to defeat the vampire. Along the way, players also have to fight a dragon. At the beginning of the game, each player has ten lives and whenever players are defeated by the dragon or the vampire, they lose a life. A record of lives is kept on a game card which has ten boxes, one for each life. In the event of a loss, one box is coloured in (see Figure 11.1).

Figure 11.1   The game board and the game card for Lego Vampire Battle

The topic that caused the most discussion was implementing the desired fighting element in the game. Children's interest in media-related fighting themes and role play has been found to be a problematic topic in educational contexts, and educators are often dismissive of anything fight-related (Lehtikangas and Mulari, 2016; Wohlwend, 2017). Ultimately, the group opted for a solution where one facet of the dice was coloured black. If a player threw the dice and it landed black-side-up, that player had to fight the dragon. The fight comprised of throwing the dice, with a larger number resulting in winning the battle. The dragon was a tangible monster built of cardboard and during the fight one player (taking a turn) threw the dice on behalf of the dragon. The battle against the dragon took one round, but in the 'boss battle' (which refers to fighting a significant enemy [the boss], and it is often seen as the climax of a whole game or a section in a game; most often, the bosses are harder to defeat than other enemies faced during the game) against the vampire, it took five rounds to resolve the winner. This illustrates that, with pedagogical guidance, fighting can be reconstructed as non-violent symbolic battles, which still respect children's media-culture interests.

In summary, the game project example drew on children's digital media-cultural interests, knowledge and enthusiasm, but it also enriched their experiences and agency from a consumer position towards active ownership and design. With careful pedagogical planning and guidance, it also aimed to enhance children's understanding of digital media as cultural products that are shaped by makers' choices. Designing and building board games in small groups also had the potential to contribute to children's learning relative to social competences, arts and crafts, as well as practising 'traditional' literacy and numeracy. Within this project, digital tools were utilised in making and printing the game cards and documenting the project. However, building tangible game boards instead of programming digital games was seen as being beneficial for several educational purposes. As Alper (2013) states, in developmentally appropriate new media literacy education, children and teachers should be able to discern between tools and to use digital tools when they are the best solution available. This project provides an inspirational example but is not a 'one size fits all' solution to be copied as such. The pedagogical value and meaningfulness of projects are always contextual.

REFLECTIVE TASKS

- Observe a typical day in an early childhood education setting. Reflect how media (new and traditional media devices, themes of play and discussion, toys and other spinoffs, etc.) are present in the everyday life of children and adults.
- How many of the media phenomena identified are based on digital devices and content, how many are non-digital and how many combine digital and non-digital practices?

SUMMARY

This chapter has discussed some of the central aspects that create the foundation for planning and implementing high-quality digital media education from the perspective of early childhood education. It aimed to broaden our understanding of early childhood educational professionalism from technical mastery to a wider educational approach. In short, the underlying idea of the proposal has been that early childhood media education should follow the core principles of early childhood education and be based on educational consciousness, educational goals and values in the prevailing media culture.

KEY POINTS TO REMEMBER

- It is worth encouraging educators to draw on those media-cultural aspects already present in everyday early childhood education, explored in the following chapters in this book, which are important and inspiring for children, as well as part of their cultural capital (see also Wohlwend, 2017).
- Instead of debating the inclusion of digital media education, educators should consider its potential in goal-orientated everyday practices within the field of early childhood education.
- As suggested by Mertala (2017a), by building on the cornerstones of early childhood education, digital media-educational competence becomes an extension of educators' existing proficiency, rather than being a new and peripheral area of expertise.

POINTS FOR DISCUSSION

- What are the age-appropriate skills children should have in order to most benefit (e.g. to learn, enjoy and express themselves) from the media present in everyday early childhood education?
- Could the skills that relate to digital media literacy also contribute to other forms of learning?
- In addition to drawing from children's everyday media-cultural interests, what kind of experiences could broaden their understanding about the world and the media? Are children already familiar with, for example, journalism, media arts or digital maps and navigation software?
- How do I/we as early years professional(s) articulate our media-educational goals and methods to parents and guardians?

FURTHER READING

Danby, S. J., Fleer, M., Davidson, C. and Hatzigianni, M. (eds) (2018) *Digital Childhoods: Technologies and Children's Everyday Lives*. Singapore: Springer.

Harviainen, J. T., Meriläinen, M. and Tossavainen, T. (eds) (2015) Game Educator's Handbook, revised international edition. Available at: www.pelikasvatus.fi/gameedu catorshandbook.pdf. This ebook is intended as an aid for all types of game educators. The target group consists of parents, schools, libraries and anyone with connections to children, adolescents or adults that play digital games.

USEFUL WEBSITE

www.mediataitokoulu.fi/resources – the website of the Finnish National Audiovisual Institute provides media-educational lesson plans and resources for practitioners working with children and young people.

REFERENCES

Alper, M. (2013) Developmentally appropriate new media literacies: supporting cultural competencies and social skills in early childhood education. *Journal of Early Childhood Literacy, 13* (2): 175–196.

Aufderheide, P. (ed.) (1993) *Media Literacy*. A report of the national leadership conference on media literacy. Washington, DC: Aspen Institute.

Blackwell, C. K., Lauricella, A. R. and Wartella, E. (2016) The influence of TPACK contextual factors on early childhood educators' tablet computer use. *Computers and Education, 98*: 57–69.

Buckingham, D. (2007) *Beyond Technology: Children's Learning in the Age of Digital Culture*. Cambridge: Polity Press.

Buckingham, D. and Burn, A. (2007) Game literacy in theory and practice. *Journal of Educational Multimedia and Hypermedia, 16* (3): 323–349.

Chaudron, S. (2015) *Young Children (0–8) and Digital Technology: A Qualitative Exploratory Study across Seven Countries*. Luxembourg: Publications Office of the European Union.

Dong, C. and Newman, L. (2016) Ready, steady... pause: integrating ICT into Shanghai preschools. *International Journal of Early Years Education, 24* (2): 224–237.

Finnish National Board of Education (FNBoE) (2016) *National Core Curriculum Guidelines for Early Childhood Education*. Helsinki: FNBoE.

Ingleby, E. (2015) The impact of changing policies about technology on the professional development needs of early years educators in England. *Professional Development in Education, 41* (1): 144–157.

Kupiainen, R. and Sintonen, S. (2009) *Medialukutaidot, Osallisuus, Mediakasvatus. [Media Literacies, Participation, Media Education]*. Palmenia: Helsinki University Press.

Kupiainen, R., Niinistö, H., Pohjola, K. and Kotilainen, S. (2006) Mediakasvatusta alle 8-vuotiaille. Keväällä 2006 toteutetun Mediamuffinssi-kokeilun arviointia. [Media education for under 8s: 'Mediamuffin' project evaluation.] Tampereen Yliopisto, journalismin tutkimusyksikkö.

Lehtikangas, A. and Mulari, H. (2016) 'Mä en oo kattonu mut mä vaan tiiän ne': Havainnointi, medialeikit ja eronteot päiväkodissa. ['I haven't seen them, I just know them': observation, mediaplay and distinctions in kindergarten.] In H. Mulari (ed.) *Somukohtia: Näkökulmia lasten mediakulttuurien tutkimusmenetelmiin ja mediakasvatukseen.* [*Viewpoints to research on children's media cultures and media education.*] Nuorisotutkimusverkosto/Nuorisotutkimusseura Verkkojulkaisuja, *103*, pp. 55–78.

Livingstone, S. (2009) *Children and the Internet.* Cambridge: Polity.

Mertala, P. (2016) Fun and games: Finnish children's ideas for the use of digital media in preschool. *Nordic Journal of Digital Literacy, 10* (4): 207–226.

Mertala, P. (2017a) Wag the dog: the nature and foundations of preschool educators' positive ICT pedagogical beliefs. *Computers in Human Behavior, 69*: 197–206.

Mertala, P. (2017b) Wonder children and victimizing parents: preservice early childhood teachers' beliefs about children and technology at home. *Early Child Development and Care,* https://doi.org/10.1080/03004430.2017.1324434.

Meyrowitz, J. (1999) Understandings of media. *ETC: A Review of General Semantics, 56* (1): 44–52.

Nikolopoulou, K. and Gialamas, V. (2015) Barriers to the integration of computers in early childhood settings: teachers' perceptions. *Education and Information Technologies, 20* (2): 285–301.

Palaiologou, I. (2016) Teachers' dispositions towards the role of digital devices in play-based pedagogy in early childhood education. *Early Years: An International Research Journal, 36* (3): 305–321.

Palsa, L. and Ruokamo, H. (2015) Behind the concepts of multiliteracies and media literacy in the renewed Finnish core curriculum: a systematic literature review of peer-reviewed research. *International Journal of Media, Technology, and Lifelong Learning, 11*: 101–119.

Portaankorva, J. (2015) Tuleeko digimaailman lapsista heinäsirkkoja vai huippuosaajia? [Will the children of the digital world have grasshoppers or top experts?] Available at: http://yle.fi/uutiset/3-7811559 (accessed 24 February 2017).

Salomaa, S. (2016a) Mediakasvatustietoisuuden jäsentäminen varhaiskasvatuksessa. [Aspects of media educational consciousness in ECE.] Varhaiskasvatuksen tiedelehti. *Journal of Early Childhood Education Research, 5* (1): 136–161.

Salomaa, S. (2016b) Aspects of educational consciousness in early childhood media education. In Í. Pereira, A. Ramos and J. Marsh (eds) *The Digital Literacy and Multimodal Practices of Young Children: Engaging with Emergent Research.* Proceedings of the First Training School of COST Action IS1410, University of Minho, Braga, Portugal, 6–8 June. Available at: http://digilitey.eu

Selwyn, N. (2003) 'Doing IT for the kids': re-examining children, computers and the 'information society'. *Media, Culture and Society, 25* (3): 351–378.

Wohlwend, K. E. (2017) Who gets to play? Access, popular media and participatory literacies. *Early Years, 37* (1): 62–76.

12

TEACHERS' DIGITAL PRACTICES IN THE CLASSROOM

DEBRA HARWOOD, DANE MARCO DI CESARE AND KAREN JULIEN

CHAPTER OVERVIEW

This chapter considers research conducted in Canada in early childhood education (ECE) centres or preschools, with a specific focus on early childhood education classrooms that refer to care and education models serving children aged 2 and a half to 5 years in both for-profit and non-profit community-based programmes, including toddler programmes, preschool and before-and-after-school-care programmes. Publicly funded kindergarten classrooms within the school system were not part of the study.

The chapter aims to help you to:

- explore teacher beliefs, knowledge and training in relation to technology integration as well as actual use in ECE classrooms
- understand the complex factors (e.g. educator beliefs, efficacy, role of training and experience) that contribute to quality integration of tablet technology
- gain insight into the important role of the teacher in mediating and guiding children's use of tablets in the classroom.

INTRODUCTION

The role of technology can be misconstrued without a close observation of teachers' actual digital practices, that is how devices like tablets are taken up, conceptualised and integrated within the play and learning opportunities provided and scaffolded for young children. Even the discussion of digital technologies and young children is polarised within the literature, which is either presented as a panacea for preparing children for learning in the 21st century or vilified as a detractor from the 'real business of play' in ECE classrooms (Palmer, 2015; Plowman et al., 2010). Clearly, from an educational perspective, the question of *how* technologies should be integrated within teachers' practice is of paramount importance.

In this chapter, we highlight some of the findings from a research project on the role of tablets within ECE classrooms in Ontario, Canada. We focused our study on tablets, given the frequency with which tablets are supplied to kindergarten classrooms in Canada (Johnson et al., 2016) and the ease of the touchscreen interface that seems particularly well suited to younger children (Hourcade et al., 2015). The ways in which tablets are conceptualised, utilised, introduced or scaffolded by a teacher within the classroom is crucial to understanding the benefits for children (Edwards, 2013a, b; Harwood, 2017). Thus, the quality of this integration often relies greatly on the teacher, their beliefs, knowledge and training in relation to technology integration as well as actual use in ECE classrooms (Blackwell et al., 2014).

Part of this year-long exploratory study involved a close observation and investigation of the impact of teachers' knowledge and beliefs regarding technology on the extent and perceived impact of tablet integration in 26 Canadian ECE classrooms. The debate as to whether tablets should be integrated within ECE, we argue, should be re-focused on the question of *how integration should occur and what supports are needed* to ensure the quality of experiences for young children and effective pedagogical approaches. Clearly, for the contemporary child, play often includes a blurring of the boundaries between real and virtual, traditional Lego and digital Lego, a 'convergence of play' spaces and experiences (Edwards, 2013b; Marsh, 2010; Plowman et al., 2012). Perhaps, teachers grapple with ways in which to provoke and incite 'converged play', thus contributing to the ways in which digital play remains a 'contested activity' (Stephen and Plowman, 2014: 330) within many Canadian ECE classrooms.

DIGITAL PRACTICES IN CANADA

Relatively little information is known about the digital habits of young children (0–8 years) in Canada. Disturbingly, there is an overall lack of research and policy specifically examining and guiding the digital practices of young children, their families and teachers. The information that does exists tends to be cautionary and alarmist with little insight into children's (and their families') actual lives and the social-cultural contexts of those lives. Potentially, this disconnect between children and families' (and teachers') actual digital practices and policies is disconcerting, and contributes little to an understanding of the ways in which digital technologies and media are embedded within the ecology of children's lives.

Although definitive rates are unknown, given reported media use in the USA amongst 2–4-year-olds as escalating to 80% in 2013 (Common Sense Media), Canada, like many other Western nations, is most likely experiencing similar trends of young children engaged with digital media daily. However, much of the discourse in Canada is shaped by media reports influenced by the Canadian Paediatric Society (CPS)'s position statement and 'keeping kids away from screens' is a pervasive theme (Macleans, 2017). Regardless, what seems to be missing from any discussion is a clear understanding of how young children, (their parents and teachers), use media and digital devices and a recognition of the social-cultural context of children's digital lives (Harwood, 2017).

MediaSmarts, a Canadian not-for-profit organisation for digital and media literacy, has the largest corpus of data on older children (9 to 17 years) in grades 4 to 11 with a series of reports they started publishing in 2000. A recent report entitled *Young Canadians in a Wired World, Phase III: Life Online* (Steeves, 2014) surveyed over 5,000 young students about their digital practices, describing this age group as 'confident and enthusiastic users of networked technology' (p. 3). Overwhelmingly, these students reported universal access to the internet outside of school, with portable devices used more often than a desktop computer. The students' online activities were also reported and appear to be somewhat complex, with digital media used for accessing information, creative endeavours (e.g. digital movie making and mashups), entertainment, socialising and networking.

Unlike some large-scale US and UK studies (Ofcom, 2013; Wartella et al., 2014), a clear picture of the digital experiences of young children in Canada is largely unknown and this applies to kindergartens. Kindergarten in Canada is provincially mandated with programmes varying in terms of half-day or full-day delivery models, and the age of entry differing from 3 to 4 years. Kindergarten is not mandatory in any province within Canada. Some insights into the Canadian ECE landscape can be garnered from looking at the findings from a study of kindergarten to grade 12 teachers and school administrators (Johnson et al., 2016). Here, the researchers examined the ways in which networked technologies (defined as any device that can connect to the internet) impacted teachers and their teaching practices. Approximately 4,000 kindergarten to grade 12 teachers and school administrators participated and the findings revealed that the majority were connected to the internet, with 97% having networked devices in their classrooms. Teachers also shared a view of the importance of digital literacy and self-confidence in their own abilities to teach digital literacy skills. The report defines digital literacy as:

including searching for online information; verifying that online information is credi-
ble/relevant/accurate; understanding online privacy issues and settings; appropriate
online behaviour; staying safe online; dealing with cyberbullying; deconstruct-
ing various messages embedded in the online environment; and understanding
how organizations collect and use personal information online. (Johnson et al.,
2016: 3)

However, teachers were more likely to adopt technologies that mirror existing teaching practices (e.g. smartboards versus using social media). Teachers also reported using
networked technologies to deliver innovative content or have students create content. Few reported encouraging students to write computer code (just over 6%) and
those who reported *that writing code was not applicable* at a specific grade level escalated
from 21% at secondary level and 25% at elementary to 59% at the kindergarten level.
Importantly, Johnson and his colleagues et al. study (2016) highlights that students'
age appears to impact teachers' practices. For example, and in addition to the infre-
quent coding opportunities noted above, kindergarten teachers were also more likely
to restrict personal device use in the classroom for educational purposes. Other differences were notable in terms of the types of and frequency that various platforms
were accessed by the varied levels of teachers (e.g. few kindergarten teachers reported
using video games for students to create content), and educator confidence in teaching specific digital literacy skills. Overall, kindergarten teachers indicated the lowest
confidence levels and were less likely than elementary and secondary teachers to use
technologies to engage their students in learning. Interestingly, tablets are most often
supplied to kindergarten teachers by their schools (71%) who report a significant use of
those tablets (39% versus 30% of elementary teachers and 18% of secondary teachers).
Given the presence of tablets in many kindergarten classrooms and the abundance of
coding apps for this age group, the infrequency of coding opportunities seems somewhat surprising.

   Moreover, because some of the findings on teaching practices are generally reported
under the umbrella term elementary (kindergarten to grade 6), it is not clear *how* or *if*
pedagogies significantly differ within kindergarten (or with even younger children).
And although the MediaSmarts report provides some information on the Canadian
landscape of kindergarten to grade 12 classrooms, a comparable study on the
full spectrum of ECE classrooms does not exist. Thus, a complete understanding of
the ways in which digital technologies and tablets specifically are utilised within ECE
pedagogies is not clearly understood in Canada. What impact, if any, do teachers'
knowledge and beliefs regarding technology have on the ways in which tablets are
integrated within classrooms? Are there structural barriers in ECE that impact digital
practices?

TABLET INTEGRATION AND EDUCATORS' PERCEPTIONS

Several frameworks are used to examine the ways in which technology integration occurs within educational contexts. Some of these frameworks focus on examining teachers' levels of technology integration, such as Puentedura's (2009) Substitution, Augmentation, Modification and Redefinition (SAMR) model. The SAMR model helps to examine whether technology is being used to enhance or transform teaching practices, and some researchers indicate that teachers tend to use iPads for enhancement more so than transforming lessons (Geer et al., 2017). However, the iPad is still considered somewhat of a 'new technology' and perhaps the innovative ways in which tablets can be combined with authentic student-centred learning have not yet been fully explored (Harwood et al., 2015; Murray and Olcese, 2011).

Another often used framework, the TPACK, places Lee Shulman's idea of pedagogical content knowledge within a technological context (Shulman, 1986, 1987). The TPACK examines teachers' knowledge in terms of a technological, pedagogical and content knowledge framework (Koehler and Mishra, 2009). TPACK supports the understanding that to make optimal use of technology in the classroom, teachers need a dynamic knowledge not only of teaching (pedagogical knowledge) and of their topic areas (content knowledge), but also of the technology they will be using, and the capabilities and limitations of that technology. TPACK also builds on the three strands of knowledge to encompass the connections and interactions between them, and how teachers apply them in the classroom (Koehler and Mishra, 2009).

Teachers who have completed their training prior to the current generation of technology may find it challenging to develop adequate technological knowledge and digital pedagogical expertise. Additionally, a 'one-size-fits-all' approach for integrating technology is not appropriate (Koehler and Mishra, 2009), given that the use of technology needs to be customised to the children, the environment and the budget of the classroom.

What specific knowledge is needed to prepare for teaching with technology? Researchers suggest that teachers need the ability to critically select software and hardware that has the capability of supporting their curricular goals, as well as an understanding of how they will benefit from gaining personal experience with the technology they intend to use (Blackwell et al., 2016; McKenney and Voogt, 2017). Thinking critically about the use of technology, the formats in which the technology will be used (e.g. small groups, individually, teacher-child), the implementation to support learning for diverse children, the opportunities for augmenting learning provided by technology, and the theory behind integrating the technology, are also key skills for technology integration (McKenney and Voogt, 2017).

Teachers' belief in the value and usefulness of technology for supporting children's learning is one of the strongest predictors of the use of technology (Blackwell et al., 2016; Liu et al., 2016). Thus, teachers' attitudes towards technology, openness to change, confidence, professional development and school or institutional support for the use of technology are significant factors (Blackwell et al., 2016; Vannatta and Fordham, 2004).

REFLECTIVE TASK

- Reflect on your current tablet/digital technology integration. Consider the level of TPACK your pedagogy falls within. Devise methods to move toward increasing your technology pedagogical and content knowledge.

CASE STUDY 12.1: THE IMPACT OF TEACHERS' BELIEFS AND PRACTICES ON THE USE OF DIGITAL TECHNOLOGY IN THE CLASSROOM

Teachers act as a gateway for the many experiences that unfold within ECE classrooms. Principally, teachers' perceptions of the role of digital technologies within children's learning experiences directly impact on how technology gets 'taken up' in practice. Quality practices matter. Our goal was to examine the beliefs and practices of teachers in varied ECE classrooms throughout a region of southern Ontario, Canada. We were curious about beliefs and actual practices as well as the potential of extrinsic barriers such as limited budgets and resources that might factor into technology integration within ECE classrooms (only the findings related to beliefs and practices are discussed in this chapter). Certainly, previous research has established that teachers' positive beliefs about children's learning from technology have a significant influence on the actual use of technology within early years classrooms (Blackwell et al., 2014). Our project entailed providing tablets and professional development training for ECE teachers, a new experience for many of the 26 educators.

Over the period of a year, we surveyed the teachers, completed three one-hour observational visits of their classrooms and encouraged the teachers to share stories and reflections on a secure blog site. The first survey was informed by the work of Blackwell et al. (2014); as such, we queried the teachers' existing digital practices, comfort levels with technology and existing beliefs in relation to technology and children's learning. The second survey was implemented toward the end of the study and at this point we hoped to gauge teachers' (perhaps changed) practices and perceived effectiveness with integrating tablets in their classrooms after the year. Once again, some of these final questions were informed by Blackwell et al.'s study, whilst others queried things such as whether teachers developed digital policies throughout the year, and how effective were the training and support components we provided as part of the project. Additionally, several questions were purposefully utilised as a means of unearthing what quality integration practices entail, that is enhancement of teaching practices or transformation (e.g. how children were engaged with the tablet, what digital practices benefitted the children).

Project budgetary constraints meant only one tablet with pre-selected apps was provided to each of the teachers, thus the ratio of tablets to children was low in most of the classrooms (e.g. one tablet for upwards of 8 to 12 children). And although some teachers reported having one or two tablets already present in their classrooms, typically these devices were used by the teachers for administration and reporting purposes or as rewards for children's behaviour. Only one teacher reported using the tablets consistently with children at the outset of the project. However, the initial observational visit to this class revealed that the tablet contained low-level gaming apps and more of a chaotic pedagogical approach (e.g. apps were chosen because they were free and not for any instructional or intentional purpose). The apps provided on the project tablets were pre-selected by the research team. These apps tended to be open-ended and creative with clear instructional goals (e.g. Explain Everything, Sock Puppets, Garageband). This start-up app package and any additional apps that were provided throughout the year were similarly vetted, utilising specific criteria to determine quality (Harwood, 2014).

The observational component of the study involved two of the researchers conducting three one-hour classroom visits throughout the year in each of the 26 teachers' classrooms (i.e. September–October, February and May). During these visits, digital photos of the classroom environment were taken and a checklist was administered. Here, we focused our observations on all technologies, thus we scanned the environment for all digital practices that were evident. The checklist was devised to ensure consistency amongst the observers and required each researcher to note and provide qualifying comments related to children's access to technology, specific activities where technology was incorporated, children's learning domains where digital technologies were incorporated, and any use of digital technologies for administrative support (e.g. communicating with parents). Teachers were also invited to participate on a secure blog site where they could share ideas and stories, and ask questions of one another and the research team.

As part of the study, teachers were also provided with a series of ongoing professional development and training sessions, such as tablet orientation, teaching

(Continued)

(Continued)

approaches to integrating tablets, using advanced features of the tablet within teaching, enhancing language and literacy skills using tablets, and sustainability protocols (e.g. finding and evaluating apps, data management and organisation). Teachers also had access to ongoing support from an educational technology specialist throughout the entire project year.

TEACHERS' BELIEFS IMPACT PRACTICE

At the outset of the project, most teachers self-narrated a pedagogical approach that was centred on co-constructing and partnering children's learning, development and play. Given the policy frameworks guiding Ontario teachers of young children and the explicit focus on play and child-directed learning within those documents (Ontario Ministry of Education, 2007, 2014, 2016), it is not surprising that most teachers, like Sasha here from our study (all names are pseudonyms), reported feeling like a competent expert in co-constructed and partnership-learning approaches:

> Learning opportunities can be created in every part of the day and during every activity throughout the day. The best lessons are not planned, but stumbled upon during play when a question is asked. A teacher can foster these learning opportunities by creating a caring, inclusive and explorational environment. (Sasha)

Interestingly, similar confidence with digital practices was not evident in the teachers' responses at the outset of the study:

> I would definitely need tech support, learning how to download the apps, etc. I am concerned that the children will rely on the iPad instead of interacting with others during play. (Jan)

These 26 classrooms and teachers had little exposure to digital technologies within their respective programmes, and most shared that their existing equipment (often a lone computer) tended to be outdated or in disrepair. Within their respective teaching practices, most described themselves as a novice or comfortable beginner with respect to using 'new technologies' within pedagogy (e.g. social media sites such as Tumblr, Facebook, Twitter, Pinterest, etc. and/or technological tools such as tablets, smartphones). Use of any technology, even digital cameras, tended to be conducted on an ad hoc basis and was not always clearly connected to overall curricular and learning goals. At the outset of the project, many teachers narrated somewhat cautionary views on the role of technology within ECE:

> Currently we do not use technological tools in our age group but [if we did] it would have to be with strict adult guidance when introduced. (Allison)

After the year-long use of tablets within teaching practices, the teachers shared a common view of a technology-infused world as being part of young children's current reality. Many of the teachers foresaw a general need for digital technologies and pedagogies that were facilitated and supported within ECE classrooms. The teachers shared that the advantages of integrating tablets into the classroom included access to unlimited information, learning benefits for children in curricular areas such as literacy, language and maths, and benefiting children's problem-solving skill development. Teachers also reported that children learned negotiating skills and self-regulation capabilities, particularly in relation to having to wait for a turn with the tablet or create classroom rules on ways of sharing the device. The primary caution disclosed by the teachers was a concern that 21st-century technologies (such as the tablet) could detract children from other types of play and social interaction:

> The children cannot read yet and some do not have access to this technology making them feel inadequate. We do not want it to be consuming all our time with the children. Play with peers is so important and an iPad tends to be a 'one person' thing. It is hard to share. (Izzy)

Overwhelmingly, teachers reported feeling more comfortable using technologies within their practice as the year progressed, but remained somewhat cautious about the idea of technology integration in ECE classrooms.

> I think it's great that children are getting the opportunity to get familiar with technology but there needs to be a fine balance between regular play and technology. (Kathy)

SHIFTING DIGITAL PRACTICES

Throughout the year-long project, the degree of integration of the tablet within teaching practices varied greatly amongst the 26 teachers. The teachers who had developed higher levels of comfort with the tool displayed the greatest degree of integration of the device within teaching practice. These teachers tended to view technology most favourably and adapted strategies such as keeping the tablets always accessible to the children, encouraging independent child use of the tablet, and integrating the device within all curricular and play opportunities.

By way of illustration of transformative practices, one teacher introduced her 3- and 4-year-old children to stop-motion animation using the tablet midway through the project. Another teacher experimented with Quick Response (QR) codes to connect a family's heritage and pictures of their travels to Saudi Arabia to the children's explorations in the classroom. Some teachers were more experimental than others, flexibly responding to the children within their classrooms:

(Continued)

(Continued)

> Children loved to explore the apps on their own and often went through phases of which apps they preferred the most. The iPad was also used as a tool to document the children's learning opportunities in the classroom. We often used the iPad to enhance children's enquiries, for example looking up videos on how things were made, etc. The iPad was also very helpful when working with children that were new to the programme and ESL [English as a second language] children because it was a familiar tool to them. (Sierra)

Other teachers reported finding specific uses for the tablet to facilitate communication with families, integrate new children to a classroom, support learning for a child with special needs, or to connect home languages (e.g. various Indigenous languages, French, Hindi) to the dominant literacies of the classroom (i.e. English). Irrespective of these examples of shifting practices, overwhelmingly teachers remained rooted to integrating the tablet within practices that focused on language and literacy, as well as mathematical thinking and numeracy. Perhaps, this is reflective of the apps included or the nature of the professional development sessions provided. And conceivably, digital practices that encompass the arts, social studies, health and well-being, scientific thinking, and so on, may require a concerted focus in teacher training and research. However, the finding does hint at the challenges and complexities with shifting digital practices within early childhood education and the continued pedagogical separation of play and digital play (Edwards, 2013a).

Another way in which digital practices changed was evidenced within the classroom environment itself. In general, a positive perception of the role of technology in children's learning and play impacted how the tablet was positioned in the classroom. For example, Jaclyn foresaw a role for technology within all aspects of learning and play, positioning the tablet centrally within her classroom and inviting children to access the device at their discretion (Figure 12.1).

Figure 12.1   Jaclyn's classroom

Conversely, educators with more cautionary views of technology within ECE contexts tended to prefer teacher-directed activities and more structured pedagogical approaches; teaching practices were somewhat modified or augmented with the tablet. Thus, within these classroom environments the tablet was often out of reach of children until such time that an activity was initiated. For example, at the end of the year-long project, Sasha emphasised her use of the tablet for documenting children's learning, individualising instruction, and alluded to the difficulties of managing children's conflicts that arose over the tablet. Sasha reported that she preferred most often using the tablet within teacher-directed/guided activities where the educator makes most of the decisions related to the tablet and controls its use (Figure 12.2). Perhaps, once again, the environment itself was reflective of the teachers' ideological separation of play and digital play, and new ways of thinking about play as a hybrid (Marsh, 2010) of online/offline, concrete/virtual, formal/informal engagements is needed.

Figure 12.2   Sasha's approach

REFLECTIVE TASKS

- Using the SAMR framework, create a model of a modified or redefined task. For example, create a digital narrative using digital storytelling software (e.g. iMovie, Toontastic-3D, Puppet Pals) and combine video, audio, text and/or music. Then, devise ways for your students to replicate the task.
- Rebrand the role of the tablet in the classroom. Introduce it as a tool for learning, for enquiry. Make the device accessible to your students; try utilising the tablet for more student-centred activities. Use your tablet to capture students' learning in the classroom.

SUMMARY

This chapter provided some insight into how Canadian ECE teachers, when supported, can develop authentic and valuable means of implementing tablets into their programmes. Overall, the integration of tablets did foster new ways of teaching and learning, especially for those teachers who perceived great value in using digital technologies within young children's lives.

In these ECE classrooms, few teachers had prior exposure to tablet use. Although the teachers narrated a view of technology as being part of the 21st-century child's context, these classrooms could be characterised as 'missing the boat' regarding technology integration (Parette et al., 2010). Like Leonard's (2013) dissertation study of two educators' journey of integrating tablets, we also found a cautious approach to integration amongst the teachers, one that was focused on somewhat narrow curricular areas (i.e. literacy and maths) and a need for continual support. Play, learning and digital play were often construed as separate constructs.

Time constraints (e.g. a lack of time for teachers to learn or play with new apps), poor internet connectivity and a lack of resources (e.g. low number of tablets, insufficient funds to purchase apps) acted as barriers to digital practice. Yet, despite these barriers, with prolonged involvement with the devices and ongoing professional development and coaching, the teacher's own efficacy in utilising tablets within their teaching practice improved.

The study was limited in terms of the self-report method and limited hours of observations conducted by the researchers. Thus, a more fulsome picture of actual teaching practices is needed to fully understand the relationship between tablets and ECE pedagogies. Still, what we offer here are exploratory insights and an insider view of teachers' thoughts, beliefs and actual experiences as they navigated the integration of tablets within pedagogies. Given that the teacher is the greatest influence on technology integration (Liu et al., 2016), understanding these complex and concomitant factors is greatly needed and would help to challenge some of the existing assumptions about tablets and young children (Kucirkova, 2014). Technology integration in ECE is complex and worthy of further exploration to examine how the context, the teacher's perceptions, beliefs and experiences intermingle to impact digital practices.

KEY POINTS TO REMEMBER

- When introducing iPads or similar devices to ECE contexts, it is important to develop an infrastructure for their implementation.
- Educator beliefs surrounding technology impact the ECE pedagogical approaches taken with tablets.
- Tablets offer opportunities for novel ways to provoke children's interests and learning, support their individual learning needs and connect with families.

POINTS FOR DISCUSSION

- In terms of tablet integration, what supports are needed to ensure quality experiences for young children?
- What steps can you take to bypass potential barriers to tablet integration in early childhood contexts and settings?
- How can you build a support network for ongoing tablet training, professional development and mentoring?

FURTHER READING

Aronin, S. and Floyd, K. K. (2013) Using an iPad in inclusive preschool classrooms to introduce STEM concepts. *Teaching Exceptional Children*, 45 (4): 34–39.

Cheung, W. S., Hew, K. F. and Chua, S. L. (2016) What information communication technology (ICT) had been used in preschool education during the recent decade? In *Proceedings of EdMedia: World Conference on Educational Media and Technology*, pp. 914–920, Vancouver, June. Waynesville, NC: Association for the Advancement of Computing in Education (AACE).

Fleer, M. (2017) *Digital playworlds* in an Australian context: supporting double subjectivity. In T. Bruce, P. Hakkarainen and M. Bredikyte (eds) *The Routledge International Handbook of Early Childhood Play*. Oxon: Routledge, pp. 289–304.

USEFUL WEBSITES

Kathy Schrock's iPads4Learning: www.ipads4teaching.net
Media Smarts: http://mediasmarts.ca
ReBrand Digital Citizenship: www.tanyaavrith.com

REFERENCES

Blackwell, C., Lauricella, A. and Wartella, E. (2014) Factors influencing digital technology use in early childhood education. *Computers and Education, 77*: 82–90.

Blackwell, C., Lauricella, A. and Wartella, E. (2016) The influence of TPACK contextual factors on early childhood educators' tablet use. *Computers and Education, 98*: 57–69.

Edwards, S. (2013a) Digital play in the early years: a contextual response to the problem of integrating technologies and play-based pedagogies in the early childhood curriculum. *European Early Childhood Education Research Journal, 21* (2): 199–212.

Edwards, S. (2013b) Post-industrial play: understanding the relationship between traditional and converged forms of play in the early years. In A. Burke and J. Marsh (eds) *Children's Virtual Worlds: Culture, Learning and Participation*. New York: Peter Lang, pp. 10–25.

Geer, R., White, B., Zeegers, Y., Au, W. and Barnes, A. (2017) Emerging pedagogies for the use of iPads in schools. *British Journal of Educational Technology*, 48 (2): 490–498.

Harwood, D. (2014) The digital world and young children. *ChildLinks*, 3: 2–8.

Harwood, D. (ed.) (2017) *Crayons and iPads: Learning and Teaching of Young Children in the Digital World*. London: Sage.

Harwood, D., Bajovic, M., Woloshyn, V., Di Cesare, D. M., Lane, L. and Scott, K. (2015) Intersecting spaces in early childhood education: inquiry-based pedagogy and tablets. *The International Journal of Holistic Early Learning and Development*, 1: 53–67.

Hourcade, J. P., Mascher, S. L., Wu, D. and Pantoja, L. (2015) Look, my baby is using an iPad! An analysis of YouTube videos of infants and toddlers using tablets. In CHI' 15: Proceedings of the 33rd Annual ACM Conference on Human Factors in Computing Systems, pp. 1915–1924, Seoul, April.

Johnson, M., Riel, R. and Froese-Germain, B. (2016) *Connected to Learn: Teachers' Experiences with Networked Technologies in the Classroom*. Ottawa, ON: MediaSmarts/Canadian Teachers' Federation. Available at: http://mediasmarts.ca/research-policy/young-cana-dians-wired-world-phase-iii-connected-learn (accessed 27 June 2017).

Koehler, M. and Mishra, P. (2009) What is technological pedagogical content knowledge? *Contemporary Issues in Technology and Teacher Education*, 9 (1): 60–70.

Kucirkova, N. (2014) iPads in early education: separating assumptions and evidence. *Frontiers in Education*, 5: 1–3.

Leonard, J. A. (2013) *How early childhood educators are initially integrating tablet technology in the curriculum*. PhD thesis, Saint Louis University.

Liu, M., Navarrete, C. C., Scordino, R., Kang, J., Ko, Y. and Lim, M. (2016) Examining teach-ers' use of iPads: comfort level, perception, and use. *Journal of Research on Technology in Education*, 48 (3): 159–180.

McKenney, S. and Voogt, J. (2017) Expert views on TPACK for early literacy: priorities for teacher education. *Australasian Journal of Educational Technology*, 33 (5): 1–14.

Macleans (2017) Keep kids away from screens, experts urge. *The Canadian Press*, 1 June. Available at: www.macleans.ca/news/keep-young-kids-away-from-screens-experts-urge (accessed 27 June 2017).

Marsh, J. (2010) Young children's play in online virtual worlds. *Journal of Early Childhood Research*, 8 (1): 23–39.

Murray, O. T. and Olcese, N. R. (2011) Teaching and learning with iPads, ready or not? *TechTrends*, 55 (6): 42–48.

Ofcom (2013) *Children and Parents: Media Use and Attitudes Report*. London: Ofcom. Available at: http://stakeholders.ofcom.org.uk/market-data-research/other/research-publications/childrens/children-parents-oct-2013 (accessed 27 June 2017).

Ontario Ministry of Education (2007) *Early Learning for Every Child Today: A Framework for Ontario Early Childhood Settings*. Toronto, ON: Queen's Printer for Ontario.

Ontario Ministry of Education (2014) *How Does Learning Happen? Ontario's Pedagogy for the Early Years*. Toronto, ON: Queen's Printer for Ontario.

Ontario Ministry of Education (2016) *Full Day Early Learning Kindergarten Program*. Toronto, ON: Queen's Printer for Ontario.

Palmer, S. (2015) *Toxic Childhood: How the Modern World is Damaging Our Children and What We Can Do About It* (new edn). London: Orion.

Parette, H. P., Quesenberry, A. C. and Blum, C. (2010) Missing the boat with technology usage in early childhood settings: a 21st century view of developmentally appropriate practice. *Early Childhood Education Journal, 37* (5): 335–343.

Plowman, L., Stephen, C. and McPake, J. (2010) *Growing Up with Technology: Young Children Learning in a Digital World*. London: Routledge.

Plowman, L., Stevenson, O., Stephen, C. and McPake, J. (2012) Preschool children's learning with technology at home. *Computers and Education, 59* (1): 30–37.

Puentedura, R. R. (2009) SAMR: A contextualized introduction. Available at: www.hippasus.com/rrpweblog/archives/2013/10/25/SAMRAContextualizedIntroduction.pdf (accessed 27 June 2017).

Shulman, L. (1986) Those who understand: knowledge growth in teaching. *Educational Researcher, 15* (2): 4–14.

Shulman, L. (1987) Knowledge and teaching: foundations of the new reform. *Harvard Educational Review, 57* (1): 1–22.

Steeves, V. (2014) *Young Canadians in a Wired World, Phase III: Life Online* (report). Ottawa, ON: MediaSmarts. Available at: http://mediasmarts.ca/research-policy (accessed 27 June 2017).

Stephen, C. and Plowman, L. (2014) Digital play. In L. Booker, M. Blaise and S. Edward (eds) *The Sage Handbook of Play and Learning in Early Childhood*. London: Sage.

Vannatta, R. and Fordham, N. (2004) Teacher dispositions as predictors of classroom technology use. *Journal of Research on Technology in Education, 36* (3): 253–271.

Wartella, E., Rideout, V., Lauricella, A. R. and Connell, S. L. (2014) Parenting in the age of digital technology (report). *Centre on Media and Human Development, School of Communication, Northwestern University*. Available at: http://cmhd.northwestern.edu/wp-content/uploads/2015/06/ParentingAgeDigitalTechnology.REVISED.FINAL_.2014.pdf (accessed 27 June 2017).

13

MULTIMODAL MEDIA PRODUCTION

CHILDREN'S MEANING MAKING WHEN PRODUCING ANIMATION IN A PLAY-BASED PEDAGOGY

MARI-ANN LETNES

CHAPTER OVERVIEW

This chapter is based on a research project on digital literacy in Norwegian kindergartens (see Chapter 5 for information on the Norwegian context). The focus of this study was the qualities related to children's play with aesthetic form and content during the creation of multimodal media products, such as animated films using digital tools. Data was collected in a kindergarten with six boys aged between 5 and 6 years, and two staff members (practitioners) collaborating to create an animated film. The research employed participant observations to provide a detailed and qualitative description. The chapter discusses three aspects of the study where children and adults created three multimodal texts based on different encounters with art using digital tools. The texts are a picture book, a digital story and an animated film.

This chapter aims to help you understand:

- a methodology that enables practitioners to use digital technology in creative projects in play-based pedagogy
- how to differentiate five different key aspects of children's multimodal media production: re-presentation, preparation, art meeting, story board and editing (Figure 13.1)
- how play and playfulness are important in developing children's creative processes
- how children can produce media products, like animated films, in light of their interest in these products, with the appropriate support.

INTRODUCTION

Creating and experiencing cultural expression is a dialogical process involving meaning making. This experience provides material for children's play, education and learning throughout their lifetime. Through self-expression, we gain a sense of self-awareness that strengthens our faith in our abilities. In a digital age, gaining the knowledge and skills to use digital tools for play is a central part of children's lives. In English literature, and media, digital technology is frequently associated with the concept of literacy, which involves the ability to read and write and the ability to use language proficiently (Marsh, 2016). Meaning is created, distributed, received, interpreted and reformulated through various forms of representation and communicative modes, and not merely through verbal language. As a result, a field addressing digital and multimodal expression has emerged through which children create meaning (Kress and Jewitt, 2003). Early childhood education represents the starting point for what is described as a lifelong learning process, and it is important and interesting to explore how early childhood education can include the use of digital tools in children's play-based pedagogical practice. Furthermore, through art, children have the opportunity to create, to be inspired and to express themselves. Encountering art expression is therefore an important catalyst in children's own cultural expression. Thus, this chapter is based on Norwegian early childhood education where playful learning, experiencing media products, digital technology and art expressions are of fundamental importance, and examines the following question:

> How do children negotiate meaning when they play with form and content in the process of making an animated film?

This project is based on a *socio-cultural* approach to play, knowledge, education and learning. In that sense, it is proposed that when a child collaborates to make an animation, s/he plays an active role in the social interaction, working with practitioners and peers to create a mutual construction of meaning. Using this approach, children and practitioners build a mutual understanding that leads to a shared knowledge base and this is done through socially situated collaboration. In addition to this, the children try out and play with tools and signs to mediate the meaning they want to communicate to the world.

PLAY AND PLAYFULNESS

All play practitioners share an intuitive belief that play benefits children (Howard and McInnes, 2013). In working with children, it is easy to see, when they play, that they are often happy, active, socialise with other children, practise different skills and problem solve – all valuable skills for children at this point in time and in informing their later life. To define and conceptualise play and the distinctions between different categories of play in general is difficult. Play has been endlessly debated, with a unified definition yet to be agreed (Howard and McInnes, 2013; Sandseter, 2010). However, a common characteristic of play is that it is inner directed and that the activity is a process of greater significance than the end goal. Another important aspect of play is that the activity gives children the experience of arousal, experimentation, fun, joy and lightheartedness (Sutton-Smith, 1997). Sutton-Smith (1997) defines seven terms that cover the different types of strategies used to talk about and through play: play as progress, play as fate, play as power, play as identity, imaginary play, play as frivolous, and the rhetoric of the self. When children play, they create their world in the moment, often along with other children, with their body, with materials and objects around them, with sounds and singing, movement, words and stories (Hovik, 2014). In many ways, play creates a way for the child to make sense of their world (Dau, 1999). The internal, affective qualities of play can be the most important perspective in terms of development and learning (Howard and McInnes, 2013). Key terms in this respect include enthusiasm, motivation and a willingness to engage in play.

AESTHETIC EXPERIENCE

Both the production and reception of art or multimodal media products involves *aesthetic experience* in one form or another. Aesthetic experience can be generated by two aspects of the activity. One concerns the experience the child gains using art, whilst the other is about the aesthetic experience the child gains when expressing themselves through creative activities. The aesthetic experience assimilated by creative activities is a transformative process. According to Dewey, experience is about our interaction with nature and the environment and is something we 'do and review' (Dewey, 1934). Dewey is primarily associated with activity pedagogy, a pedagogy that argues that the child must be active in order to learn. Dewey had a strong focus on experience as the fundamental aspect of our construction of knowledge. With Dewey, knowledge is proactive and anticipates and guides our adaptation to future experiences and interactions with the environment. He is frequently associated with the phrase, 'learning by doing, and reflecting'; and he believed that the interaction between the child's activities and the results of this activity informs the child's experience and is the basis for knowledge construction.

MULTIMODALITY

When we communicate and interact with each other, we use different modes to communicate meaning; we don't just communicate through writing (which is one mode) but also through speaking, gesture, gaze and visual forms (which are many modes). Meaning making extends beyond the written and spoken word and this enhances the semiotic process, offering a multimodal opportunity to communicate meaning. Kress and van Leeuwen (2001) argue that the different modalities appearing in a multimodal text must be seen in context with each other. Kress and van Leeuwen claim that digital tools offer opportunities to consider whether to use a single modality or a multimodal approach to express and communicate meaning. They argue that, in traditional linguistics, which work through double articulation, when a message is articulated as a form and as a meaning, multimodal texts offer multiple articulations.

Undoubtedly, children consume a great number of multimodal media products. They watch animated films, look at picture books and play videogames. Consequently, it is important that children experience how to make multimodal media productions in order to understand the process. In this way, children get to be a producer and a consumer of a multimodal media product.

ANIMATION WORKSHOP: CHILDREN'S ENGAGEMENT IN MEDIA PRODUCTION

Storytelling has several functions in educational practice (Klerfelt, 2007). Multimodal media products are complex in nature. The production process for multimodal stories must be demonstrated to children in stages. By segmenting the process, children focus on stages of the process rather than on the product. Dividing up the creative process into smaller units requires a practitioner to master each part of the whole. In this way, the practitioner explains and guides the child through each stage. The practitioner can then structure the tasks to reduce its complexity, and assist the child with structuring resources. Through this research project, the model 'Children's multimodal media production' was designed. This model shows five main aspects with several supportive features in a transformation circle. The five main aspects of children's production of multimodal media products are: preparation, art meeting, storyboard, editing and representation (see Figure 13.1).

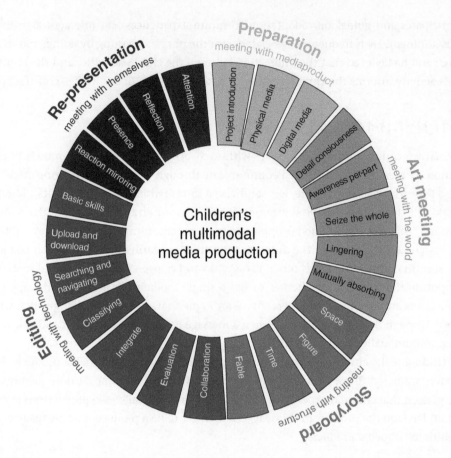

Figure 13.1   Five main aspects in children's multimodal media production (Letnes, 2014)

In the following, I would like to present these five aspects and include examples of how children construct and discuss the different components of the story they are creating.

PREPARATION: MEETING WITH MULTIMEDIA PRODUCTS

Practitioners' preparation for children's play and learning is about offering children various media and resources as tools to use as they wish. By using audio, pictures, video and text, children can be inspired and engaged in different ways. The goal for the activities may be modified, extended and/or reoriented by both the children and the practitioner (Selander and Kress, 2012). Motivation is crucial for children's dedication, perseverance and endurance in different activities. It is important that there is sufficient preparation time for projects and that the children can participate in the preparation stage. By allowing the children to participate in this early stage, they get the opportunity to shape the project in a way that is meaningful and relevant to them. In preparation for the animated film, the children initially worked with the theme 'pirates'. In the narrative in case study 13.1, the conversation is centred around what is needed for a pirate movie.

CASE STUDY 13.1: PIRATES

Eric and the other children are gathered in a small group in the middle of the room to work on the animation project. They gather in front of a piece of white cardboard that the practitioner has placed in front of the children. She asks them what she has with her, and the children shout out that they can see that it is *a stage.*

'That's right', Mari-Ann says and smiles at them. 'Maybe we should make a pirate movie?' The children nod.

'What we need is a stage', Mari-Ann continues, whilst pointing at the stage.

'We should create one like that.' Tara is smiling and pointing to a little figure made of a roll of toilet paper, a ball and pipe cleaners that Mari-Ann is holding in her hand.

'Yes, all of you have to make your own pirate', says Mari-Ann, nodding her head and smiling at the children.

'That's what I knew.' Tara is smiling and looking confidently at the other children.

'But do you think that this little figure is similar to a pirate?' Mari-Ann asks the children, whilst holding the cardboard figure up so the children are able to see it better.

'No', the children say in unison whilst shaking their heads.

'He has no sword and you haven't painted him black as a pirate', Eric says.

'No, I haven't done that', Mari-Ann responds and smiles at Eric.

'And he has no hat, pirates do have pirate hats', Vidar eagerly explains.

'We need to paint a pirate ship', Vidar proposes, whilst pointing at the stage background.

'Indeed, we need a pirate ship, but we need to make a pirate ship', Mari-Ann says.

In the conversation in case study 13.1, the practitioner talks to the children about what is needed to create an animation about pirates. Already, the children, aged 5, have genre expertise. The children play with the idea of a pirate movie and their play becomes an imaginary (Sutton-Smith, 1997) activity. They know which colours are dominant in a pirate movie, which effects and props you need and how the scenery should be designed for the pirate theme. Note that colours also communicate meaning and the children participate in discussions related to colour and meaning. The children are eager to tell the practitioner what is needed in a pirate film, and the practitioner wants the children to make everything they need themselves.

With this introduction to the film-making process, the children get aesthetic experi-ence and play with form and content in order to communicate that this is a 'pirate movie' (see Figure 13.2).

Figure 13.2   Props for the pirate movie

REFLECTIVE TASK

Reflect on case study 13.1 and consider:

a   The role of the adult in the process, with an emphasis on how the adult allowed the
     children to participate in the preparation stages of the project.
b   How children were given the opportunity to shape the project in a direction that is
     meaningful and relevant to them.

ART MEETING: MEETING WITH THE WORLD

The different artistic expressions that served as inspiration for the media products that the children made during the research project were in a range of different modalities: vis-ual, auditory and texts of our cultural heritage. An art meeting is an event where children and art interact in a broad sense (Letnes, 2013; Tollefsen et al., 1997). A meeting with art embodies a complex relationship between the creator of the work, the artwork itself and an interpretation of the worldly phenomena that the art work represents. Such a meeting generates aesthetic reflection as the children construct meaning whilst they experience the expression of art. Letting children meet with and talk about art as a basis for their own expressions, creates a situation where art opens up children's encounters with the world. Each child feels their own individual and personal experiences in the guise of various forms of art. As part of this project, the kindergarten went on an excursion to a music museum named 'Rockheim', the national museum of popular music which presents Norwegian pop and rock. When the children walked around the museum, they talked about and recognised the different moods and emotions that music expresses. The children discussed how scary music sounds, how nice calm music sounds, and so on. In this example, sound was the mode of discussion, with the children playing with different sound effects in the museum's workshop. The children were allowed to make music with computers and garage bands. People experience art in the context of their own lives. When children hear and interpret different forms of musical expression, they do so with their own life experiences in mind. The music offered a form of engagement and inspiration for the film-making process that lay ahead.

CASE STUDY 13.2: STORYBOARD – MEETING WITH STRUCTURE

In working with storyboards, children have a way to structure and create an outline for their story. The purpose is to structure different elements in a story to make it work logically and to be communicative. In an animated film, different elements from different semiotic sign systems are brought together and structured in a meaningful whole.

In the verbal structuring process, the children gain an experience with narrative structure, dialogue and plot. The visual aspect of the film is about form, shape, direction, colour, views, size, light, motion and the composition of these. The process regarding the auditory modality is about tempo, tone, rhythm, volume and composition of these elements. Using multimodal media, children play with different aesthetic tools, creating an animated film that is about six pirates who find some treasure. By letting children play with, see and discuss how these components are composed as a whole, they get the opportunity to experience the complexity behind a multimodal media production. Children engage in this process using a playful and imaginative approach. They playfully try out different approaches to progress the story. A visual storyboard offers a tool for the children to create the story for the animation. In this session, the practitioners placed special emphasis on fable, shape, space and time. The storyboard that they worked with was made of brown paper with plastic sleeves (Figure 13.3).

(Continued)

(Continued)

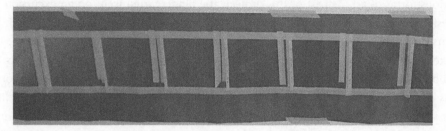

Figure 13.3   The children's brown paper storyboard with plastic sleeves

In this way, the children work dynamically with the storyboard and change the narrative back and forth. In addition to the dynamic element of the storyboard, the plastic pockets offer a visual modality for children who don't yet read and write. By using photographs of different scenic combinations, figures and props, pre-literate children were able to make, create and work with storyboards and scripts. In the narrative below, the six boys discuss the plot of their animation as they look through photographs of the scenes, figures and props. After a while, the practitioner asks what happens at sea and how the pirates find the treasure:

'We must have a map', Vidar says; he looks at the practitioner and then he gets an idea.

'and we must have a bad pirate ship too', he continues as he takes up an image of the pirate ship.

'Yes, we must', the other children answer in a choir; they are very eager. The practitioner also thinks this is a good idea, and she wonders what happens when the bad pirate ship arrives.

'Then we shoot him, bang, bang', Kristian says whilst he is jumping around in the room shooting with an imaginary rifle. The boys are laughing.

In scene 2, they meet another pirate ship and the practitioner summarises the situation – 'this is super dramatic' – the plot's conflict occurs when another pirate ship arrives.

'And that's the bad guy', Vidar explains.

'What's the bad guy's name?' the practitioner wants to know.

'How about cruel ...?' The practitioner waits a moment to let the children finish the sentence.

'Snake Man', Vidar suggests and looks at the other boys.

The practitioner pretends to use a pair of binoculars and says in a feigned voice – 'oh no, oh no, cruel ...

''Snake Man is in sight', Vidar completes.

Figure 13.4 The children's developing storyboard

Through dialogue and interaction, the boys create excitement and add critical points to their story. They discuss the way the movie should start and move forward. They know that almost every movie has a protagonist (hero of the story), and that this protagonist often has an antagonist (an opponent). The antagonist represents or creates the challenge for the protagonist to overcome. This is a common structure in any drama. In the boys' animated film, the six small pirate figures represent six protagonists and cruel Snake Man represents the antagonist that the pirates must overcome.

REFLECTIVE TASK

Reflecting as a researcher on case study 13.2, the story and the main plot are set. The plot should evolve from the ideas of the children, but it is an advantage for the practitioner to ask open-ended questions such as: Where are they? What's happening? Is there someone else? In this way, children can, in a playful way, discuss and progress and create an intriguing story.

Discuss other ways that children may create playful stories using digital devices.

CASE STUDY 13.3: EDITING – MEETING WITH TECHNOLOGY

The boys vary the mood of the film by showing the pirates' journey night and day, at sea and on land, in war and at a party. To create the film's various scenes, different digital tools are used. In this part of the project, the various resources of meaning are brought together through a digital editing process resulting in a composition. It is the digital technology which enables the assembly of the various modalities within a multimodal

(Continued)

(Continued)

media product. Although the plan for the story already exists as an idea in a storyboard, the different elements in the story were changed when the different modalities were brought together.

The boys had more ideas and extended the story as they progressed the work. This is clear in the next narrative. Victor, age 6, and David, age 5, are working together to edit the animation. The practitioner helps them create their animation using a MacBook, iStopMotion and a webcam. The boys are sitting in front of the scene, and create an animated story where two pirate ships have a hostile encounter. One of the ships contains six pirates who represent the six boys, whilst the other ship belongs to cruel Captain Snake Man. Victor looks at the practitioner and shouts out – 'the cruel Captain Snake Man has arrived'; he looks at the storyboard and sees that, in scene two, cruel Snake Man is arriving. Victor smiles and eagerly moves the figures into the film's frame, whilst David takes pictures in iStopMotion (see, for example, Figure 13.5). This activity involves reversible and/or repetitive processes. Through active use of the storyboard, the children get countless opportunities to change the plot and story in the film. They construct meaning again and again. In this way, they reconstruct the film's meaning a number of times.

Figure 13.5   A scene from the pirate movie

'Look, Victor's pirate does like this', David says and bends his head backward to show how the little pirate is standing.

'Yes, he is looking up to see if there is an air plane coming.' Mari-Ann (the practitioner) laughs and looks at the boys when she talks.

'Yes, the plane is about to land on the ship.' David is laughing together with Mari-Ann; Victor takes his pirate and bends his head so the little pirate is looking straight ahead.

'Maybe cruel Snake Man should climb up the ladder', Mari-Ann suggests, and points to the mast in the LEGO ship. Victor moves Cruel Snake Man to the ladder.

'Yea, he climbs up to the top.' Mari-Ann smiles to the boys and points to the lookout tower on the LEGO boat. Victor agrees; he moves cruel Snake Man little by little, whilst David takes the pictures with iStopmotion. The boys film Cruel Snake Man climbing up the ladder. Mari-Ann helps them – 'Oh, now he is hanging by one arm', Mari-Ann says, laughing.

'He almost fell into the ocean', David says and suddenly he freezes. 'Wait a minute', he says, 'why can't somebody fall into the ocean?' He looks directly at Mari-Ann.

'YES, Nils can fall overboard', Victor replies, whilst eagerly stretching the pirate that represents Nils.

'No, it would be wrong', Mari-Ann responds with a serious voice. 'It should be someone who is present now; perhaps Nils will be upset if his character falls into the water. What about your character, David? Maybe your character could fall into the water?' Mari-Ann looks directly at David. David wrinkles his nose a bit; he doesn't want his character to fall into the water.

'OK then, I think we should drop it', Mari-Ann says in a strict voice. David stops for a minute then he changes his mind: 'on the other hand, my pirate can fall into the water' – he pauses and then proceeds – 'because I didn't see where I was walking, so I stumbled and fell into the water', he says, whilst smiling at the others.

The narrative above portrays the boys playing with the story and the characters. They try out different ideas to create an interesting story. Whatever the boys are creating is rooted in their understanding of reality. If somebody falls into the water, it is important to know why he falls in. When David allows his pirate to fall into the water, he constructs a viable explanation of why this is happening. The explanation that makes sense to David is that, if you don't see where you are walking then you could fall and if you are on a boat then you risk falling into the water. This is an example of children's meta-communication during play. The children engage in a playful approach to the creation of their animated film. One minute, the children are playing with their figures and the pirates are flying through the air; the next, the children are deeply focused on film making and stick to the storyboard they created with the rest of the group. They are playful and creative in their suggestions; for example, the idea that a pirate should fall into the water or climb up the ship's mast is both fun and imaginative.

When the children take pictures in iStopmotion, they need guidance from the practitioner. This is an element that the child can't solve for themselves, but may master with guidance from an adult or a more knowledgeable other. Vygotsky (1978) underlines the importance of social interaction in children's learning. He uses the term 'zone of proximal development' for the support and facilitation that an experienced other may give a child to help them move from one developmental stage to another (Vygotsky, 1978). The term is often translated as being a supportive scaffold. The concept of scaffolding can be extended to include children gaining experience with digital tools.

REFLECTIVE TASK

Reflect on case study 13.3 and consider other ways supportive scaffolding may be used to help a child develop their understanding of digital devices.

RE-PRESENTATION: MEETING WITH THEMSELVES

In communicating their re-presentation (in this case an animated film) through various forms of meta-reflection, the children's meta-reflective conversations appear. The animated film was presented to an audience, thus giving the children a voice and the opportunity to 'speak' and to be 'heard'. When the children showed their animated film to the rest of the kindergarten, they were proud and excited. They discussed the different parts of the movie with the audience, pointing at the screen. In this way, they created meaning for themselves and others when they saw the finished product together with their peers. This forms part of a meta-reflective process, with the children communicating what they think about the different parts of the film and how the film was created. It also enables the children to view the film through the eyes of their audience and to gain a sense of mastery and self-efficacy. From an artistic stance, the conversation about the children's artistic creation is of great importance. How this conversation is situated determines children's interpretation of the quality of their product from the audience's perspective, and the audience's reaction to the cinematic experience created by presenting the film on a large screen using a projector.

SUMMARY

The narratives presented above demonstrate that children's meaning making appears in both the animated film and in the conversations and reflections around the creation of the text. Halliday (1978) explores language from an ecological perspective and, through the study of language, he argues that it is language that makes humans social beings. Through social practices, we enter into social relationships. As part of a social practice, the human may reflect on actual and imagined realities and construct several levels of meaning. As a basic principle, interactions with children require adults to recognise their input and to be aware, interested, question and ponder, and to position them as agentic participants in the process.

KEY POINTS TO REMEMBER

- When children play with different ideas in their creation of an animated film, they create their world in the moment. The animation is the children's product, whilst the practitioners' role is to help and guide the children in translating their stories into film.
- By creating an animated film, the children receive experience and knowledge in animation production and processes. This knowledge involves media experience, playing with form and content and developing aesthetic awareness.
- In this, the children are beginning to build their own digital literacy, and finally the children, through the distribution of the animated film, get what might be called *subject-in-the-world knowledge*.

POINTS FOR DISCUSSION

- Discuss how you might contribute to children's digital literacy by using a playful introduction to the creative process.
- Discuss how you might contribute to children's play using different multimodal projects.
- Undertake some one-to-one play sessions with the goal of playing and creating digital multimodal expressions, and some group play sessions with the same goal:
  a   How did these experiences differ?
  b   Identify the benefits and challenges of each multimodal project.

FURTHER READING

Fleer, M. (2016) Theorising digital play: a cultural-historical conceptualisation of children's engagement in imaginary digital situations. *International Research in Early Childhood Education*, 7 (2): 75–90.

This work collectively illustrates a range of play behaviours where a number of important understandings about how young children engage in virtual contexts are given. However, little theoretical work has been directed at determining whether what children do on these devices would constitute play. This article seeks to examine this literature and present a theoretical discussion on what might characterise a cultural-historical conception of digital play, where the essence of digital play for children aged 3–5 years is considered. The analysis and theoretical discussion presented draw attention to the special nature of digital play, as including an imaginary digital situation, the emergence of special forms of digital talk, digital placeholders and digital pivots to support imaginary play, and the intermeshing of digital play and social pretend play.

Thomson, R., Berriman, L. and Bragg, S. (2018) Everyday childhoods: time, technology and documentation. In *Researching Everyday Childhoods: Time, Technology and Documentation in a Digital Age*. London: Bloomsbury, pp.vii–xi.

Researching Everyday Childhoods begins by asking what recent 'post-empirical' and 'post-digital' frameworks can offer researchers of children and young people's lives, particularly in researching and theorising how the digital shapes childhood and youth. The key ideas of time, technology and documentation are then introduced and woven throughout the book's chapters. Research-led, the book is informed by two state-of-the-art empirical studies – 'Face 2 Face' and 'Curating Childhoods' – and links to a dynamic multimedia archive generated by the studies.

Vygotsky, L. S. (1967/2016) Play and its role in the mental development of the child. *Soviet Psychology*, 5: 6–18; *International Research in Early Childhood Education*, 7 (2).

This article by Vygotsky is devoted to the development of play in early childhood. In the original Russian text, Vygotsky uses the word *doshkol'nik* (дошкольник)/preschooler which, according to the Russian educational system, refers to the age of 3 to 6 years. The Russian terms 'preschool' and 'kindergarten' refer to the same age period and therefore are different from the English/Australian usage which refers only to the last year before school. In the text, 'preschool age' and 'preschool child' mean a child aged 3 to 6 years, whilst a 'very young child' is from birth to 3 years.

USEFUL WEBSITES

www.sheffield.ac.uk/education/research/csnl/digilitey
www.sheffield.ac.uk/education/research/csnl/makerspaces
These websites are based on two European-funded research projects and offer a number of ways that technology can be used with young children.

REFERENCES

Dau, E. (1999) *Child's Play: Revisiting Play in Early Childhood Settings*. Sydney, NSW: MacLennan and Petty.

Dewey, J. (1934) *Art as Experience*. New York: Berkley Publishing Group.

Halliday, M. A. K. (1978) *Language as Social Semiotic: The Social Interpretation of Language and Meaning*. London: Edward Arnold.

Hovik, L. (2014) *De røde skoene: et kunstnerisk og teoretisk forskningsprosjekt om teater for de aller minste [The red shoes: an artistic and theoretical research project on theatre for toddlers]*

(Vol. *157*). Trondheim: Norges teknisk-naturvitenskapelige universitet [Norwegian University of Science and Technology].

Howard, J. and McInnes, K. (2013) *The Essence of Play*. Hoboken, NJ: Taylor & Francis.

Klerfelt, A. (2007) *Barns multimediala berättande: en länk mellan mediakultur och pedagogisk praktik*. [*Children's multimedia narrative: a link between media culture and pedagogical practice*.] Gothenburg: Acta Universitatis Gothoburgensis.

Kress, G. and Jewitt, C. (2003) *Multimodal Literacy*. New York: Peter Lang.

Kress, G. and Van Leeuwen, T. (2001) *Multimodal Discourse: The Modes and Media of Contemporary Communication*. London: Arnold Hodder.

Letnes, M.-A. (2013) Barnehagebarns kunstmøte i digitalestetisk praksis. [Preschool children's meeting with art in digital-aesthetic practice.] In A. L. Østern, G. Stavik-Karlsen and E. Angelo (eds) *Kunstpedagogikk og kunskapsutvikling*. [*Art Education and Knowledge Development*.] Oslo: Universitetsforlaget (i produksjon).

Letnes, M.-A. (2014) *Digital dannelse i barnehagen: barnehagebarns meningsskaping i arbeid med multimodal fortelling*. [*Digital building in kindergarten: children's perception of working with multimodal stories*.] Trondheim: Norges teknisk-naturvitenskapelige universitet [Norwegian University of Science and Technology].

Marsh, J. A. (2016) The digital literacy skills and competences of children of pre-school age. *Media Education: Studi, Ricerche, Buone Practice, 7* (2): 197–214.

Sandseter, E. B. H. (2010) *Scaryfunny: A Qualitative Study of Risky Play among Preschool Children*. Trondheim: Norges teknisk-naturvitenskapelige universitet.

Selander, S. and Kress, G. (2012) *Læringsdesign: i et multimodalt perspektiv*. [*Learning design: in a multimodal perspective*.] Frederiksberg: Frydenlund.

Sutton-Smith, B. (1997) *The Ambiguity of Play*. Cambridge, MA: Harvard University Press.

Tollefsen, T., Syse, H. and Nicolaisen, R. F. (1997) *Tenkere og ideer: filosofiens historie fra antikken til vår egen tid*. [*Thinkers and ideas: the history of philosophy from antiquity to our own time*.] Oslo: Ad notam Gyldendal.

Vygotsky, L. S. (1978) *Mind in Society: The Development of Higher Psychological Processes*. Cambridge, MA: Harvard University Press.

14

MOBILE LEARNING AND THE OUTDOORS

GARY BEAUCHAMP, NICK YOUNG AND RUBY PRICE

CHAPTER OVERVIEW

The outdoor environment has the potential to offer invaluable benefits to children's learning and development; not only the obvious physical benefits often associated with outdoor play, but also social, creative and personal skills are developed through real-world problem solving and experiences (DCELLS, 2008; Figueiredo et al., 2016). The features of the outdoors, the availability of space and open areas, lend themselves to a child-directed play experience (Bilton, 2010), where children are free to learn about their world through self-directed interactions with their environment: learning about nature, through nature, in nature. It is suggested that the 'educative potential of the [outdoors]' (p. 28) is created from freedom, space and the creation of meaningful experiences (Waters and Maynard, 2014). Exploration is key to realising this educative potential, which includes using effective 'scaffolding', building on children's curiosity and imagination (Watts, 2013). Again, given young children's growing technical competence and confidence, technology can contribute to, and help scaffold, more independent learning. This chapter will focus on the use of mobile technologies in the early years outdoor learning environment in Wales.

This chapter aims to help you develop an understanding of:

- the developmental and educational benefits of mobile learning within devices
- the particular features of mobile technologies that make them suitable for use in early childhood education in outdoor settings
- effective pedagogic practice for early years practitioners.

LEARNING THROUGH PLAY OUTDOORS IN WALES

Learning outside of the classroom is an essential feature of successful early years education in many countries, particularly in the Foundation Phase [FP] in Wales, where children aged 3–7 years of age currently 'learn through first-hand experiential activities with the serious business of "play" providing the vehicle' (DCELLS, 2008: 4). This emphasis on play is common to many early years curricula, but Rogers and Lapping (2012) remind us that we need to exercise some caution in the way we use and interpret this apparently simple signifier, as it is actually used in many different complex, but sometimes uncritical, ways in the policy discourse. This policy discourse varies between countries, both within the United Kingdom (UK) and around the world. This has resulted in early years practitioners adopting what Miller et al. (2012) label a 'signature pedagogy', where 'underpinning the distinctive nature of early years methodology is a set of values and beliefs about the nature of childhood and the purpose of education' (p. 228). There is a growing interest in how technology integrates within these values and beliefs, particularly outside of the classroom.

The Welsh Government guidance suggests that the FP environment 'should promote discovery and independence and a greater emphasis on using the outdoor environment as a resource for children's learning' (DCELLS, 2008: 4). This emphasis is comparable to official guidance in both Scotland and Northern Ireland (see 'Useful websites' below and Chapter 2 (Scotland), Chapter 9 (Northern Ireland)). This reflects the devolved nature of education within the UK, as these devolved governments have taken advantage of their ability to develop curricula which reflect their own specific culture and heritage. This is particularly obvious in the early years of education in Wales, where the 'radical potential' (Wincott, 2005: 466) of the FP has resulted in a 'playful pedagogy' (Wainwright et al., 2016) with an emphasis on the use of the outdoors. In this context, 'outdoors' will be interpreted as anything from a school playground to a woodland to an outdoor museum. Although Davies and Hamilton (2018) highlight the pressure put on outdoor learning by assessment policies, Estyn (2011: 1), the Welsh inspectorate, has judged that for children under 5:

Most schools and settings are making at least adequate use of the outdoors and children's learning generally benefits from this. In most cases, children's enjoyment, well-being, behaviour, knowledge and understanding of the world, and their physical development improve as a result of using the outdoors.

We should, however, be cautious when considering the *potential* benefits of learning out-doors as 'being outside does not automatically mean that there are worthwhile educational outcomes' (Waite et al., 2017: 52). Indeed, there is a big difference between 'learning out-doors' and 'outdoor learning', as 'outdoor learning' is not just taking existing learning out of the classroom. As we will see below, this also applies to using mobile technologies out-side of the classroom in the early years (for play outdoors with technology, see Chapter 4).

A review of the curriculum in Wales by Donaldson (2015) – who had previously led a similar review in Scotland – recommended a new curriculum based on Areas of Learning and Experience (AoLE), which will continue the focus of using the outdoors. Donaldson highlights similar national (Scotland and Northern Ireland) and international trends, cit-ing examples in New Zealand (eight areas of learning) and the Netherlands (six broad areas). This recommendation, for all school ages, with no key stages – with a broader focus on areas of learning, explicitly integrated with each other (Beauchamp with Purcell, 2016) – was adopted by the Welsh Government and is currently in the early stages of implementation. The AoLE are:

- expressive arts
- health and well-being
- humanities
- languages, literacy and communication
- mathematics and numeracy
- science and technology.

In addition:

 literacy, numeracy and digital competence should be Cross-curriculum Responsibilities for all teachers and people who work with children and young people. (Donaldson, 2015: 40)

We will consider the implications of this below, but, before we do this, we need to briefly consider any associated risk of implementing this curriculum, including the use of tech-nology, outside of the classroom.

RISK AND OUTDOOR LEARNING

Although the benefits of learning outdoors are widely recognised internationally (Aasen et al., 2009; Maynard and Waters, 2007; Thorburn and Allison, 2017), in all outdoor activities there is an element of both explicit and implicit risk (Beauchamp with Purcell, 2016). Risk taking in general can be defined as 'any behaviour in which there is uncer-tainty about the outcomes of the behaviour' (Little, 2006: 142), but it is in the early years that it is perhaps most often encountered in the context of play. Risky play 'often involves letting go of control and overcoming fear' (Sandseter, 2009: 6), but this risk is 'a positive and necessary aspect of children's physical, emotional and social development' (Waters and Maynard, 2010: 475). Indeed, Little et al. (2011) found that Australian children's mothers and EY practitioners thought that risky play was an important part of learning and should be encouraged. It is unfortunate, therefore, that if practitioners cannot find a balance between providing appropriate risk-taking opportunities and ensuring safety, the children may not gain as much from a learning situation as they might have done (Stan and Humberstone, 2011). This means that the benefits of risky play are not always perceived and 'in response to litigation concerns over managing "risk", some schools are limiting out-of-school activities, therefore eliminating potentially rich learning experiences for children' (Malone, 2008: 5).

Some of this risk taking, in this case by practitioners, is also associated with using technology outside the classroom, such as the device not working properly (risking the success of the learning activity) or the perceived risk of damaging expensive devices. Reassuringly, however, evidence from studies in Scotland (Burden et al., 2012) and Wales (Beauchamp and Hillier, 2014) shows that many primary teachers are not concerned about pupils damaging equipment.

MOBILE LEARNING AND PLAY

As Howard et al. (2012: 176) rightfully point out, 'it is important to understand how ICT, play and learning can be integrated to best effect'. One way of integrating effectively is to make sound judgements about what ICT is good at, and to use these features in a wide range of contexts, including the outdoors. In recent years, the growing availability and sophistication of mobile technologies, especially tablet devices, have facilitated new learning opportunities in outdoor settings. The advent of a wide range of powerful mobile ICT devices and 'the wide availability of these portable, powerful, networked technologies has changed how we work, learn, spend our leisure time, and interact socially' (McNaughton and Light, 2013: 107). These devices can take many forms, but the key principle is that they are handheld and portable, small enough to be carried conveniently, 'enabling the learner to be "on the move", providing anytime anywhere access for learning' (Price, 2007: 34). Beauchamp (2017: 88) suggests that this results in learners being able to make decisions about '*where* they learn, *what* resources they use to help them learn, *how* they learn and even *who* they learn with'.

The concept of 'mobile learning', however, is not a single entity, but instead remains only one part of a complex set of learner interactions between young learners and their environment, both physical and virtual. In this context, mobile learning is part of an ecology of resources, which Luckin (2008: 451) defines as 'a set of inter-related resource elements, including people and objects, the interactions between which provide a particular context'. In outdoor learning, this can include mobile devices, children, adults and features of the outdoor setting. Some of these interactions will be *initiated* by, *stimulated* by or *facilitated* by the technology, whilst others (between children, between children and adults, and between children and the environment) will not use technology at all. Others may be stimulated by the environment, but then *enhanced* by technology. To allow for a range of interactions using technology, however, pupils need to have the necessary confidence and competence to use the technology, as well as being allowed to make decisions about *what* technology they use and *when* and *how* they use it. It is therefore even more important than usual for practitioners to allow pupils to use the many existing digital skills they already have.

PRACTITIONERS LEARNING TO USE TECHNOLOGY: THE ROLE OF PLAY

There are, of course, some practical considerations which can both facilitate and restrict the effective use of mobile technologies outside the classroom, such as cost, access to a network and robustness of the hardware. Many decisions regarding these factors, however, are beyond the control of the practitioner and sometimes even the setting. Some of the more pragmatic concerns, such as the purchasing of hardware and software, can be addressed by schools, but others are reliant on local authority or even government funding. What is harder to change, perhaps, are early years practitioners' pedagogic practice and confidence. This is important as Ingleby (2014: 144) suggests that 'recent research has identified a significant gap in early years practitioners' knowledge and their understanding of pedagogical practice in relation to technology'. Teacher confidence has traditionally been addressed by providing extra training, often by external providers. Recent research, however, has shown that pupils may also be a very good (or even better!) source of confidence building and training, as early years and primary practitioners are willing to learn from their pupils when using mobile devices (Beauchamp et al., 2015). As one teacher said, 'All my pupils had used one [mobile device] and were better at using them than me ... They explained it to me in words I could understand so it was brilliant' (2016: 170). For this co-construction of knowledge to happen, however, practitioners will need to adopt a much more 'symmetrical power relationship' (2016: 170) with their pupils – which actually fits very well with early years pedagogy.

This approach to learning to use technology also accords with the concept of 'digital play' (Marklund and Dunkels, 2016). Indeed, in a study of primary teachers in Wales and Scotland, Beauchamp et al. (2016: 161) found that teachers adopted 'a diverse range of experiential, informal and playful strategies contrasting sharply with traditional models underpinning professional development which emphasize formal courses and events led by "experts" conducted in formal settings such as the school'. One of the most effective strategies was to take the device home (often over a holiday period) and 'play' with it, often with their own children helping. In summary, however confidence in using technology is developed, 'we need to make digital devices available as tools that extend possibilities for children as part of their play' (Palaiologou, 2016: 307).

REFLECTIVE TASK

Reflect on your own use of digital devices and consider the following questions:

- How do you develop your own confidence in using mobile technologies?
- Even if you are very confident now, how would you master a new device or app if you had never seen it before?
- Are you happy to learn from pupils?

WHY BOTHER WITH MOBILE TECHNOLOGY?

Having examined the pragmatic and pedagogic issues, we will now consider the potential of mobile technologies in general, and more specifically outside of the classroom. Following a detailed literature review, Hassler et al. (2016: 139) concluded that mobile devices have the potential to 'enhance, extend and enrich the concept of learning in a number of ways:

1. contingent mobile learning and teaching (where learners can respond and react to their environment and changing experiences, and where learning and teaching opportunities are no longer predetermined);
2. situated learning (where learning takes place in surroundings that make it more meaningful);
3. authentic learning (where learning tasks are meaningfully related to immediate learning goals);
4. context-aware learning (where learning is informed by the history, surroundings and environment of the learner); and
5. personalised learning (where learning is customised for the interests, preferences and capabilities of learners).'

REFLECTIVE TASK

On your own, or in a group, think of one example of how mobile technologies could be used outdoors for each of Hassler et al.'s (2016) listed suggestions. Remember that 'outdoors' covers everywhere from your own playground to a visit to a museum or other place of interest.

These findings are reinforced by Burden and Maher (2014: 176), who suggest that:

one of the liberating features of mobile technologies is their portability, which allows them to be taken into the field to support pupils' gathering of data that can then be used back in the classroom to further their understanding of the focus of the investigation. In this way the devices support pupils' learning in authentic settings.

In such learning, young children are increasingly able to influence the direction of their learning and mobile devices provide a multimodal 'hub' (for instance, the ability to record speech, sound, moving and still images and text in one place) in outdoor settings. This not only allows learning to become more user-centred, but also allows it to take place anywhere, both in the school grounds and beyond.

CASE STUDY 14.1: NATURAL HABITATS AND NATURE DETECTIVES

RESOURCES

Simple school grounds map drawn up by the teacher
iPads (x2 per group)
Magnifying glasses
Apps used: Puppet Edu, QR Code
Website: www.leaf-ID.com

As part of a 'Natural Habitats' topic, a Year 2 class began with pupils being asked what animals and plant life they thought lived on our school grounds. The objectives of the following lesson were 'To observe and identify the animals and plant life that lived in certain areas of the school grounds'. Learners were split into mixed-ability 'learning groups' with a maximum of four learners in each group. Pupils were informed that they were going to be 'nature detectives' and were going to explore who lived on 'our school grounds'. Each group had four magnifying glasses, two iPads and a laminated map of the school grounds. First, as a whole-class input, children were shown the school grounds map on an interactive whiteboard and were set brief questions to familiarise themselves with the map. Each group was designated an area chosen by the class teacher, which was identified on the map with a shaded colour. The areas being explored varied, with two groups exploring parts of the 'Forest School' area, one group exploring a strip of grass next to the main yard and the final group exploring an area on the main playground next to a partitioning wall.

The teacher modelled how to scan QR codes and how to take pictures on the iPad before the groups were set off on their tasks. Accompanied by an adult, each group first identified the correct area they had to explore and clarified their position on the map. Each area had a quick response (QR) code, which learners needed to find and scan. This code contained a link to a video recording of the class teacher (recorded and saved on YouTube) issuing the next set of instructions for the learners. The learners were asked in the video to explore the areas and to use the iPad camera to 'capture' the nature living in this area. Once it was collectively decided by the group that each item was living, pupils were encouraged to identify the living creatures or plants and then to take a picture.

The groups were given 10 minutes to explore their areas and to capture all the living creatures and plant life that inhabited this area. Groups then had to reflect on the pictures they took, using the website www.leaf-ID.com to help identify the leaves they had found. Next, they opened the app 'Puppet Edu' (an app which collates selected pictures and allows for narration, text and music to be added to these pictures to create a short presentation). They had used this before and had to complete a short 'Puppet Edu' presentation with pictures and a narration over the top of each picture, explaining what nature they found living in their area. The adults working with the groups probed with questioning to get the children to reflect on why these animals or plant life lived in the area (access to sunlight or shade, access to food, etc.) and this information was included in some of the presentations. Some groups also included brief text overlays of their pictures.

Later in the week, the groups saved their presentations to YouTube and shared them with the rest of the class. Discussion was promoted on how the areas varied and why certain creatures or plants lived in differing areas. In the next series of lessons, groups had to create their own QR code linking to their Puppet Edu video, and to put this QR code in the area they had explored, so in the future pupils walking past could scan this QR code and watch the presentation. The class teacher reported that 'learners were really engaged with the activity, the use of mobile devices contributed to a better reflection on what the learners had found, as they were able to research after using google images and leaf-ID to clarify what they had found'. One learner stated that 'it was great sharing what we had found. My older brother is in year 6 and could watch my video with the QR code'.

DIGITAL COMPETENCE FRAMEWORK IN WALES

As part of the ongoing curriculum developments in Wales, a Digital Competence Framework was developed by practitioners from Pioneer Schools, supported by external experts. At the very first meeting of this group of practitioners, it became obvious that a key challenge facing everyone was the high level of existing skills that a 4-year-old child brought with them when they started school. Not only did the new curriculum have to cater for a pupil aged 4, it also had to build in progression for the next 12 years of schooling. This highlights a fundamental challenge facing practitioners in the early years, which is that they must not underestimate the digital skills and confidence of the children they teach.

REFLECTIVE TASK

Reflect on your own context and, on your own or in discussion with others, discuss and then make a list of the digital skills that a 2-year-old child and a 5-year-old child would reasonably be expected to possess when they enter a setting. Next:

- If necessary, look at your national curriculum framework for suggested headings or suggestions.
- Consider which of these are particularly relevant or useful in outdoor learning.

Having established that young children bring many digital skills to a setting from a very early age, it is vital that they are allowed to use them. This may mean using programmes and apps that *they* are familiar with, if they can be adapted into a strong pedagogical framework – not just because they are there or are 'fun' – such as in case study 14.2.

CASE STUDY 14.2: 'POKEMON GO' AS A WHOLE-CLASS ACTIVITY

RESOURCES

iPad, iPod, interactive whiteboard, paper grid maps.

CONTEXT

Glan Usk Primary School is a large three-form entry primary school of 690 pupils. The lesson was with a Year 2 class of 30 mixed-ability pupils. Pupils had previously learnt directional language in mathematical development and were learning instructions such as quarter turn, half turn and full turn.

LESSON

A class teacher decided that she wanted to offer the learners practical experience with tangible objects to reinforce this newly acquired vocabulary. Through a series of Assessment for Learning strategies, the class teacher had identified a common class interest in the popular mobile application 'Pokemon Go', which is a location-based augmented reality app available on most smart devices from phones to tablets. Players use the mobile device's GPS capability to locate, capture and battle virtual creatures, called Pokemon, who appear on the screen as if they were in the same real-world location as the player.

The lesson introduced 'Pokemon Go' as a whole-class activity through the interactive whiteboard and excitement grew amongst the learners as they were informed that they had to identify the Pokemon and locate them on the school grounds. As a starter activity, pupils were set into pairs and the first partner was given the application and asked to locate the nearest Pokemon. They were then asked to give directions orally to their partner to find the Pokemon using the mathematical vocabulary they had learnt to help to direct their partners.

During the teacher-directed activities, pupils used the school's iPads to locate these Pokemon, which were dotted across the school grounds, and were asked to highlight where the Pokemon were and write clear directions to these targets on a paper grid map of the school. Once highlighted and located on the map grids, pupils were encouraged to go out into the outdoor environment to hunt and capture the Pokemon, which added to their enthusiasm for the activity.

At the end of the lesson, pupils reflected on the session. One noted that 'we could have just used paper maps like we did in Year 1, but this was more fun'. A teaching assistant highlighted the fact that 'the app engaged the learners and brought directions to life, with learners using mathematical vocabulary to direct each other more efficiently'.

SUMMARY

From everything we have seen above, there are key ideas which need to be considered in the developing use of technology in outdoor learning. In Wales, the concept of outdoor play as a means of learning has long been established, but the recent advent of a new curriculum and an associated digital competence framework has refocused attention on the unique contribution that technology can make. This is allied to a growing awareness of the high level of skill that even very young children bring to a setting and how this can best be realised outdoors. Most importantly, this means giving young learners a high level of autonomy to choose the direction of their learning and what tools they will use, both digital and non-digital, including tablets and digital cameras, as well as bits of wood and mud! There are inevitable infrastructure challenges that may arise, such as a lack of Wi-Fi, equipment costs, as well as changes in pedagogy, and some elements of risk (that equipment may get damaged or lessons may not go well). But none of these should prevent the potential of technology (or better still, technologies) being exploited in outdoor learning in the early years.

KEY POINTS TO REMEMBER

- Even very young children arrive at settings with a high level of skill in using technology.
- Practitioners need to give young learners a high level of autonomy to choose the direction of their learning and what tools they will use, especially outdoors.
- Practitioners should not let concerns about damaging technology put them off using it outside.
- Mobile technologies are part of an ecology of resources in outdoor learning, including mobile devices, children, adults and features of the outdoor setting. Interactions between these can be *initiated, stimulated, facilitated* or *enhanced* by the technology, whilst others will not use technology at all.

POINTS FOR DISCUSSION

- How can practitioners record the use of mobile learning taking place outside of the classroom? (Including the use of mobile technology to do this!)
- Sometimes the media blames mobile technology for the decline in children playing outside. Is this fair?

FURTHER READING

Beauchamp, G. with Purcell, N. (2016) Current developments in education. In D. Wyse and S. Rogers (eds) *A Guide to Early Years and Primary Teaching*. London: Sage, pp. 45–66.

Davies, R. and Hamilton, P. (2018) Assessing learning in the early years' outdoor classroom: examining challenges in practice. *Education 3–13*, 46 (1): 117–129.

USEFUL WEBSITES

Digital Competence Framework (Wales) – http://learning.gov.wales/resources/browse-all/digital-competence-framework/?lang=en. This link contains a range of videos and resources to explain and use the DCF, including a curriculum mapping tool.

Learning and Teaching Scotland (2010) *Curriculum for Excellence through Outdoor Learning* – www.outdoorlearning.org/Portals/0/Region%20Documents/Scotland/14.5.2010. cfeoutdoorlearning.pdf

Welsh Assembly Government (WAG) (2009) *Foundation Phase Outdoor Learning Handbook* – http://learning.gov.wales/docs/learningwales/publications/140828-foundation-phase-outdoor-learning-handbook-en.pdf

REFERENCES

Aasen, W., Grindheim, L. T. and Waters, J. (2009) The outdoor environment as a site for children's participation, meaning-making and democratic learning: examples from Norwegian kindergartens. *Education 3–13, 37* (1): 5–13.

Beauchamp, G. (2017) *Computing and ICT in the Primary School: From Pedagogy to Practice*, 2nd edition. London: David Fulton/Routledge.

Beauchamp, G. and Hillier, E. (2014) *An Evaluation of iPad Implementation across a Network of Primary Schools in Cardiff*. Cardiff: Cardiff Metropolitan University. Available at www.cardiffmet.ac.uk/education/research/Documents/iPadImplementation2014.pdf (accessed 5 May 2017).

Beauchamp, G. with Purcell, N. (2016) Current developments in education. In D. Wyse and S. Rogers (eds) *A Guide to Early Years and Primary Teaching*. London: Sage, pp. 45–66.

Beauchamp, G., Burden, K. and Abbinett, E. (2015) Teachers learning to use the iPad in Scotland and Wales: a new model of professional development. *Journal of Education for Teaching: International Research and Pedagogy, 41* (2): 161–179.

Bilton, H. (2010) *Outdoor Learning in the Early Years: Management and Innovation*. London: Routledge.

Burden, K. and Maher, D. (2014) Mobile technologies and authentic learning in the primary school classroom. In S. Younie, M. Leask and K. Burden (eds), *Teaching with ICT in the Primary School*. London: Routledge, pp. 171–183.

Burden, K., Hopkins, P., Male, T., Martin, S. and Trala, C. (2012) *iPad Scotland Evaluation*. Hull: University of Hull, Faculty of Education.

Davies, R. and Hamilton, P. (2018) Assessing learning in the early years' outdoor classroom: examining challenges in practice. *Education 3–13, 46* (1): 117–129.

DCELLS (2008) *Foundation Phase: Framework for Children's Learning for 3- to 7-Year-Olds in Wales*. Cardiff: WAG.

Donaldson, G. (2015) *The Donaldson Review of Curriculum and Assessment*. Cardiff: The Welsh Government.

Estyn (2011) *Outdoor Learning: An Evaluation of Learning in the Outdoors for Children under Five in the Foundation Phase*. Cardiff: Estyn.

Figueiredo, M., Gomes, C. and Goncalves, N. (2016) *'Going outside': discussing the connection between pedagogical practices with digital tools and outdoor education in early childhood and primary education.* Paper presented at EDULEARN16, Barcelona, July.

Hassler, B., Major, L. and Hennessy, S. (2016) Tablet use in schools: a critical review of the evidence for learning outcomes. *Journal of Computer Assisted Learning, 32* (2): 139–156.

Howard, J., Miles, G. E. and Rees-Davies, L. (2012) Computer use within a play-based early years curriculum. *International Journal of Early Years Education, 20* (2): 175–189.

Ingleby, E. (2014) The impact of changing policies about technology on the professional development needs of early years educators in England. *Professional Development in Education, 41* (1): 144–157.

Little, H. (2006) Children's risk-taking behaviour: implications for early childhood policy and practice. *International Journal of Early Years Education, 14* (2): 141–154.

Little, H., Wyver, S. and Gibson, F. (2011) The influence of play context and adult attitudes on young children's physical risk-taking during outdoor play. *European Early Childhood Education Research Journal, 19* (1): 113–131.

Luckin, R. (2008) The learner centric ecology of resources: a framework for using technology to scaffold learning. *Computers and Education, 50* (2): 449–462.

McNaughton, D. and Light, J. (2013) The iPad and mobile technology revolution: benefits and challenges for individuals who require augmentative and alternative communication. *Augmentative and Alternative Communication, 29* (2): 107–116.

Malone, K. (2008) Every Experience Matters: An evidence-based research report on the role of learning outside the classroom for children's whole development from birth to eighteen years. Available at: www.face-online.org.uk/face-news/every-experience-matters (accessed 5 April 2015).

Marklund, L. and Dunkels, E. (2016) Digital play as a means to develop children's literacy and power in the Swedish preschool. *Early Years, 36* (3): 289–304.

Maynard, T. and Waters, J. (2007) Learning in the outdoor environment: a missed opportunity? *Early Years, 27* (3): 255–265.

Miller, D., Robertson, D., Hudson, A. and Shimi, J. (2012) Signature pedagogy in early years education: a role for COTS game-based learning. *Computers in the Schools, 29* (1/2): 227–247.

Palaiologou, I. (2016) Teachers' dispositions towards the role of digital devices in play-based pedagogy in early childhood education. *Early Years, 36* (3): 305–321.

Price, S. (2007) Ubiquitous computing: digital augmentation and learning. In N. Pachler (ed.) *Mobile Learning: Towards a Research Agenda.* London: WLE Centre, Institute of Education, pp. 33–54.

Rogers, S. and Lapping, C. (2012) Recontextualising 'play' in early years pedagogy: competence, performance and excess in policy and practice. *British Journal of Educational Studies, 60* (3): 243–260.

Sandseter, E. (2009) Characteristics of risky play. *Journal of Adventure Education and Outdoor Learning, 9* (1): 3–21.

Stan, I. and Humberstone, B. (2011) An ethnography of the outdoor classroom: how teachers manage risk in the outdoors. *Ethnography and Education, 6* (2): 213–228.

Thorburn, M. and Allison, P. (2017) Learning outdoors and living well? Conceptual prospects for enhancing curriculum planning and pedagogical practices. *Cambridge Journal of Education, 47* (1): 103–115.

Wainwright, N., Goodway, J., Whitehead, M., Williams, A. and Kirk, D. (2016) The Foundation Phase in Wales: a play-based curriculum that supports the development of physical literacy. *Education 3-13*, 1–12.

Waite, S., Rutter, O., Fowle, A. and Edwards-Jones, A. (2017) Diverse aims, challenges and opportunities for assessing outdoor learning: a critical examination of three cases from practice. *Education 3–13, 45* (1): 51–67.

Waters, J. and Maynard, T. (2010) 'What's so interesting outside?' A study of child-initiated interaction with teachers in the natural outdoor environment. *European Early Childhood Education Research Journal, 18* (4): 473–483.

Waters, J. G. and Maynard, T. (2014) *Exploring Outdoor Play in the Early Years*. Maidenhead: Open University Press.

Watts, A. (2013) *Outdoor Learning through the Seasons: An Essential Guide for the Early Years*. London: Routledge.

Wincott, D. (2005) Reshaping public space? Devolution and policy change. *British Early Childhood Education and Care: Regional and Federal Studies, 15* (4): 453–470.

15

DIGITAL MANIPULATIVES AND MATHEMATICS

ZOI NIKIFORIDOU

CHAPTER OVERVIEW

Preschoolers learn about and understand basic mathematical concepts and skills through explorative and interactive experiences with materials, manipulatives, peers and teachers. The role of tangible manipulatives has been underlined by many traditional theorists (e.g. Bruner, 1966) who explain how physical objects and small-world objects can bridge complex, abstract ideas with the real world. With the integration of technology in children's lives today, we have in place novice-type 'digital manipulatives'. The aim of this chapter is to argue that the debate on the physical *or* digital distinction is not so straightforward. Digital and tangible manipulatives give children diverse opportunities to make connections between their perceptions, cognitions and motor actions, especially in early mathematics. Such implications are discussed in how both digital and tangible manipulatives can support early mathematics and be part of an effective pedagogy in early childhood education.

This chapter aims to help you:

- explore the usefulness of manipulatives in the development of children's mathematical thinking

- examine differences and similarities in the affordances of digital and tangible manipulatives
- address pedagogical aspects of implementing digital and tangible manipulatives in practice.

INFORMATION COMMUNICATION TECHNOLOGY AND EARLY CHILDHOOD EDUCATION

Given the emerging close relationship between children and information communication technology (ICT), there has been extensive interest in exploring the nature, quality and challenges raised by this relationship. Children not only grow up in a world that contains technology but also in a world that increasingly is shaped by it (Siraj-Blatchford and Whitebread, 2003). The original notion of children as digital natives (Prensky, 2001), the net generation (Tapscott, 2009), the millennials (Howe and Strauss, 2000), emphasises this relationship but there is also a need to consider issues concerning the ways in which young people are using new technologies (Helsper and Eynon, 2010). The fact that technology is an integral part of children's lives doesn't necessarily mean that it is always present in effective, efficient, productive ways. Immersion in technology, especially in educational settings, from early ages, needs to address aspects of pedagogy and curriculum, as well as children's home digital patterns and habits (Palaiologou, 2016).

Historically, there has been a transition from 'learning about ICT' to 'learning through ICT'. ICT nowadays is incorporated in many early childhood educational practices worldwide and offers new opportunities that strengthen many aspects of early childhood experiences (Plowman and Stephen, 2005). Computers have been found to support the teaching and learning process by enhancing knowledge, skills and competencies in many ways (e.g. Plowman, 2016; Siraj-Blatchford and Siraj-Blatchford, 2006; Yelland, 2011). Research supports the contention that children at a young age show advanced cognitive capacities through computer-based activities as they develop their memory, attention, literacy abilities, storytelling, mathematical thinking, motivation to learn, creativity, problem-solving capacities and consequently their school achievement (Chung and Walsh, 2006; Evans Schmidt and Vandewater, 2008; Sarama and Clements, 2009; Skantz Åberg et al., 2014). Furthermore, a recent UNESCO (Kalaš, 2012) policy brief states that overall ICT supports the following key areas of learning in early childhood education and care: 'communication and collaboration, cognitive development, creativity, socio-dramatic play, and learning to learn' (2012: 2).

Hayes and Whitebread (2006) mention that ICT can make a contribution in diverse areas of learning in early childhood, if the approach used recognises and respects how children learn and become confident and creative thinkers. Playful, positive experiences with computers are fundamental for children. Howard et al. (2012) found in their study in 12 Welsh early years settings that the blend of continuous, enhanced and focused provision is an effective means of integrating computer use within a play-based curriculum. Yet Edwards (2013) argues that there is still a separation between play and technology in the early childhood curricula, and suggests that children's digital play should be seen as a part of socio-cultural meaning making and not as a singular artefact.

Papert (1987: 23) used the term 'technocentrism' to capture the tendency to give a centrality to a technical object, such as computers or other technological devices. This raises particular questions, including 'what is the effect of the computer on cognitive development?' However, Papert feels that such an approach to the use of technology ignores the 'most important components of educational situations – people and cultures' (p. 23). He also argues that the context for human development is not the technology, but instead culture, and that in order to understand or influence change the point of focus should be on the culture and not on the technology.

TANGIBLE (CONCRETE) MANIPULATIVES

Experiences with materials, peers and teachers encourage personal involvement and construction, as well as collaboration and the exchange of ideas. Such experiences play a key role in active learning, 'learning by doing', where 'doing is a good way to learn. And it is made better by talking and thinking' (Papert, 1999: xiii). Manipulatives are resources that provide opportunities for exploration, discussion, manipulation and conceptualisation. These could be blocks, puzzles, different props, coins, balance scales, objects, cubes or beads. They offer ways through which children, in the case of mathematics, can connect mathematical ideas to real-world experiences (McNeil and Jarvin, 2007). Moving manipulatives enhances the connection between children's senses and their spatial, kinaesthetic, causal thinking. Manipulatives are transitional objects that encourage learners to move from concrete, hands-on experimentation to more abstract thinking and understanding. The sensory nature of these physical objects enhances meaningful learning (Martin, 2009), where doing and thinking –action and perception – interact explicitly. A mathematical manipulative is an object 'that can be handled by an individual in a sensory manner during which conscious and unconscious mathematical thinking is fostered' (Swan and Marshall, 2010: 14).

Manipulatives have a long history in children's mathematical learning. Montessori (1964) believed that education consists of developing the senses and relating them to language and intellect. Therefore, she created a series of materials that would support children in gaining knowledge from the outside world. Besides sensory education, her educational approach had exercises about practical life, basic academic skills, language, and muscular development. The children independently worked with manipulative materials that facilitated their learning of basic academic skills, including mathematics. For example, in teaching young children how to write, they first outlined geometric figures such as circles, squares, triangles, ellipses, rhombuses and pentagons (Balfanz, 1999). Then children learned letter shapes. Both Montessori and Froebel believed that education was an individual activity that included self-discipline, independence and self-direction. However, Montessori focused on sensory education, whereas Froebel focused on symbolic education (Saracho and Spodek, 2006).

Froebel (1912) designed educational play materials known as 'gifts'. These were geometric shapes, which included structural-design toys, pattern recognition and building blocks. The gifts were underpinned by the cornerstones of unity, respect and play. According to Manning (2005), the aim of the gifts was to make children feel familiar and comfortable in using them, thus accelerating and enhancing their learning experience. He even introduced rules for teachers to follow, whilst applying gifts in the classroom. Wiggin and Smith (1896) list the following rules:

1. Use all the materials in order to keep the idea of the relation of parts to a whole.
2. Give names to each object constructed, bringing it into relation with the child's experience.
3. The younger the child, the more you should talk about the thing that you will construct.
4. When the play is designed to be individually oriented, do not allow the child to rely on the materials of his playmates in his building project.
5. Intentional group work or 'united building' should be frequently introduced during these exercises. (pp. 54–56)

REFLECTIVE TASK

Reflect on Froebel's ideas about early childhood education and the notion of gifts. Imagine if he had produced 'digital' gifts. Do you think his suggested five rules would apply and why? If you were exploring the theme 'shapes', how would you consider these five rules in practice? Can you think of examples? Can you think of any possible limitations?

However, the physicality of manipulatives per se does not necessarily lead to mathematical thinking. Carbonneau et al. (2013) found in a meta-analysis of 55 studies that manipulatives only elicit learning under certain conditions. For example, the content being taught makes a difference to whether the use of manipulatives is beneficial or not; manipulatives were more advantageous for learning about fractions than for learning arithmetic. The presence of manipulatives is not sufficient in ensuring meaningful learning. Their effectiveness depends on how they are embedded in comprehensive, well-planned, instructional settings (Sarama and Clements, 2009). Thus, the manipulatives do not carry the meaning of the mathematical idea explored; it is the active, sensori-motor engagement of the learner within a wider pedagogical context that does. According to McNeil and Uttal (2009), what matters is whether and how learners gain insight into the meaning and purpose of what they are learning through the use of materials.

Therefore, Laski et al. (2015) propose that manipulatives in early childhood need to meet the following four general principles: (a) consistent use of manipulatives, over a long period of time; (b) a progressive move from highly transparent concrete representations to more abstract ones; (c) avoidance of manipulatives that look like everyday objects; and (d) explicit explanation of the relation between the manipulatives and the mathematical concept. These principles are supported by findings from cognitive science and could inform practice and instruction. Through manipulation, children might build initial meanings but they then need to reflect on their actions in order to reach the underpinning mathematical idea (Sarama and Clements, 2009).

DIGITAL (VIRTUAL) MANIPULATIVES

Innovations in technology, the prevalence of the internet and the increasing accessibility of computers in classroom and home environments, have led to the development of more contemporary types of manipulatives: the computer-based, digital manipulatives. Computer manipulatives, according to Sarama and Clements (2009), provide unique affordances for the development of knowledge; they offer great control and flexibility and facilitate the development of mathematical thinking. Virtual manipulatives are digital, interactive, web-based and software-based 'representations of a dynamic object that presents opportunities for constructing mathematical knowledge' (Moyer et al., 2002: 373).

Nowadays, digital mathematics manipulatives are increasingly used. Some of them replicate the physical, concrete manipulatives in a virtual environment, whereas others allow learners to explore concepts that would be difficult to explore in the physical world (Bujak et al., 2013). In considering comparisons between physical and digital manipulatives, Sarama and Clements (2009) recommend that seven key affordances make computer manipulatives more advantageous than other resources. Computer manipulatives, for example, provide immediate feedback, provide space for direct changes and alterations (e.g. size of shapes, number of patterns) and the opportunity for repetition and the recording of actions. They also enable mathematical ideas and processes to be reached at an explicit level of awareness (Clements and Sarama, 2007). When using physical manipulatives, a child might turn, flip or slide them intuitively without conscious awareness of the geometric motions that relate to these movements. In a similar condition, on a computer, these movements would be made with more precision and exactness and the 'action on objects' would be more obvious to the user. For example, decomposing a hexagon into other shapes is easier with a computer manipulative than with a tangible one (Sarama and Clements, 2009).

Sometimes, when using physical manipulatives, children might find it difficult to understand the relationship between the manipulative and the mathematical concept represented (Bujak et al., 2013). A possible reason for this mismatch is the dual representation concept (DeLoache, 2000; Uttal et al., 2009). Manipulatives have a dual nature; they are objects in their own right but also representations of something else. Dice have their own physical properties, like size, colour, texture, mass, but they also have a representational nature if they are used in probabilistic games where the likelihood of getting a 2 is 1:6. Sometimes this dual representation might lead to misunderstandings in young children. Hence, Sarama and Clements (2009) suggest that computer-based manipulatives reduce the demands of dual representation by enabling users to pay less attention to onscreen objects and more attention to the connections derived.

Another reason why virtual manipulatives might be more attractive in classroom practice relates to the practical aspects of curricular design. For example, they do not require lengthy set-up and clean-up time (Moyer et al., 2002). Once accessed, they can be manipulated through a mouse or a finger and the activity terminates when the device is switched off. Also, in terms of resource allocation per student, it is easier to have groups of children observing and interacting with the virtual manipulative at the same time, than using physical manipulatives that require turn taking (Bujak et al., 2013). In the same way, virtual manipulatives can become more personalised as children can be creative in using them; for instance, by setting the background of the screen or by adding effects.

Novack and Goldin-Meadow (2015) underline the role that hands play in teaching and learning – not only as part of gestures or non-verbal communication but also as mediators of tactile interactions with various objects and technological devices. As such, the role of children's hands, whilst exploring tangible and/or digital manipulatives, changes. In the case of physical manipulatives, through their senses children would *feel* and *embody* the consequences of their manipulation. If they spin a disc at high speed, they then can see and feel the consequences of their direct manipulation. Thus, in a similar digital case, the phase of embodiment becomes more distant. Children would press a key on a keyboard or click on a mouse in order to provoke the spinning but without controlling the force and speed. In this case, it would be harder for users to experience the spinning and understand that the nature of the input manipulation (initiation of spinning) can lead to diverse outputs (less force, shorter time of spinning). Mangen (2010) outlines the difference in sensory, perceptual, cognitive and phenomenological experience afforded by digital technology and real-world materials. She questions the *intangibility* of the digital stimuli and calls for a more multidisciplinary approach in considering how ICT can be handled theoretically, methodologically and pedagogically in early childhood.

CASE STUDY 15.1: CHILDREN'S INTERACTIONS WITH DIGITAL/ CONCRETE MANIPULATIVES – THE CASE OF PROBABILITIES

One of the mathematical areas investigated recently in preschool education is the notion of probability. Research has shown that children at the age of 4 possess a minimal understanding of randomness, as they recognise notions like possible, impossible, certain, uncertain, sample space and can make predictions and inferences (i.e. Nikiforidou et al., 2013; Schlottmann and Wilkening, 2011). In this study, children between 4 and 6 years of age (N = 40) in a nursery in Greece explored the likelihood of events with the use of digital (Condition 1) and concrete (Condition 2) manipulatives. In groups of three, the children participated in three repeated probabilistic games and their responses, time reactions and discussions were recorded. The findings suggested that in both conditions, physical and digital, children engaged with the probabilistic tasks in different ways.

METHODOLOGY

After written consent from their parents, their headteacher and themselves, children participated in play-based activities exploring the probability of an event. Children were allocated randomly to one of two conditions; in Condition 1 they engaged in activities through the use of computer-based animal cards (designed in PowerPoint) and in Condition 2 they interacted with concrete animal cards (Figure 15.1). In both conditions, children were introduced to the cards and the distribution of the sample space (being always 8) by counting and observing the animals depicted; in case 1 5:3, in case 2 5:2:1 and in case 3 5:1:1:1. They were then asked to turn the cards over and mix them up. In Condition 1 children used a laptop's mouse to make the movements, whereas in Condition 2 they directly manipulated the cards. The researcher asked them, by randomly pointing at a card: 'Which animal do you think is more probable to be under this card? Why?' The same process was repeated five times.

Children in both conditions were given specially designed sheets where they could record their estimations as well as the actual findings. As they participated in small groups, their discussions were recorded.

FINDINGS

It was found that as the complexity of the sample space increased, the children were unable to take into account all the odds and make correct predictions. Thus, in case 1 (two sets of animals) 68.8% responded correctly, in case 2 (three sets of animals) 34.8%

Figure 15.1   Example of cards (digital and concrete) used in case 3 (5:1:1:1)

and in case 3 (four sets of animals) 26.6% gave the correct answer. The condition (digital vs concrete) wasn't found to be a significant factor in the accuracy of these predictions. However, it was observed that children in Condition 2 (concrete) engaged in more dialogue and discussion whilst interacting. Thus, it took them longer to predict and consider each outcome. Another observation was that in this group work children in Condition 1 would engage more with turn taking and inhibitory control in comparison to Condition 2 where they would interact with the cards at once.

PEDAGOGICAL IMPLICATIONS OF TANGIBLE AND DIGITAL MANIPULATIVES

The use of manipulatives in learning and especially in mathematics using either tangible or digital resources is not about difficulty. Instead, it is a matter of considering how manipulatives can be effectively embedded in the pedagogical process; whether and how they make meaning (Sarama and Clements, 2009). The one manipulative does not replace the other – they can be complementary – as each type can provide pedagogical experiences. It could be assumed that digital manipulatives are the evolution of tangible ones considering the vast contemporary technological advances.

Both tangible and virtual manipulatives do not of themselves encourage meaningful connections and conceptual understanding (McNeil and Jarvin, 2007). Nonetheless, it is the way they are effectively integrated in children's learning that gives them value and significance. In this way, the features of different manipulatives, the context and pedagogical implementation, the role of the teacher and wider implications should be taken into consideration (Björklund, 2014; McNeil and Uttal, 2009; Mix, 2010; Sarama and Clements, 2009).

Mix (2010) identifies four mechanisms through which manipulatives are efficient: they generate actions, they serve as conceptual metaphors, they offload intelligence and they focus attention. Through the manipulation of virtual or concrete resources, action, thinking and memory are strongly interconnected and, by engaging with semiotic tools, children can contextualise and understand abstractions (Hoyles and Noss, 2009). For example, during an addition task, children may more easily grasp that $2 + 3 = 5$ if they interact with manipulatives, count them, move them around and place them in a line, whilst verbally counting the sequence. Either this activity is done on-screen or using real beads – in both cases, children draw their attention to the task, experience how their actions and movements influence the manipulatives and develop deep levels of arithmetic thinking.

Instruction and the role of the teacher is an important factor in using manipulatives, concrete or digital, for learning purposes. Bruner (1966) underlined the importance of the role that teachers play in organising and directing students' activities. He believed that teachers can support learners in internalising information from their environment through enactive, iconic and symbolic modes of representation. He noted:

> Any set of knowledge ... can be represented in three ways: by a set of actions appropriate for achieving a certain result (enactive representation); by a set of summary images or graphics that stand for a concept without defining it fully (iconic representation); and a set of symbolic or logical propositions drawn from a symbolic system that is governed by rules or laws forming and transforming propositions (symbolic representation). (pp. 44–45)

Teachers are to scaffold students to 'wean themselves from the perceptual embodiment to the symbolic notation' (Bruner, 1966: 63). Therefore, it is suggested that the teacher, if needed, has to point out and guide the connections between representations and abstract thought (Sarama and Clements, 2009; Uttal et al., 2009). In her study with

1- and 2-year-olds, Björklund (2014) found that the teacher's discourse and directed questions can be critical in enhancing children's attention on a goal-specific learning object. The teacher's role as a guide, points, holds, demonstrates and manipulates whilst linguistically emphasising specific information, is core in promoting meaning making in the early years.

Another pedagogical factor related to the use of virtual and concrete manipulatives has to do with time and familiarity. Children need time to experiment with and solidify their responses before being introduced to an alternative manipulative that represents a similar mathematical idea (Mix, 2010). If the session is rushed or if children have limited time to interact and repeat their engagement, then learning and conceptualisation might be obstructed. Familiarity with the manipulative is another pedagogical factor. It has been found that if the same set of manipulatives is used across contexts, then discovery and learning are supported (Son et al., 2012). In such cases, children feel familiar with the manipulatives and do not spend a large amount of time trying to figure out how different manipulatives function or connect. Martin (2009) suggests that as concrete and symbolic representations of mathematical concepts co-evolve, the use of simple as opposed to highly attractive blocks and tiles can facilitate reflection and abstraction; it is a matter of material choice.

REFLECTIVE TASK

Whilst embedding virtual manipulatives in mathematics classroom activities, what aspects would you take into consideration? Are there any challenges? Any barriers?

SUMMARY

Overall, movement and the real activity of hands and body enhance learning and perceptual thinking. The interaction with tangible objects and with virtual manipulatives enables the development of abstract thought and mathematical ideas. The two types of manipulatives are equally important as they provide diverse pedagogical possibilities; in the case of tangible objects, there is a direct feeling of manipulation, whereas in the virtual case there is a screen-based mediator between the action of the hand or finger and its consequence for the object(s). Thus, instead of debating between tangible and virtual manipulatives, it will be helpful to explore the ways in which they can each play a significant role in the development of early mathematical thinking.

KEY POINTS TO REMEMBER

- Digital manipulatives, like tangible manipulatives, have a long history and are fundamental to learning mathematical ideas and concepts, if used effectively.
- Digital manipulatives differ from tangible manipulatives in that they are flexible, unique affordances that offer control, immediate feedback, space for direct changes and the opportunity for repetition and recording of actions.
- Manipulatives, in spite of their nature, can only be pedagogical if embedded in child-centred activities, scaffolded by teachers and based on children's interests and active engagement.

POINTS FOR DISCUSSION

- If a colleague or a parent asked your view on the use of virtual manipulatives in promoting maths, what would you say? Give consideration to the use of tangible manipulatives, their history and their evolution.
- Papert (1993) claimed that: 'The educator must be an anthropologist. The educator as anthropologist must work to understand which cultural materials are relevant to intellectual development' (p. 32). How do you understand this quote if the cultural materials are virtual manipulatives?

FURTHER READING

Baykal, G. E., Veryeri Alaca, I., Yantaç, A. E. and Göksun, T. (2018) A review on complementary natures of tangible user interfaces (TUIs) and early spatial learning. *International Journal of Child-Computer Interaction*, 16: 104–113.

Nikiforidou, Z. (2018) Digital games in the early childhood classroom: theoretical and practical considerations. In S. J. Danby, M. Fleer, C. Davidson and M. Hatzigianni (eds) *Digital Childhoods: Technologies and Children's Everyday Lives*. (International Perspectives on Early Childhood Education and Development 22.) Singapore: Springer, pp. 253–265.

Sarama, J. and Clements D. H. (2016) Physical and virtual manipulatives: what is 'concrete'? In P. Moyer-Packenham (ed.) *International Perspectives on Teaching and Learning Mathematics with Virtual Manipulatives: Mathematics Education in the Digital Era, 7.* Cham: Springer.

USEFUL WEBSITE

www.ixl.com/math/probability-and-statistics – this website has interesting and interactive activities for teaching maths to young children.

REFERENCES

Balfanz, R. (1999) Why do we teach young children so little mathematics? Some historical considerations. In J. V. Copley (ed.) *Mathematics in the Early Years*. Reston, VA: National Council of Teachers of Mathematics; and Washington, DC: National Association for the Education of Young Children.

Björklund, C. (2014) Less is more: mathematical manipulatives in early childhood education. *Early Child Development and Care, 184* (3): 469–485.

Bruner, J. S. (1966) *Toward a Theory of Instruction*. Cambridge, MA: Harvard University Press.

Bujak, K., Radu, I., Catrambone, C., MacIntyre, B., Zheng, R. and Golubski, G. (2013) A psychological perspective on augmented reality in the mathematics classroom. *Computers and Education, 68*: 536–544.

Carbonneau, K. J., Marley, S. C. and Selig, J. P. (2013) A meta-analysis of the efficacy of teaching mathematics with concrete manipulatives. *Journal of Educational Psychology, 105*: 380–400.

Chung, Y. and Walsh, D. J. (2006) Constructing a joint story-writing space: the dynamics of young children's collaboration at computers. *Early Education and Development, 17* (3): 337–420.

Clements, D. H. and Sarama, J. (2007) Early childhood mathematics learning. In F. K. Lester, Jr (ed.) *Second Handbook of Research on Mathematics Teaching and Learning*, Vol. 1. Charlotte, NC: Information Age, pp. 461–555.

DeLoache, J. S. (2000) Dual representation and young children's use of scale models. *Child Development, 71*: 329–338.

Edwards, S. (2013) Digital play in the early years: a contextual response to the problem of integrating technologies and play-based pedagogies in the early childhood curriculum. *European Early Childhood Education Research Journal, 21* (2): 199–212.

Evans Schmidt, M. and Vandewater, E. A. (2008) Media and attention, cognition, and school achievement. *The Future of Children: Children and Computer Technology, 18* (1): 63–85.

Froebel, F. (1912) *Froebel's Chief Writings on Education* (trans. S. S. F. Fletcher and J. Welton). London: Edward Arnold.

Hayes, M. and Whitebread, D. (2006) *ICT in the Early Years*. Maidenhead: Open University Press.

Helsper, E. and Eynon, R. (2010) Digital natives: where is the evidence? *British Educational Research Journal, 36* (3): 503–520.

Howard, J., Miles, G. E. and Rees-Davies, L. (2012) Computer use within a play-based early years curriculum. *International Journal of Early Years Education, 20* (2): 175–189.

Howe, N. and Strauss, B. (2000) *Millennials Rising: The Next Great Generation.* New York: Vintage Books.

Hoyles, C. and Noss, R. (2009) The technological mediation of mathematics and its learning. *Human Development, 52*: 129–147.

Kalaš, I. (2012) *Policy Brief: ICTs in Early Childhood Care and Education.* Moscow: UNESCO Institute for Information Technologies in Education.

Laski, E. V., Jor'dan, J. R., Daoust, C. and Murray, A. K. (2015) What makes mathematics manipulatives effective? Lessons from cognitive science and Montessori education. *SAGE Open, 5* (2): 1–8.

McNeil, N. M. and Jarvin, L. (2007) When theories don't add up: disentangling the manipulatives debate. *Theory into Practice, 46* (4): 309–316.

McNeil, N. M. and Uttal, D. H. (2009) Rethinking the use of concrete materials in learning: perspectives from development and education. *Child Development Perspectives, 3*: 137–139.

Mangen, A. (2010) Point and click: theoretical and phenomenological reflections on the digitization of early childhood education. *Contemporary Issues in Early Childhood, 11* (4): 415–431.

Manning, J. (2005) Rediscovering Froebel: a call to re-examine his life and gifts. *Early Childhood Education Journal, 32* (6): 371–376.

Martin, T. (2009) A theory of physically distributed learning: how external environments and internal states interact in mathematics learning. *Child Development Perspectives, 3*: 140–144.

Mix, K. S. (2010) Spatial tools for mathematical thought. In K. S. Mix, L. B. Smith and M. Gasser (eds) *Space and Language.* New York: Oxford University Press, pp. 41–66.

Montessori, M. (1964) *The Advanced Montessori Method.* Cambridge, MA: R. Bentley.

Moyer, P. S., Bolyard, J. J. and Spikell, M. A. (2002) What are virtual manipulatives? *Teaching Children Mathematics, 8* (6): 372–377.

Nikiforidou, Z., Pange, J. and Chadjipadelis, T. (2013) Intuitive and informal knowledge in preschoolers' development of probabilistic thinking. *International Journal of Early Childhood, 45* (3): 347–357.

Novack, M. and Goldin-Meadow, S. (2015) Learning from gesture: how our hands change our minds. *Educational Psychology Review, 27* (3): 405–412.

Palaiologou, I. (2016) Children under five and digital technologies: implications for early years pedagogy. *European Early Childhood Education Research Journal, 24* (1): 5–24.

Papert, S. (1987) Computer criticism vs. technocentric thinking. *Educational Researcher, 16* (1): 22–30.

Papert, S. (1993) *Mindstorms: Children, Computers and Powerful Ideas*, 2nd edn. New York: Basic Books.

Papert, S. (1999) *What is Logo? And Who Needs It? Introduction to Logo Philosophy and Implementation*. Highgate Springs, VT: LCSI, pp. v– xvi.

Plowman, L. (2016) Rethinking context: digital technologies and children's everyday lives. *Children's Geographies, 14* (2): 190–202.

Plowman, L. and Stephen, C. (2005) Children, play and computers in pre-school education. *British Journal of Educational Technology, 36* (2): 145–157.

Prensky, M. (2001) Digital natives, digital immigrants: Part 1. *On the Horizon, 9* (5): 1–6.

Saracho, O. N. and Spodek, B. (2006) Roots of early childhood education in America. In M. Takeuchi and R. Scott (eds) *New Directions for Early Childhood Education and Care in the 21st Century: International Perspectives*. Waterloo, IA: G and R Publishing, pp. 252–277.

Sarama, J. and Clements, D. H. (2009) 'Concrete' computer manipulatives in mathematics education. *Child Development Perspectives, 3* (3): 145–150.

Schlottmann, A. and Wilkening, F. (2011) Judgment and decision-making in young children. In M. K. Dhami, A. Schlottmann and M. R. Waldmann (eds) *Judgement and Decision-making as a Skill: Learning, Development, Evolution*. Cambridge: Cambridge University Press, pp. 55–83.

Siraj-Blatchford, I. and Siraj-Blatchford, J. (2006) *A Guide to Developing the ICT Curriculum for Early Childhood Education*. Stoke-on-Trent: Trentham Books.

Siraj-Blatchford, J. and Whitebread, D. (2003) *Supporting Information and Communications Technology Education in Early Childhood*. Buckingham: Open University Press.

Skantz Åberg, E., Lantz-Andersson, A. and Pramling, N. (2014) 'Once upon a time there was a mouse': children's technology-mediated storytelling in preschool class. *Early Child Development and Care, 184* (11): 1583–1598.

Son, J. Y., Smith, L. B., Goldstone, R. L. and Leslie, M. (2012) The importance of being interpreted: grounded words and children's relational reasoning. *Frontiers in Developmental Psychology, 3*: 1–12.

Swan, P. and Marshall, L. (2010) Revisiting mathematics manipulative materials. *Australian Primary Mathematics Classroom, 15* (2): 13–19.

Tapscott, D. (2009) *Grown up Digital: How the Net Generation is Changing Your World*. New York: McGraw-Hill.

Uttal, D. H., O'Doherty, K., Newland, R., Hand, L. L. and DeLoache, J. (2009) Dual representation and the linking of concrete and symbolic representations. *Child Development Perspectives, 3* (3): 156–159.

Wiggin, K. and Smith N. A. (1896) *Froebel's Occupations*. London: Gay and Hancock.

Yelland, N. (2011) Knowledge building with ICT in the early years of schooling. *He Kupu the World, 2* (5): 33–44.

INDEX